# FOOD IN ZONES OF CONFLICT

# THE ANTHROPOLOGY OF FOOD AND NUTRITION

Series Editor: *Helen Macbeth*, Oxford Brookes University

Eating is something all humans must do to survive, but it is more than a biological necessity. Producing food, foraging, distributing, shopping, cooking and, of course, eating itself are all deeply inscribed as cultural acts. This series brings together the broad range of perspectives on human food, encompassing social, cultural and nutritional aspects of food habits, beliefs, choices and technologies in different regions and societies, past and present. Each volume features cross-disciplinary and international perspectives on the topic of its title. This multidisciplinary approach is particularly relevant to the study of food-related issues in the contemporary world.

Volume 1
**Food and the Status Quest: An Interdisciplinary Perspective**
Edited by *Polly Wiessner* and *Wulf Schiefenhövel*

Volume 2
**Food Preferences and Taste: Continuity and Change**
Edited by *Helen Macbeth*

Volume 3
**Food for Health, Food for Wealth: Ethnic and Gender Identities in British Iranian Communities**
*Lynn Harbottle*

Volume 4
**Drinking: Anthropological Approaches**
Edited by *Igor de Garine* and *Valerie de Garine*

Volume 5
**Researching Food Habits: Methods and Problems**
Edited by *Helen Macbeth* and *Jeremy MacClancy*

Volume 6
**Consuming the Inedible: Neglected Dimensions of Food Choice**
Edited by *Jeremy MacClancy, C. Jeya Henry* and *Helen Macbeth*

Volume 7
**Liquid Bread: Beer and Brewing in Cross-Cultural Perspective**
Edited by *Wulf Schiefenhövel* and *Helen Macbeth*

Volume 8
**Food in Zones of Conflict: Cross-Disciplinary Perspectives**
Edited by *Paul Collinson and Helen Macbeth*

# FOOD IN ZONES OF CONFLICT

*Cross-Disciplinary Perspectives*

..............................................................................................................

*Edited by*

Paul Collinson and Helen Macbeth

berghahn

NEW YORK · OXFORD

www.berghahnbooks.com

First published in 2014 by
Berghahn Books
www.BerghahnBooks.com

**Library of Congress Cataloging-in-Publication Data**

Food in zones of conflict: cross-disciplinary perspectives / edited by
Paul Collinson and Helen Macbeth.

    pages cm. -- (The anthropology of food and nutrition; volume 8)
Includes bibliographical references and index.
ISBN 978-1-78238-403-8 (hardback: alk. paper) -- ISBN 978-1-78238-
404-5 (ebook) 1. Food--Social aspects. 2. Food--Political aspects.
3. War and society. 4. Food security. 5. Food supply--Political aspects.
6. Hunger--Political aspects. I. Collinson, Paul, 1969- II. Macbeth,
Helen M.
GT2850.F674 2014
394.1'2--dc23

                                       2014000988


**British Library Cataloguing in Publication Data**
A catalogue record for this book is available from the British Library


ISBN 978-1-78238-403-8 (hardback)
E-ISBN 978-1-78238-404-5 (e-book)

# CONTENTS

List of Figures      vii

List of Tables      ix

Foreword      x

Preface      xii

List of Contributors      xiv

Introduction      1
*Paul Collinson and Helen Macbeth*

1. **'Try to imagine, we didn't even have salt to cook with!':
Food and War in Sierra Leone**      27
*Susan Shepler*

2. **Landmines, Cluster Bombs and Food Insecurity in Africa**      39
*Bukola Adeyemi Oyeniyi and Akinyinka Akinyoade*

3. **Special Nutritional Needs in Refugee Camps:
A Cross-Disciplinary Approach**      53
*Jeya Henry and Helen Macbeth*

4. **Patterns of Household Food Consumption in Conflict Affected
Households in Trincomalee, Sri Lanka**      65
*Rebecca Kent*

5. **Engaging Religion in the Quest for Sustainable Food Security
in Zones of Conflict in Sub-Saharan Africa**      77
*Lucy Kimaro*

6. **Livestock Production in Zones of Conflict in the Northern
Border of Mexico**      85
*Daria Deraga*

7.  The Logic of War and Wartime Meals                                    95
    *Nives Rittig Beljak and Bruno Beljak*

8.  Nutrition, Food Rationing and Home Production in the UK
    during the Second World War                                          107
    *Helen Lightowler and Helen Macbeth*

9.  Beyond the Ration: Alternatives to the Ration for British
    Soldiers on the Western Front, 1914–1918                             123
    *Rachel Duffett*

10. Sustaining and Comforting the Troops in the Pacific War              133
    *Katarzyna J. Cwiertka*

11. Enemy Cuisine: Claiming Agency, Seeking Humanity and
    Renegotiating Identity through Consumption                           145
    *K. Felicia Campbell*

12. The Memory of Food Problems at the End of the First World
    War in Subsequent Propaganda Posters in Germany                      155
    *Tania Rusca*

13. Echoes of Catastrophe: Famine, Conflict and Reconciliation in
    the Irish Borderlands                                                171
    *Paul Collinson*

14. 'Land to the Tiller': Hunger and the End of Monarchy in
    Ethiopia                                                             185
    *Benjamin Talton*

15. Prospects for Conflict to Spread through Bilateral Land
    Arrangements for Food Security                                       197
    *Michael J. Strauss*

16. Food, Conflict and Human Rights: Accounting for Structural
    Violence                                                             209
    *Ellen Messer*

Index                                                                    225

# LIST OF FIGURES

1.1   Boy selling monkeys as food                                              30

1.2   Women using a Nigerian Peacekeeper's helmet in food
      preparation                                                               33

4.1   Average monthly incomes derived from livelihood activities
      for participating households (Tamil village with land)                    71

6.1   Map of US–Mexican Border States                                           86

7.1   Map of Croatia                                                            96

8.1   *Dig for Victory* poster                                                  110

8.2   *The Kitchen Front* booklet                                               113

8.3   Percentage of pregnant women within the normal range for
      biochemical measures of iron, protein, vitamin A, vitamin C
      and riboflavin (data from Huxley *et al.* 2000)                           118

10.1  The extent of the Japanese Wartime Empire, 1942                           135

10.2  Shipments of rice (in metric tons) from Japan for the
      Imperial Japanese Army (IJA) and the Imperial Japanese Navy
      (IJN)                                                                     137

10.3  US Parachute Glider Regiment soldiers enjoying Japanese beer
      and a meal on Japanese soil (September 1945)                              141

12.1  *Your children need peace and bread. Therefore, women vote!*,
      a poster of the Association of the German Women's
      Organization                                                             159

12.2   *'Farmers! Do your duty! The cities are starving!'* a poster
       designed by Heinrich Hönich for the Central Committee for
       Popular Education                                               160

12.3   *'What we have to lose!'*, a poster of 1919, which adopted a
       typical pre-war design                                          162

12.4   Graph showing average rate of the posters dealing with food
       according to the years when elections occurred, i.e., 1919,
       1920, 1924, 1925, 1930 and 1932                                 165

13.1   Map of North-West Ireland                                       172

# LIST OF TABLES

2.1   African countries with proven usage of APOs          44

2.2   Cost of demining activities versus national budget in selected
      African countries                                    48

3.1   Comparison of vitamin and iron content in refugee rations and
      pet food                                             56

3.2   Quantities of ingredients for the Rice–Sesame RUTF as
      quantities (%)                                       60

3.3   Nutritional composition of Rice–Sesame RUTF per 100 g and
      percentage contribution to energy                    61

3.4   Mineral analysis for Rice–Sesame RUTF                61

4.1   Characteristics of study villages and patterns of rice shortages    67

4.2   Patterns of rice storage in interviewed households    73

9.1   British Army rations 1917–1918                       124

# FOREWORD

..............................................................................................................................

This is a rare book that addresses many different aspects of food in zones of conflict, very usefully doing so from a historical and multidisciplinary perspective. Different contributors explore the politicisation and militarisation of hunger, the micronutrients needed to prevent starvation, and the persistent cultures of survival and innovation that grow up around chronic hunger.

The value of this volume is in the intimate detail it provides about hunger in armed conflicts. Hunger, it seems, is very personal. We do not just lack nutrients when we are hungry. We also miss particular tastes, gatherings, signature dishes from our family, and national dishes from our group. People also miss the process of cooking. Whether they are living off humanitarian food aid or military rations, people in war miss 'real food' that fosters their identity as well as their nutritional status, their souls as well as their bodies.

Hunger is equally personal in the way it strikes some but not others. As the Sri Lankan chapter shows, people may be living in the same war, in villages or camps only a few miles apart, but they can have very different experiences of food insecurity. While their geography is close, their access to food may differ greatly. Some may have family members earning army pay. Some may have assets or skills that are in high demand in the war economy and so enable them to survive. Others, just down the road, may have few assets, low value skills and poor social networks that mean they starve.

Several strong messages emerge from this book. One tells of the consistent use of food as a weapon in armed conflict. Hunger has routinely been engineered to defeat the enemy. Famine, hunger and rising food prices have also proved to be a critical rallying point for opposition forces seeking to bring down autocratic regimes.

Another message is about human ingenuity; in people's constant attempts to survive hunger and to humanise it somehow by adding special ingredients to minimal rations, or creating taste in hunger foods that is reminiscent of good times. In the trenches of the First World War, the displaced camps of Sierra Leone, the besieged cities of Croatia and the American barracks of occupied Iraq, people buy, beg, borrow, grow or steal to make food that both feeds and reminds. To lose hearth, these chapters suggest, is to begin to lose heart. A major part of food survival is psychological as well as nutritional. It focuses on recreating hearth as well as health.

The last strong message is how much governments can do if they determinedly set about organising food economies for the common good. Britain's extraordinary rationing programme in the Second World War left the British population with better nutritional status after six years of war than before the conflict started. Today, major advances in food science and the logistical reach of humanitarian aid stop people around the world from starving to death every day. Much of this is funded by governments. But the chapters on terrible failures of government in the Irish famine of the nineteenth century and the Ethiopian famines of the twentieth century show how catastrophic famines can be if governments look the other way.

Each chapter in this book makes clear that food is an extremely important part of any armed conflict, and needs to be respected as a right and a duty in war.

*Hugo Slim*
*Senior Research Fellow*
*Oxford Institute for Ethics, Law and Armed Conflict*
*University of Oxford*

# PREFACE

The editors of this book have long believed that the topic *Food in Zones of Conflict* should be the subject of a cross-disciplinary volume. While researchers, practitioners and writers of international reports tend to concern themselves with the literature and reports of their own academic discipline or professional field, we argue that studying the interaction between food and conflict necessarily involves consideration of factors which are of interest to a number of different specialists. Our ambition is that those interested in the food and nutritional security of those living in zones of conflict would gain a more holistic comprehension of the issues if they were able to read other perspectives encapsulated in one volume.

We are fully aware that our selection of contributors and their subjects of enquiry cannot provide even a fraction of what a complete coverage of this very broad topic would involve. However, we feel that this juxtaposition of a wide range of perspectives demonstrates linkages and provides readers with an introduction to the different angles from which to view the topic. As we expect the book to be of general interest, every effort has been made to ensure that the material in all the chapters is accessible to a broad range of readers. Specialist language has been avoided.

The editors had been able to discuss the issues with experts in different fields of study during two separate meetings. Our thanks, therefore, go to Oxford Brookes University and the International Commission on the Anthropology of Food and Nutrition [ICAF(UK)] for their support of one meeting, and to the Modern East Asian Research Centre (MEARC) at Leiden University for hosting and supporting an international conference, and to all those personnel who helped at both. We wish to acknowledge gratefully a grant from the Wenner Gren Foundation (Grant Number CONF-563), grants from the Netherlands Organisation for Scientific Research (NWO, VIDI Grant Number 276–53–003) and the Japan Foundation (Grant Number 23 RIE-RC-E11035). We thank Kat Mason warmly for help with checking references and assistance with compiling the Index of this volume. Finally, we are deeply grateful to the contributors for their chapters and for graciously responding to our requests and comments.

*PSC and HMM*
*(October 2012)*

# LIST OF CONTRIBUTORS

**Dr. Akinyinka Akinyoade**    African Studies Centre
Leiden University
Leiden
The Netherlands

**Nives Rittig Beljak**    Institute of Ethnology and Folklore Research
Zagreb
Croatia

**Dr.vet. med. Bruno Beljak**    Department of Ethnology and Cultural
Anthropology
Faculty of Humanities and Social studies
University of Zagreb
Zagreb
Croatia

**Felicia Campbell**    Food Studies Department
New York University
New York
United States of America

**Dr. Paul Collinson**    Department of Anthropology
Oxford Brookes University
Oxford
UK

**Dr. Katarzyna Cwiertka**    Institute of Area Studies
Leiden University
Leiden
The Netherlands

**Dr. Daria Deraga**    Department of Biological and Social
Anthropology
National Institute of Anthropology and
History

|                              | Guadalajara, Jalisco |
|                              | Mexico |
| **Dr. Rachel Duffett** | Department of Sociology |
|                              | University of Essex |
|                              | Essex |
|                              | UK |
| **Professor Jeya Henry** | Clinical Nutrition Research Centre |
|                              | Singapore |
| **Dr. Rebecca Kent** | Department of Geographical and Life Sciences |
|                              | Canterbury Christ Church University |
|                              | Canterbury |
|                              | UK |
| **Dr. Lucy Kimaro** | Department of Religious Studies |
|                              | The Catholic University of Eastern Africa |
|                              | Nairobi |
|                              | Kenya |
| **Dr. Helen Macbeth** | Department of Anthropology |
|                              | Oxford Brookes University |
|                              | Oxford |
|                              | UK |
| **Dr. Ellen Messer** | Department of Food Policy and Planning |
|                              | Friedman School of Nutrition Science and Policy |
|                              | Tufts University |
|                              | Boston, MA |
|                              | USA |
| **Dr. Bukola Adeyemi Oyeniyi** | Department of History |
|                              | Missouri State University |
|                              | Springfield, Missouri |
|                              | USA |
| **Dr. Tania Rusca** | Dipartimento di Storia Moderna e Contemporanea |
|                              | Universitá degli Studi di Genova |
|                              | Genova |
|                              | Italy |
| **Professor Susan Shepler** | International Peace and Conflict Resolution |
|                              | School of International Service |
|                              | American University |
|                              | Washington DC |
|                              | USA |

**Dr. Michael J. Strauss**        Centre d'Etudes Diplomatiques et
                                      Stratégiques
                                  Paris
                                  France

**Dr. Benjamin Talton**           Department of History
                                  Temple University
                                  Philadelphia
                                  USA

# INTRODUCTION

*Paul Collinson and Helen Macbeth*

## Overview

Food is essential for human life. Conflict is a persistent aspect of human life, as history shows us and the media remind us daily. This book is about food and conflict. Both are infinitely broad subjects in their own right, with perspectives discussed in many different academic disciplines. Use of the phrase 'food in zones of conflict' reflects a somewhat narrower focus. The contributions collected together in this volume are concerned with food or its scarcity in specific geographical areas in which conflict has taken place in the past or is occurring now.

Conflict here is defined in terms of a confrontation between usually armed combatants, as opposed to a more all-encompassing definition in which conflict is taken to mean almost any disagreement, from intrafamilial discord to broader social tensions which may or may not involve the use of violence or physical force. It was always intended that the scope of this volume should exclude these broader understandings of the term. Of course, armed conflict may frequently arise from such social tensions, but not all social tensions result in armed conflict.

Armed confrontation between groups of people often leads to significant upheavals in the prevailing social order and deleterious impacts on social and economic patterns of everyday life for those living within conflict zones or caught up in conflict in some other way. Despite technological advances in warfare, such as the development of precision munitions and more sophisticated intelligence capabilities, all too often the impact of warfare today is depressingly familiar in its effects on civilians (c.f. Slim 2007; Slim and Mancini-Griffoli 2008). The ability of people to grow or procure their own food is often one of the first activities to be undermined by warfare, because of disruption to the daily lives of a community, because those involved in the fighting require food for themselves, or because the fields or factories that produce food are destroyed or rendered too dangerous to work in. The ability of humanitarian agencies to deliver food is also greatly constrained in conflict zones. To this list should be added the deliberate restriction of food by one side or the other as a weapon of war.

For these reasons, the topic of food in zones of conflict generally implies the existence of some food insecurity in such areas. Although this volume is not exclusively focused on food insecurity, the issue is discussed in a majority of the chapters. However, some chapters are concerned with different aspects of food and armed conflict, such as how the meaning of food can change in the circumstances of war, how this might relate to the psychological responses to war and how food can become a symbol for something beyond its intrinsic subsistence value. How armed conflict impacts upon, and is influenced by, the responses of individuals, communities, governments and armed forces in terms of the production, supply, access to and meaning of food, therefore represents the overarching theme of this book.

## Food Security

Food security is determined by a combination of the availability of, access to and use of food. The relationship between food insecurity and conflict is, of course, one of mutual reinforcement. Conflict contributes greatly to food insecurity; food insecurity causes conflict (c.f. Cohen and Pinstrup-Anderson 1999; Messer and Cohen 2004, 2007; Messer, this volume). This serves to establish a vicious, self-reinforcing circle of conflict, food insecurity and underdevelopment, from which countries find it difficult to escape (Bora *et al.* 2010; Verwimp 2012).

Humanity has achieved some notable successes in improving food security since the 1960s. Food production worldwide has increased by one-third during this period (Nellemann *et al.* 2009: 21), a trend which has been accompanied by a marked decline in the proportion of undernourished[1] people (O'Grada 2009: 2), from around 24 percent of the world's total population in 1975 to around 13 percent today (Food and Agriculture Organization 2011: 44). However, the decline has slowed in the last ten years as the *absolute* number of hungry people has risen, from 791.5 million in 1995–1997 to an estimated 925 million in 2012 (Nellemann *et al.* 2009: 7; Food and Agriculture Organization 2012: 90), which has offset the reductions achieved during the previous two decades. The global statistics also mask significant differences between regions. Two-thirds of the world's undernourished people reside in only eight countries: India, Pakistan, Bangladesh, China, the Democratic Republic of Congo (DRC), Ethiopia and Indonesia. Forty percent live in just China and India. In Sub-Saharan Africa, there has been little progress at all, with the number of undernourished people increasing by 31 percent since the early 1990s and a drop of only four percentage points in the proportion of undernourished people as a percentage of the total population. In several countries, Botswana, Burundi, Gambia, Liberia, Madagascar, Swaziland, Tanzania, Uganda and Zambia, this proportion has increased or, in the case of Kenya, remained the same (Food and Agricultural Organization 2006, 2008, 2010, 2011, 2012).

This volume comes at a period when the international community is facing some very significant challenges in terms of addressing inequalities in access to and sustainability of global food systems. Events which have reversed some of the gains made in previous decades include the rises in global food prices between 2006 and 2008, the worldwide economic downturn since 2009, various natural disasters (most notably the East African and Sahelian droughts) and continuing conflicts in several countries. Moreover, the challenges facing the world are likely to become more pronounced in the coming decades. According to Nellemann *et al.* (2009: 6–7), by 2050, the world's population will have swelled by another 2.7 billion people; in order to feed everyone on the planet, there will need to be a fifty percent increase in global food production. However, the effects of climate change, losses of cropland, increasing urbanisation, water scarcity and environmental degradation, among many other factors, mean that production may fall short by as much as a quarter of the additional demand for food (Nellemann *et al.* 2009). All of these factors, along with a deepening inequality in access to food, are likely to increase instability and make conflict within and between countries more prevalent (Beddington 2009; McDonald 2010).

## Food and Conflict

The nature of conflict has also changed markedly in recent decades. The geopolitical certainties of the Cold War have been replaced by a plethora of localised conflicts, with civil war and internal insurgencies becoming far more important than state-on-state conflict. It is worth noting that at time of writing, with the possible exceptions of 'latent' wars such as that between North and South Korea (still in an official state of war) and the tensions between Russia and Ukraine, globally there are no direct conflicts between states. Instead, wars between countries are fought increasingly by proxy, often using insurgent or non-state actors with asymmetric rather than conventional military tactics. The diffused nature of conflict in this way has heightened the exposure of local populations to its effects, and thereby increased their vulnerability to food stress (Teodosijević 2003).

Armed conflicts, together with natural disasters, present the greatest threats to a population's food security (Sikod 2008; Food and Agriculture Organization 2012: 84). A recent study conducted by Gates *et al.* (2012), examining the effect of armed conflict on progress towards the United Nation's Millennium Development Goals, measured the extent to which conflict hinders development. The research found that an event which causes around 2,500 battle deaths leads in affected populations to, on average, a ten percent increase in infant mortality, a 3.3 percent increase in undernourishment and a reduction in life expectancy of one year. Specific examples of this from around the world are legion. In the case of the civil war in Burundi, which lasted from 1993 to 2005, for example, D'Haese *et al.* (2010: 14) found that between 1996 and 2007 the agricultural productivity of households in two northern provinces fell from over 4,000 to around 1,500 calories per person per day. The authors concluded that the ability of farming families in this region to recover from conflict is very low. In the Central African Republic, the displacement of the population by rebel activities during 2012 meant that many people were unable to cultivate their crops; a study carried out by a non-governmental organisation (NGO) in the north east of the country found that 21 percent of local children were suffering from acute malnutrition after their families had returned home (reported in Green 2012). The civil war in Syria which began in 2010 has greatly affected access to food in many areas of the country, with disruption to supplies (both domestic and imported), endemic unemployment, large numbers of internally displaced people and significant price rises for staples, all contributing to the problem. By October 2013, 5.2 million Syrians – over twenty percent of the country's pre-war population – were receiving assistance from the World Food Programme (WFP) both in Syria itself and in neighbouring countries (World Food Programme 2014b).

In 2010, the Food and Agriculture Organization (FAO) identified twenty-two countries, seventeen of which are in Sub-Saharan Africa, as being in a state of 'protracted crisis', defined as those which had suffered from an extended period of political crisis or conflict, either internally or in confrontation with another country (or countries). These were: Afghanistan, Angola, Burundi, the Central African Republic, Chad, Congo-Brazzaville, Côte d'Ivoire, the DRC, Eritrea, Ethiopia, Guinea, Haiti, Iraq, Kenya, Liberia, North Korea, Sierra Leone, Somalia, Sudan, Tajikistan, Uganda and Zimbabwe (Food and Agriculture Organization 2012: 86). Forty percent of their combined populations were undernourished, and together they accounted for twenty percent of the world's global population of undernourished people (Food and Agriculture Organization 2012: 84). These countries roughly correspond with those classed by the Chronic Poverty Research Centre (CPRC), among others, as 'fragile states' (Chronic Poverty Research Centre 2008, 2010), being those in which there is a close correspondence between the state's inability or unwillingness to deliver basic services to the population, and the levels of poverty (and food insecurity). The CPRC notes that conflict is the principal reason why chronic poverty is so endemic in fragile states (CPRC 2010: 2–3; see also Collinson *et al.* 2008; Jaspars and Maxwell 2009).

The number of forcibly displaced persons in the world was 45.2 million at the end of 2012 (up from 37.5 million in 2005), of whom 15.4 million were refugees, 937,000 were asylum seekers, and 28.8 million were internally displaced persons (International Organisation for Migration 2012; United Nations High Commissioner for Refugees 2013a) – an eighteen-year high. Self-evidently, when people are unable to remain in their own homes, they are unable to grow their own food, whether to consume or to sell, to maintain agricultural self-sufficiency or to plan for the future. For example, the ongoing conflicts in the Central African Republic, Somalia, South Sudan and Sudan have in recent years had a devastating impact on the local populations, with millions of people forced to leave their home areas and go into displacement camps locally or refugee camps in neighbouring countries. There, they usually become entirely dependent on humanitarian aid. With food production in these countries severely curtailed, it will take many years for indigenous populations to re-establish a basis for sustainable livelihoods. Displacement can also cause conflict with the populations of the host area or country, as some recent examples have demonstrated (e.g., Ghimire *et al.* 2010, in the case of Nepal; Porter *et al.* 2008 and Codjoe *et al.* 2013, in the case of Liberian refugees in Ghana; Burns 2010, in the case of Somali refugees in Kenya; Chatty and Mansour 2011, in the case of Iraqi refugees in Syria; and Loveless 2013 in the case of Syrian refugees in Lebanon).

Thus, the reverse relationship, the role of food insecurity in causing conflict, is also a very strong one. One obvious manifestation of this is in the form of food riots, the most recent examples being those which occurred in a number of countries (notably Burkina Faso, Cameroon, Côte d'Ivoire, Egypt, Mauritania, Morocco and Senegal) following the 2007–2008 global food price rises (Brinkman and Hendrix 2011: 7; Lagi *et al.* 2011). In a globalised world, both consumers and producers in developing countries are increasingly vulnerable to shocks in global market prices, and it is likely that the relative significance of this as a trigger for conflict will continue to deepen as globalisation accelerates (Messer and Cohen 2007; Berazneva and Lee 2013). Economics can also play a major role in large-scale internal conflicts. A study of Besley and Persson (2008), for example, demonstrated how the risk of civil war increases as the prices of food imports rise. Similarly, the work of Miguel (Miguel *et al.* 2004; Miguel 2007) highlights the links between fluctuations in economic growth and conflict. The control placed by many governments on food prices, and therefore on availability, is also important; protests in Sudan in 2012 and 2013, for example, were prompted in part by the lifting of government subsidies on a number of key staples. The recent phenomenon of the long-term leasing of agricultural land in developing countries by external companies and countries has introduced another important dimension to the impact of the globalised economic system on food security (see Daniel 2011; Strauss, this volume).

As mentioned above, natural disasters are also likely to lead to food insecurity, and they thereby increase the likelihood of conflict (e.g., Brancati 2007;

Nel and Righarts 2008; Hilhorst 2013). With its link to many individual natural disasters, climate change is surely the most significant environmental problem currently facing the world. The effects of climate change on food insecurity and conflict have been a major research theme over the past decade, and the association between climate change induced environmental stress and civil strife has been demonstrated empirically in numerous different studies (e.g., Homer-Dixon 1991; Nordås and Gleditsch 2007; Raleigh and Urdal 2007; Ingram *et al.* 2010; Akokpari 2012; Hendrix and Salehyan 2012; Scheffran *et al.* 2012). Localised competition over scarce resources – long recognised as an important trigger for warfare (e.g., Ember and Ember 1992) – has also become one of the major factors behind many current conflicts. This is particularly the case in Central and East Africa where violent conflict between tribal groups has been fuelled in part by territorial pressures over cattle grazing. The relationship has been attributed partly to a reduced ability of the population to adapt to environmental pressures, which have resulted in food shortages and rising mortality rates, particularly among women and young children (Gray *et al.* 2003; Jabs 2007; Meier *et al.* 2007, Rowhani *et al.* 2011; Cheserek *et al.* 2012; Njiru 2012; Terefe 2012). In the words of a Sudanese pastoralist, 'when there is food, there is no cattle-raiding' (quoted in Schomerus and Allen 2010: 55).

Another aspect of how conflict has a negative affect on food security is in relation to unexploded ordnance, which reduces the availability of agricultural land to grow crops and presents a risk to those who work in the fields, as discussed by one contribution in this volume. Furthermore, munitions, even from a past era, can also poison the soil, as is the case, for example, due to chemical leakages from disintegrating First World War bombs and mustard gas canisters in Belgium and northern France, or due to radioactivity following the dropping of atomic bombs in Japan and atomic bomb testing in the Pacific Islands.

However, shortage of food *per se* is only one part of the problem. Neo-Malthusian approaches which fail to take into account the importance of socio-political factors underlying food shortages are necessarily missing a critical explanatory element and can therefore be grossly misleading (c.f. Scanlan *et al.* 2010). As Amartya Sen (1981) emphasised over thirty years ago, the relationship between food insecurity and the environment is not a simple one, with the political mechanisms governing food 'entitlement' being more important than the amount of food produced in determining the human impact of shortage and famine. In this way, access to food – who gets what – is, for Sen, always the result of instrumentalist political decisions which prioritise the needs of some groups over others. In Sub-Saharan Africa, such access to food is usually a product of access to land, with land reform programmes instituted by governments often leading to conflict by redistributing land from weaker to more powerful groups, with bureaucratic inefficiency, corruption, human-wildlife conflicts and international political pressure also contributing to perceived injustices (e.g., Peters 2004; Bob 2010). Some commentators argue that the International Criminal Court should recognise the denial of food or the deliberate manipulation of its access and distribution by governments and other organisations as crimes against humanity (e.g., Ratip 2011; see also de Waal 1997, in relation to a similar argument regarding the Geneva Convention).

The critical importance of the relationship between conflict and (under) development was recognised officially by the United Nations (UN) in May 2013, when the UN's High Level Panel on the Post-2015 Development Agenda published its findings (High Level Panel 2013). The panel's report sets forth an agenda for creating peaceful and stable societies as a key to resolving underdevelopment and reducing poverty and food insecurity; it establishes goals for reducing violence, increasing the capacity of countries' security and justice sectors and preventing external shocks. It has been described as a 'milestone' in the creation of a new worldwide development framework (Denney 2013).

## Humanitarian Intervention

It could reasonably be argued that a failure to appreciate fully the relationship between conflict and food insecurity has been a key impediment in the effectiveness of humanitarian and development interventions in the past. This point has been vociferously asserted by de Waal, who has demonstrated how the difficulty of indigenous populations to adapt to new conditions can often be precipitated by poorly thought-out external interventions from governments, international organisations and agencies. His seminal work on the famine in Darfur in 1984, published as *Famine That Kills* (1989) was at once a superbly detailed ethnographic treatment on the causes of famine, highlighting the importance of political factors in triggering it, and an indictment of methods used by external humanitarian actors, which, he contended, often ignore political realities. He took this latter point further in his subsequent work, *Famine Crimes* (1997), in which he argued that the humanitarian 'industry' has contributed to, not solved, the problem, by preventing local populations from developing their own responses to food crises. In his view:

> Humanitarian agencies can be a genuine instrument of change in the international system for responding to large-scale human tragedies. . .[yet] most current humanitarian activity in Africa is useless or damaging and should be abandoned. (de Waal 1997: xvi)

However, the aid and development sectors have improved in the past two decades, and this type of criticism is almost certainly less valid in 2014. There is now a wealth of literature on the policies, doctrines, practices and practicalities of humanitarian intervention, which encompasses a vast range of disciplinary perspectives, not least from the social sciences. One of the reasons for the improvement in the effectiveness of international development and aid strategies is that humanitarian actors are now far more willing to incorporate perspectives offered by social scientists, which prioritise the 'bottom-up' model of development and place a premium on the voices, opinions and needs of local populations (Pottier 1999). The importance of recognising the adaptability of local populations has been highlighted by the UK's Overseas Development Institute, which examined the response of communities to threats to livelihood in Chechnya, Darfur, the Occupied Palestinian Territories (OPT) and Sri Lanka. This research found that in the study locations, local populations had developed several strategies which reduced their exposure to risk and enabled them to remain in their home areas. In terms of food production, this included choosing different crops to cultivate, which required less maintenance and were less likely to be destroyed by armed actors; in the cases of Darfur and the OPT, this included forming self-defence groups and paying for 'protection' (Jaspars 2010; Jaspars and O'Callaghan 2010).

In addition, the vast majority of programmes and projects implemented by international donors, agencies and NGOs are subject to meticulous evaluation of their impact on local populations, with lessons learned fed back into the design of future schemes. Despite the significant advances made in the professionalisation of the aid and development sectors over the past two decades, however, there is still room for improvement in the way international intervention is carried out, as shown by Bell (2008), Messer (2009, this volume) and Anderson *et al.* (2012), among many others (see also, as examples, Anderson 1999; Clover 2003; Barrett and Maxwell 2005; Baro and Deubel 2006; Andrews and Flores 2008).

Part of the problem, of course, is the sheer logistical challenge of operating in conflict zones, with NGO and international agency staff increasingly subject to attack by armed protagonists. According to the Aid Worker Security Database (AWSD), the number of attacks on aid workers worldwide has almost trebled during the past decade, from 63 incidents (affecting 143 workers) in 2003 to 170 (affecting 331 workers) in 2013 (Aid Worker Security Database 2014). A recent case in point was the targeting of Médecins Sans Frontières staff in Somalia in 2013, which led to the charity closing its programmes and withdrawing all its staff from a country where it had been operating continuously since 1991. In Syria, 32 members of the Syrian Arab Red Crescent (SARC) were killed from the beginning of the conflict in 2011 to 2013 (International Committee of the Red Cross 2013). In some cases, humanitarian actors are unable to operate at all because of political constraints – for example, in rebel-controlled areas of southern Sudan and South Sudan.

Finally, a less obvious aspect of the links between food and conflict is in relation to the subsistence of armed protagonists. In the social sciences, this is an under-researched area, although some studies have focused on a historical perspective. This volume contains three contributions on this important topic (see below).

It will be clear from the above discussion that understanding the links between armed conflict, food insecurity, poverty, underdevelopment, humanitarian and developmental intervention, environmental change and political factors is crucial for fully appreciating the issues surrounding food in zones of conflict. This book pursues this objective.

## The Approach of this Book

Social scientists have written extensively about food and conflict (e.g., de Waal 1989, 1997; Richards 1996; Pottier 1999; Alinovi *et al.* 2008; Geissler and Prince 2010; Magdoff and Tokar 2010), but the two subjects have never, as far as we are aware, been combined across so many disciplines in one volume. Yet, as the previous volumes in this series testify, the many perspectives on food, if one is to study the subject fully, make such a multidisciplinary approach essential. One might say the same about conflict.

Food is often studied in the context of development and humanitarian aid and the locations are also frequently zones of conflict; therefore, just as armed conflict creates food insecurity, it also disrupts the delivery of aid. From microscale research on local conflicts and their impact on production and consumption patterns to macro-scale treatments of the international politics of food aid (and food denial), scholarship on this covers a whole range of different disciplinary areas and practitioner methodologies. However, only rarely are these brought together in a multidisciplinary or interdisciplinary manner.

Related to all these aspects of food insecurity are the nutritional and medical effects of hunger and starvation due to conflict. There are articles concerning nutritional conditions and effects in specific historical and contemporary conflict situations, but they are scattered in disparate journals over separate topics, from micronutrient details of specific conditions to mortality, from the care of military personnel to the malnutrition of children. In contrast, some authors (e.g., Young *et al.* 2004; Egal 2006; Rossi *et al.* 2006; Young 2007; Pike *et al.* 2010) have incorporated cross-disciplinary perspectives. Egal (2006) writes of the need for nutritionists to collaborate more with government institutions and NGOs, to review and advise in conflict situations, 'promoting integrated interventions at community level' (2006: S18), while she recognises that this 'would call for a shift from a scientific/dietetic approach to nutrition' (2006: S18).

In the 'softer' social sciences, sociology and social anthropology, conflict is considered as a 'social fact', with civil wars and international armed conflict being viewed in similar terms and studied in similar ways to local conflicts taking place at a community or even family level. Furthermore, social anthropologists and sociologists try to understand the meaning of conflict from the point of view of those affected rather than only from that of the researchers; this provides an added dimension to the perspectives discussed above.

They also consider the symbolic and social roles of food, examining the way in which food can be used as a mechanism to bind communities together, to promote reconciliation, to formulate social identities and to distinguish different groups from one another.

In view of the above, probably the most potent analyses are those which combine perspectives from different theoretical and disciplinary viewpoints, demonstrating the role of environmental, social, political, economic, institutional and governmental factors in triggering food shortages in particular places at particular points in time (c.f. Devereux and Maxwell 2001; Oniang'o 2009; Ogola and Sawe 2013).

This volume includes perspectives from anthropology, sociology, international relations, political science, history, nutrition and religious and development studies. Most chapters are based on empirical research in conflict zones, with some of the authors recounting their own experiences of being caught up in a zone of conflict, either passively, or, in one case, as a member of the armed forces. Other contributions adopt a historical perspective, examining modes of subsistence in past conflicts among civilians and combatants, and the relationships between food, politics and conflict. Taken together, we hope that the sixteen essays collected here do justice to our original aspirations, to demonstrate the benefits of illuminating the topic of food in zones of conflict from several different disciplinary perspectives in order to promote fuller understanding.

Several themes weave through the diverse chapters in this volume. As we have emphasised, one of the most significant topics is food scarcity: this includes the ways in which conflict creates scarcity as well as how scarcity, or even the memory of scarcity, can promote conflict and political change. The relationship between conflict, (under)development and food stress is prominent in several contributions. The nature of food itself is the focus elsewhere, its intrinsic qualities and nutritional value and how it is enculturated from raw to cooked states are subjects examined by a number of the authors. From how to provide and prepare food in conflict situations when ingredients are limited to the role of war in altering subsistence patterns, several chapters highlight the adaptability of human beings in situations of hardship and scarcity. Another theme discussed is the intersection of food and politics and the instrumental use of food – or denial of food – by governments.

Finally, the cultural meaning of food is discussed in many of the essays. The importance of food's symbolic value and its social functions, and how they relate to everyday life is highlighted, which reminds us that the meaning of food often extends far beyond its role in providing subsistence. A theme that runs through several chapters is the way in which the symbolic characteristics of food might alter in conditions of conflict. From the collective remembrance of past famines to 'food wars', in which food is used as a weapon, the meaning of food in a particular context is formed from multiple layers of social and cultural associations which are constantly shifting. This also serves as a reminder that the production and consumption of food are often highly politicised activities exploited by governments and other powerful groups.

## Introducing the Chapters

The basic themes discussed above provide a framework for the contributions to this volume, demonstrating the need for and the benefits of a multidisciplinary approach. While the contributions represent a broad spectrum of perspectives, from the 'hard' to the 'soft' ends of the human sciences and the humanities, and from archival study to the experiences of those 'in the field', we have not attempted to separate the chapters by discipline. This is in order to emphasise how themes discussed above can be discerned from different theoretical angles and within different material, geographic and temporal contexts. We argue strongly that the collection of these diverse perspectives into one volume provides an important contribution to the subject, enabling those interested in any one aspect to gain insight into other dimensions for a more holistic understanding of the issues.

The contributions start with Shepler's 'discovery' of the importance of food in the narratives of her interviewees in Sierra Leone when asked about their experiences during their civil war of the 1990s and early 2000s. 'What emerges', she argues, 'is the centrality of hunger to their experience of the war', a point echoed throughout many of the chapters of this volume. Because Shepler found that food issues had been mentioned so often, her focus is on the meaning of food for local populations during conflict, both its material role as sustenance, and, more importantly, its symbolic meaning, with implications for networks of hierarchy, power and gender, as well as for wider social relations. Shepler demonstrates the way that the war prompted the introduction of innovations in food preparation and consumption, with displaced populations, for example, becoming agents of change when they returned to their home villages (a point also reflected in Beljak and Beljak's chapter in this volume). She concludes by emphasising that it is often the innovation and adaptability of local people which is the most important factor in how countries reconstruct themselves in the post-conflict period, and may assist them in future periods of subsistence stress. Echoing the approach of Alex de Waal (1989, 1997), human adaptability is a key theme that runs through many of the contributions to this volume.

The focus of the following chapter, by Oyeniyi and Akinyoade, is on the impact of unexploded ordnance and mines on food production in Africa, and the often harrowing effects of their accidental detonation. The authors note how many governments in Africa are failing to ratify or implement international treaties which they have signed, and instead continue to stockpile and deploy Anti-Personnel Ordnances (APOs). Drawing on the oral testimonies of civilian victims in Africa, the chapter demonstrates how devastating the impact of APOs can be at individual, family and community levels, and advocates a more concerted international focus on the problem. The impact on food procurement due to danger in accessing fields for cultivation and harvest, identified in this chapter, is reflected elsewhere in this book, as is the international concern about such problems.

The office of the United Nations High Commissioner for Refugees (UNHCR) is one such vehicle of international concern for the victims of conflict. In Chapter 3, Henry and Macbeth show how the nutritional value of food aid for refugee camps has often been inadequate in the past, with some rations for refugees providing less micronutrient value than an average can of pet food in a developed nation. The chapter advocates that as local water sources may be contaminated, there are benefits in providing refugees in camps with ready to use therapeutic foods with well-balanced nutrients which do not require pre-preparation. If these can be produced locally there are not only micronutrient advantages, but also local socioeconomic benefits. Examples of such foods developed by Henry and colleagues are given. The authors conclude by noting the benefits of a holistic approach to interventions such as this, with researchers from different areas of applied human science working together to shape the most appropriate solutions, an argument which reflects a key aim of this volume.

The relevance of international concern is also shown in Chapter 4. The work of a French NGO, Action Contre la Faim, stimulated the research that Kent reports on regarding certain villages of different ethnic composition in conflict-torn north-eastern Sri Lanka. The research includes a detailed analysis of the food available to different households, in order to assist the NGO identify the strategies for moving from aid delivery through rehabilitation to development. Using established evaluation methods she shows that answers could be provided to the basic question of who was hungry, how and why, all of which varied considerably between village communities of different ethnic composition in the study area. In concluding, Kent argues that the research demonstrates that in certain circumstances, interventions which improve the education about food and nutrition may be more effective than those which simply focus on improving health, sanitation and care.

The significance of international concern is again implied in the following chapter by Kimaro, who presents a passionate defence of the role of Christian NGOs in alleviating food insecurity in helping countless thousands of people over recent decades. She reminds us, first of all, how central conflict is in causing food insecurity and ill-health in Sub-Saharan Africa. The chapter uses interview data to examine the relationship between religious practices and food sustainability, and, by interweaving the testimonies of her informants with the main themes of her essay, she argues that a decline in traditional religious beliefs is reducing local mechanisms for conflict resolution and so contributes to subsistence stress in a number of ways.

As in Chapters 4 and 5, Chapters 6 and 7 are about the effects of internal conflict on food security in a specific geographic area. Deraga describes a situation in northern Mexico and along the border with the US where ongoing drug wars have had a seriously deleterious effect on livestock production and lifestyles in general. Acknowledging the difficulties of generating statistics concerning this problem, the author uses an ethnographic approach to describe how cattle ranchers and horse breeders have been finding increasing difficulties in transporting livestock to markets both within Mexico and across the border into or from the US. Thefts of livestock on ranches and during transport have become more common. Furthermore, the growing instability in the region in recent years has led to a rise in personal violence against local food producers and retailers.

The following chapter by two Croatian anthropologists, Beljak and Beljak, provides an interesting insiders' perspective on the effects of conflict on food consumption. The principal focus for their essay is on the impact of the war in the Balkans during the 1990s on the Croatian population, and the responses of the latter to increasing food stress and water shortages. This included relearning methods of food preparation used in earlier times, and adopting some new dietary regimes to cope with a shortage of staple foods. The authors pay particular attention to the importance of bread in the traditional Croatian diet, not only for its role in subsistence, but also for its symbolic relationship with 'home and hearth'. With a shortage of yeast, the population was forced to adopt new, alien methods of preparing bread or bread substitutes. This chapter again reminds us of the resilience and adaptability of human beings in conditions of drastic change, such as occur during wars and other conflicts.

The effects of war on food consumption and life patterns are also exemplified in Lightowler and Macbeth's chapter on feeding the British population during the Second World War, and the often-reported beneficial nutritional consequences of government intervention at all levels, including the rationing introduced in 1940. The authors begin by detailing the measures introduced by the Ministries of Food and of Agriculture, planned before the food shortages became significant. Encouraged by the government's 'Dig for Victory' campaign, abandoned farmland, public and private gardens, railway land and embankments, verges, etc., as well as pre-existing allotments, were cultivated for food. A complete governmental reorganisation of the provision and distribution of food had been planned, with the then recent scientific understanding of nutrition firmly included in the holistic overview. Lightowler and Macbeth explore how successful this policy was as regards the general nutrition and health of the whole British population during the war years and consider if there have been subsequent health effects.

Governmental provisioning is also fundamental to the next three chapters, which consider the provision of food to military personnel deployed in foreign locations during the twentieth century. In Chapter 9, basing her research on data such as letters home from the front, Duffett focuses on soldiers' rations during the First World War. Although she compares these favourably with those of the French or German soldiers, she comments on the difficulties in some situations and the limited understanding at the time of micronutrients and not just calories. Her essay represents an important contribution to the understanding of how the British infantry fighting on the Western Front supplemented their rations by sourcing other means of subsistence. One of the most common ways they achieved this was through 'scrounging' from the local environment and the local population. Soldiers also received parcels from their families in Britain, which represented both an important source of additional food and an emotional reminder of home. Furthermore, Duffett notes the significance of the rituals surrounding the procurement, sharing and consumption of food in helping to forge strong bonds between the soldiers themselves.

In Chapter 10, Cwiertka draws on her archival research on the experiences of US and Japanese troops fighting in the Pacific during the Second World War. She compares the official subsistence regimes of each country's armed forces, whereby the distribution to US forces was centred in the US, whereas the Japanese army relied far more on locally sourced food, wherever their forces were based, supplementing rations erratically from Japan. The latter became very unreliable, particularly towards the end of the war, leading to food shortages among the Japanese army to the point of starvation; it is estimated that more than half of the Japanese soldiers who died between 1937 and 1945 died from malnutrition or starvation. Cwiertka cites a diary entry from a Japanese soldier revealing that starving Japanese troops resorted to cannibalism of the bodies of dead US soldiers. The role of the 'PX' system in providing US troops with a comforting 'taste of home', even at the Front Line, is compared with the Japanese *Shuho* facilities with a similar objective. Since both armies supplemented their rations with 'enemy food', this chapter, as with earlier chapters, draws attention to cultural changes in food habits engendered by war.

As Chapter 11 starts 'I remember', we are immediately introduced to a forceful, personal account of the experience of military provisioning, the symbolic role of food and the acquisition of change. Campbell was deployed with the US Army's 101st Airborne Division in the early days of the Iraq War in 2003, and is now conducting research on Iraqi cuisine and national identity. She describes the dry ration packs provided to the US armed forces in Iraq and how, despite their balanced nutritional value, she and her fellow soldiers quickly became bored with the monotonous and processed nature of their contents. This led them to explore and develop a taste for the local cuisine, which Campbell describes as becoming a 'craving' for basic Iraqi foods, such as chicken and flatbread. In a highly thoughtful passage, Campbell describes how this established feelings of what might be described as 'cognitive dissonance' on the part of herself and her colleagues, as they consumed the cuisine of a conceptually dehumanised 'enemy'. Food became an agent of changed attitudes, as through food the humanity of the Iraqi people was revealed. Drawing on interview data, Campbell also details the way that this taste for

Iraqi food lingered among veterans after they had returned to the US, sometimes to civilian life. Her concluding comment that 'war is filled with many paradoxes' is one which is reflected in several chapters in this book.

The more deliberate use of food in attempts to influence attitudes is the theme of Chapter 12, as Rusca recounts how memories of famine were manipulated in political posters during the Weimar Republic in Germany (1919–1933). Rusca shows how the propaganda of different political factions used food extensively in their visual and textual imagery to support the objectives of their party, either by instilling fear with warnings of a return to starvation with the policies of their opponents, or by suggesting hope and food through the benefits of their own policies, as well as exhortations to work and not strike. Rusca uses detailed content analysis of the political posters at the time to demonstrate how this policy was put into practice, and how sophisticated some of these posters were in playing on the population's psychological vulnerabilities. Her chapter highlights how food can be of great political importance, especially when memories of famine and severe malnutrition are played upon. As other contributors to this volume have noted, she refers in her conclusion to the use of food and concepts about food as a weapon of war.

That past famine can be a powerful political symbol and a focus for galvanising political rhetoric is also demonstrated in Chapter 13 by Collinson. He examines the role of the Irish Famine of the 1840s in creating the social and political upheavals in Ireland during the nineteenth and early twentieth centuries, as well as its legacy today. Tracing the changes wrought in the Irish diet by the Famine, the author considers the important relationship between subsistence, land ownership and political change, which was brought together instrumentally by the Irish Land League in the latter half of the nineteenth century, leading to conflict with landlords and the British government. Drawing on his fieldwork in Ireland, Collinson goes on to discuss what this historic Famine means to the present-day population, noting the way in which recent memorial events have been used as a way of reconciling formerly divided communities. In the final section of the chapter, the use of partisan images from the Famine in Republican murals in Northern Ireland is contrasted with the current role of food used in promoting cross-border development on the isle of Ireland.

The political use of publicising famine and hunger is central to Chapter 14 by Talton, which highlights the important relationship between food stress and political change. His chapter focuses on Ethiopia during the early 1970s, and specifically the way in which the famine in 1972–1974, which killed an estimated 40,000 to 60,000 people, galvanised political protest within the student movement in Ethiopia and abroad against Emperor Haile Selassie's government. While the government prioritised the delivery of food to urban areas and even food exports, exacerbating the lack of access to food among rural communities, the Ethiopian students intervened directly to provide food aid to the starving. The student movement thereby created the political space which was then usurped by the armed forces to manoeuvre against the government, leading to the coup of 1974 and then the overthrow of the monarchy. As Talton states, 'hunger . . . served as the cornerstone of Ethiopia's revolution', but he also shows how attitudes from outside Ethiopia played a significant role.

In the following chapter, Michael Strauss is also concerned with how external conditions can affect the potential for conflict in or between nations. He details a relatively recent macro-level response to potential food stress, which has significant implications for international relations, that of land leasing. This phenomenon involves multinational corporations or national governments taking over vast areas of agricultural land, largely in Africa, in order to protect the long-term food security of the lease-holding nation. In 2010, there were reportedly 177 such arrangements covering 27 African countries. Strauss convincingly emphasises the dangers of land leasing in this way, where there is no transfer of sovereignty, and yet the territories leased may come to be viewed as *de facto* territory of the lease-holding nation. In a conflict situation, this introduces the possibility of a third country being drawn into a conflict between two nation states in order to protect its own investments. Strauss provides an example of the way in which the South Korean corporation, Daewoo, was involved in an arrangement in 2008 which would have leased up to half of Madagascar's cultivable agricultural land for 99 years, in return for payments and investments of up to US$6 billion. A coup in Madagascar prevented the deal going ahead, in which Strauss speculates that North Korea may have had a role.

Because of its interdisciplinarity, we use as our concluding chapter of this volume the broad and detailed coverage of the topic by Messer, who emphasises the important role that anthropologists can play in understanding and promoting the complex ways in which food, agriculture and conflict are interconnected with social, geographic, political, economic, ethnic and religious factors and forces operating at regional and global levels. She draws on her extensive research on western development policies and responses to food insecurity to provide a critique of the approaches adopted by global institutions and aid agencies, focusing in particular on the concept of 'food wars'. These she defines as 'situations of organised armed political violence where combatants on one or both sides use hunger as a weapon, and where destruction of farming populations, infrastructure, waterworks and markets results in disruptions to agricultural production, food markets, health services and human nutrition long after formal fighting had ceased'. While this definition covers aspects in every one of the preceding chapters of this volume, her own chapter contains detailed information on the efforts to provide aid by different organisations, constantly reminding readers of the need for attention to the full context of each situation. She notes that the WFP and the FAO are moving towards a model that marries development and relief, emphasising the establishment of sustainable modes of livelihood as well as the delivery of aid.

## Conflicts Continue

Time has passed since we had the initial idea for this volume, and during that time several new conflicts have emerged around the world.

*In Mali*, a Tuareg rebellion in the north of the country and a coup among the country's armed forces was exploited by Islamists, who captured several towns during 2012. A further advance south towards the capital Bamako in early 2013 prompted a French military intervention, which succeeded in ousting the Islamists from their urban strongholds, and enabled the delivery of aid to the population, which had been internally displaced due to the instability. The WFP described the humanitarian situation in Mali as 'critical' in April 2013, with twenty percent of households in the northern areas of the country facing extreme food shortages (World Food Programme 2013).

*In the Central African Republic*, to the south east, a rebel coalition overthrew the government of François Bozizé in March 2013 after advancing from the north east of the country. The coalition was itself ousted from power when its leader, Michel Djotodia, was persuaded to step down by regional leaders in January 2014. The country experienced an almost complete breakdown in law and order during 2013. Over 465,000 internally displaced persons and refugees have been created as a consequence, with a concomitant rise in demand for food aid and pressures on surrounding countries; around half of the population are in need of humanitarian assistance. The targeting of Muslim populations by militia groups during 2014 has been described as 'ethnic cleansing' by Amnesty International (2014). A French and African force was deployed to the country in 2013 to help stabilise the security situation.

*In Sudan*, continuing violence in the border region with South Sudan, since the latter's secession in 2011, has created an estimated 300,000 refugees who are residing in camps in South Sudan, Kenya and Ethiopia, and has forced a further 250,000 to leave their homes. These problems are compounded by the limited humanitarian access in parts of southern Sudan. Meanwhile, the conflict in Sudan's Darfur region has intensified in 2013 and 2014, adding to the already substantial aid-dependent population, estimated to amount to around 1.5 million people (Department for International Development 2013).

*In South Sudan*, conflict between different sections of the armed forces erupted in December 2013 and led to a significant humanitarian crisis in the country. As of March 2014, 932,000 people had been forced from their homes and were internally displaced or residing as refugees in, primarily, Ethiopia, Kenya, Sudan or Uganda (UNICEF 2014). Three million people, almost a third of the population, were estimated to be food insecure (United Nations News Centre 2014), with the rainy season in 2014 predicted to add to this number

and complicate the delivery of aid. The speed at which the crisis emerged
provides a stark illustration of the impact of armed conflict on already vulnerable populations.

*In Syria*, the most serious crisis over the past two years has once again focused
the world's attention on the Middle East. The civil war in Syria has torn the
country apart and had an enormous impact on the population. As of March
2014, 2.5 million people were living as refugees in surrounding countries,
with around 4.3 million internally displaced, figures which together represent
over one third of the country's pre-war population (United Nations High
Commissioner for Refugees 2014); around 9 million people required humanitarian assistance (Guardian 2014). The situation has been described by the
United Nations High Commissioner for Refugees, António Guterre, as 'a
disgraceful humanitarian calamity with suffering and displacement unparal-
leled in recent history'. It is probably the most significant crisis international
agencies and NGOs have faced since the end of the Cold War, the effects
of which will be felt for several generations to come (United Nations High
Commissioner for Refugees 2013b; Guardian 2013a; Guardian 2013b).

To these conflicts many others could be added, for example the serious
riots in Venezuela in early 2014 over high inflation and shortage of staple
foods, continuing violence and food deprivation in Iraq (United Nations
Development Programme 2013), and the situation in Afghanistan, where over
a quarter of the population faced crisis or emergency levels of food insecurity
in November 2013 (World Food Programme 2014a).

## Conclusion

Despite the huge challenges which the global community faces in alleviating
the suffering of the populations affected by conflict, Shepler's chapter at the
start of this volume, applied on a broader scale, may be viewed as something
of a beacon of hope for humanity in coming years. Innovation – scientific,
technical, agricultural, developmental, socioeconomic and, critically, political – will hopefully hold the key to overcoming many of the threats to human
food security, as it has in previous decades. It is worth reminding ourselves of
the tremendous progress which has been forged over the past thirty years or
more in reducing poverty and hunger throughout the world; innovation has
played a critical role in this. However, the international community must work
as much as possible with local populations, recognising the latter's inherent
adaptability and resourcefulness, rather than attempting to impose scientific
and technical solutions from above, as has happened too often in the past.

Yet, there is also the argument that the growing environmental pressures
caused by climate change are so great that they have the potential to undermine or even wipe out the gains of recent years – not least because they may

well significantly increase levels of conflict around the world (c.f. Burke *et al.* 2009). Nevertheless, of the different forms of innovation which are likely to be needed, political innovation, with sound leadership, could be the most pressing and the most important in terms of suppressing future levels of conflict.

Many of the contributions collected together in this volume emphasise the relationship between political contexts and actions and the food security of human populations. This relationship can be deleterious – as in Ethiopia in the 1970s, Bosnia in the 1990s or in parts of Sub-Saharan Africa today – or positive, as in the case of Britain's rationing programme during the Second World War. Political innovation and leadership will undoubtedly be required in the coming decades at a global level, so that a more concerted effort from governments and international organisations can be achieved to address inequalities in food access, which, as they deepen, have the potential to exacerbate existing conflicts, cause new ones to emerge, and, perhaps in time, threaten the future of us all.

## Note

1   Undernourishment is defined in terms of a minimum calorific energy intake relative to size and body weight (Food and Agriculture Organization 2011: 51, no 2).

## References

Aid Worker Security Database (AWSD) (2014) *Major attacks on aid workers: Summary statistics (2003–2013)*. Published at: https://aidworkersecurity.org/incidents/report/summary. Accessed on 16th March 2014.

Akokpari, J. (2012) Environmental Degradation and Human Insecurity in Sub-Saharan Africa, *Journal of Human Security*, 8(1): 24–46.

Alinovi, L., Hemrich, G. and Russo, L. (2008) *Food Security in Protracted Crisis*, Practical Action Publishing, Rugby.

Amnesty International (2014) Central African Republic: Ethnic cleansing and sectarian killings, *Amnesty International News*. Published at https://www.amnesty.org/en/news/central-african-republic-ethnic-cleansing-sectarian-violence-2014–02–12. Accessed on 18th March, 2014.

Anderson, M.B. (1999) *Do No Harm. How Aid Can Support Peace – Or War?*, Lynne Rienner, Boulder, Colorado.

Anderson, M.B., Brown, D. and Jean, I. (2012) *Time to Listen: Hearing People on the Receiving End of International Aid*, CDA Collaborative Learning Projects, Cambridge, Massachusetts.

Andrews, C. and Flores, M. (2008) *Vulnerability to Hunger: Improving Food Crisis Responses in Fragile States*, United Nations University Research Paper No. 2008/42 UNU Wider, Helsinki.

Barbieri, K., and Levy, J. S. (1999) Sleeping with the Enemy: The Impact of War on Trade. *Journal of Peace Research*, 36(4): 463–479.

Baro, M. and Deubel, T.F. (2006) Persistent Hunger: Perspectives on Vulnerability, Famine, and Food Security in Sub-Saharan Africa, *Annual Review of Anthropology*, 35: 521–538.

Barrett, C.B. and Maxwell, D.G. (2005) *Food Aid After Fifty Years: Recasting Its Role*, Routledge, Oxford.

Beddington, J. (2009) Food security: contributions from science to a new and greener revolution, *Philosophical Transactions of the Royal Society (Biological Sciences)*, 365 (1537): 61–71.

Bell, E. (2008) The World Bank in Fragile and Conflict-Affected Countries. 'How', Not 'How Much', *International Alert*. Published at: http://www.international-alert.org/sites/default/files/publications/WBank_in_fragile_and_conflict-affected_c.pdf. Accessed on 4th March 2014.

Berazneva, J. and Lee, D.R. (2013) Explaining the African Food Riots of 2007–2008: An Empirical Analysis, *Food Policy*, 39: 28–39.

Besley, T. and Persson, T. (2008) *The Incidence of Civil War: Theory and Evidence*, National Bureau of Economic Research Working Paper No. 14585, Cambridge, Massachusetts.

Bob, U. (2010) Land-related conflicts in Sub-Saharan Africa, *African Journal of Conflict Resolution*, 10(2): 49–64.

Bora, S., Ceccacci, I., Delgado, C. and Townsend, R. (2010) Food Security and Conflict, *World Development Report 2011 Background Paper*, Agriculture and Rural Development Department, World Bank, Washington, D.C.

Brancati, D. (2007) Political Aftershocks: The Impact of Earthquakes on Intrastate Conflict, *Journal of Conflict Resolution*, 51(5): 715–743.

Brinkman, H.-J. and Hendrix, C.S. (2011) *Food Insecurity and Violent Conflict: Causes, Consequences, and Addressing the Challenges*, Occasional Paper no 24, World Food Programme.

Burke, M., Satyanath, S., Dykema, J. and Lobell, D. (2009) Warming increases risk of civil war in Africa, *Proceedings of the National Academy of Sciences*, 106(49): 20670–20674.

Burns, A. (2010) Feeling the Pinch: Kenya, Al-Shabaab, and East Africa's Refugee Crisis, *Refuge: Canada's Journal on Refugees*, 27(1): 5–15.

Chatty, D. and Mansour, N. (2011) Unlocking Protracted Displacement: An Iraqi Case Study, *Refugee Survey Quarterly*, 30(4): 50–83.

Cheserek, G.J., Omondi, P. and Odenyo, V.A.O. (2012) Nature and Causes of Cattle Rustling among some Pastoral Communities in Kenya, *Journal of Emerging Trends in Economics and Management Sciences (JETEMS)*, 3(2): 173–179.

Chronic Poverty Research Centre (CPRC) (2008) *The Chronic Poverty Report 2008–9*, CPRC, Manchester.

Chronic Poverty Research Centre (CPRC) (2010) Fragile States, Conflict and Chronic Poverty, *Policy Brief*, 24, CPRC, Manchester.

Clover, J. (2003) Food Security in Sub-Saharan Africa, *Africa Security Review*, 12(1): 5–15.

Codjoe, S.N.A., Quartey, P., Tagoe, C.A. and Reed, H.E. (2013) Perceptions of the Impact of Refugees on Host Communities: The Case of Liberian Refugees in Ghana, *Journal of International Migration and Integration*, 14(3): 439–456.

Cohen, M. and Pinstrup-Anderson, P. (1999) Food Security and Conflict, *Social Research*, 66(1): 375–416.

Collinson, S., Elhawary, S. and Muggah, R. (2008). States of fragility: stabilisation and its implications for humanitarian action, *Humanitarian Policy Group Working Paper*, Overseas Development Institute, London.

Daniel, S. (2011) Land Grabbing and Potential Implications for Global Food Security. In Behnassi, M., Shahid, S.A. and D'Silva, J. (eds) *Sustainable Agricultural Development*, Springer, The Hague: 25–42.

Denney, L. (2013) *Consulting the Evidence. How Conflict and Violence Can Best Be Included in the Post 2015 Development Agenda*, Overseas Development Institute, London. Published at http://www.odi.org.uk/sites/odi.org.uk/files/odi-assets/public ations-opinion-files/8486.pdf. Accessed on 4th March 2014.

Department for International Development (2013) *Featherstone: Breaking Darfur's dependency on aid*. Published at: https://www.gov.uk/government/news/featherstone-breaking-darfur-s-dependency-on-aid. Accessed on 27th April 2013.

Devereux, S. and Maxwell, S. (2001) *Food and Security in Sub-Saharan Africa*, Intermediate Technology Development Group (ITDG), London.

de Waal, A. (1989, 2005) *Famine That Kills: Darfur, Sudan*, Oxford Studies in African Affairs, Oxford University Press, Oxford.

de Waal, A. (1997) *Famine Crimes. Politics and the Disaster Relief Industry in Africa*, James Conway, Oxford.

D'Haese, M.F.C., Speelman, S., Vandamme, E., Nkunzimana, T., Ndimubandi, J. and D'Haese, L. (2010) *Recovering from conflict: an analysis of food production in Burundi*. Poster presented at the Joint 3rd African Association of Agricultural Economists (AAAE) and 48th Agricultural Economists Association of South Africa (AEASA) Conference, Cape Town, South Africa, September 19–23, 2010. Published at: http://purl.umn.edu/96829. Accessed on 4th March 2014.

Egal, F. (2006) Nutrition in Conflict Situations, *British Journal of Nutrition*, 96 Suppl.1: S17–S19.

Ember, C.R. and Ember, M. (1992) Resource Unpredictability, Mistrust, and War. A Cross-Cultural Study, *Journal of Conflict Resolution*, 36(2): 242–262.

Food and Agricultural Organization (2006) *The State of Food Insecurity in the World 2006*, Food and Agricultural Organization of the United Nations, Rome.

Food and Agricultural Organization (2008) *The State of Food Insecurity in the World 2008*, Food and Agricultural Organization of the United Nations, Rome.

Food and Agricultural Organization (2010) *The State of Food Insecurity in the World 2010*, Food and Agricultural Organization of the United Nations, Rome.

Food and Agricultural Organization (2011) *The State of Food Insecurity in the World 2011: How does international price volatility affect domestic economies and food security?* Food and Agricultural Organization of the United Nations, Rome.

Food and Agricultural Organization (2012) *FAO Statistical Yearbook 2012*, Food and Agricultural Organization of the United Nations, Rome.

Gates, S., Hegre, H., Nygård, H.M. and Strand, H. (2012) Development Consequences of Armed Conflict, *World Development*, 40(9): 1713–1722.

Geissler, P.W. and Prince, R.J. (2010) *The Land is Dying. Contingency, Creativity and Conflict in Western Kenya*, Berghahn, Oxford.

Ghimire, A., Upreti, B.R. and Pokharel, S. (2010) Livelihood strategies of internally displaced people in Western Nepal: Some observations. In Upreti, B.R. and Müller-Boker. U. (eds) *Livelihood Insecurity and Social Conflict in Nepal*, Kathmandu: South Asia Regional Coordination Office, Swiss National Centre of Competence in Research (NCCR), North-South Kathmandu, Nepal: 217–256.

Gray, S., Sundal, M., Weibusch, B., Little, M.A., Leslie, P.W. and Pike, I.L. (2003) Cattle-raiding, cultural survival, and adaptability of East African pastoralists, *Current Anthropology*, 44 Supplement: S3–S30.

Green, A. (2012) The Central African Republic's Silent Health Crisis, *The Lancet*, 380 (9846): 964–965.

Guardian newspaper (2013a) Wars push number of internally displaced people to record levels. Published at: http://www.guardian.co.uk/global-development/2013/apr/29/record-levels-internally-displaced-people. Accessed on 1st May 2013.

Guardian newspaper (2013b) Half of Syrian population 'will need aid by the end of the year'. Published at: http://www.guardian.co.uk/world/2013/apr/19/half-syrian-population-aid-year. Accessed on 1st May 2013.

Guardian newspaper (2014) Syria crisis: what we've learned three years on. Published at: http://www.theguardian.com/global-development/guardianwitness-blog/2014/mar/14/syria-crisis-what-weve-learned-three-years-on. Accessed on 16th March 2014.

Hendrix, C.S. and Salehyan, I. (2012) Climate change, Rainfall, and Social Conflict in Africa, *Journal of Peace Research*, 49(1): 35–50.

High Level Panel of Eminent Persons on the Post-2015 Development Agenda (2013) A New Global Partnership: Eradicate Poverty and Transform Economies Through Sustainable Development. The Report of the High Level Panel of Eminent Persons on the Post-2015 Development Agenda. United Nations Publications, New York. Published at: http://www.post2015hlp.org/wp-content/uploads/2013/05/UN-Report.pdf. Accessed on 4th March 2014.

Hilhorst, D. (2013) Disaster, conflict and society in crises: everyday politics of crisis response. In Hilhorst, D. (ed.) *Disaster, conflict and society in crises: Everyday politics of crisis response*, Routledge, Abingdon: 1–16.

Homer-Dixon T.F. (1991) On the threshold: environmental changes as causes of acute conflict, *International Security*, 16: 76–116.

Ingram, J., Ericksen, P. and Liverman, D. (eds) (2010) *Food Security and Global Environmental Change*, Earthscan, London.

International Committee of the Red Cross (2013) The International Red Cross and Red Crescent Movement deplores the death of another aid worker in Syria. Published at: http://www.icrc.org/eng/resources/documents/statement/2013/11–18-syria-death-aid-worker.htm. Accessed on 16th March 2014.

International Organisation for Migration (2012) *Facts and Figures*. Published electronically at: http://www.iom.int/jahia/Jahia/about-migration/facts-and-figures/lang/en.

Jabs, L. (2007) Where Two Elephants Meet, the Grass Suffers: A Case Study of Intractable Conflict in Karamoja, Uganda, *American Behavioral Scientist*, 50(11): 1498–1519.

Jaspars, S. (2010) Coping and change in protracted conflict: The role of community groups and local institutions in addressing food insecurity and threats to livelihoods. A case study based on the experience of Practical Action in North Darfur, *Humanitarian Policy Group Working Paper*, Overseas Development Institute, London.

Jaspars, S. and Maxwell, D. (2009). Food security and livelihoods programming in conflict: a review, *Humanitarian Practice Network*, Paper 65, Overseas Development Institute, London.

Jaspars, S. and O'Callaghan, S. (2010). *Challenging choices: protection and livelihoods in conflict*, HPG Policy Brief 40, Overseas Development Institute, London.

Lagi, M., Bertrand, K.Z. and Bar-Yam, Y. (2011) *The Food Crises and Political Instability in North Africa and the Middle East*, Social Science Research Network Working Paper (15 August 2011). Published at: http://papers.ssrn.com/sol3/papers.cfm?abstract_id=1910031 or http://dx.doi.org/10.2139/ssrn.1910031. Accessed on 4th March 2014.

Loveless, J. (2013) Crisis in Lebanon: camps for Syrian refugees? *Crisis*, May 2013: 66–68.

McDonald, B.L. (2010) *Food Security*, Polity Press, Cambridge.

Magdoff, F. and Tokar, B. (2010) *Agriculture and Food in Crisis: Conflict, Resistance and Renewal*, Monthly Review Press, New York.

Meier, P., Bond, D. and Bond, J. (2007) Environmental influences on pastoral conflict in the Horn of Africa, *Political Geography*, 26: 719–735.

Messer, E. (2009) Rising Food Prices, Social Mobilizations, and Violence: Conceptual Issues in Understanding and Responding to the Connections Linking Hunger and Conflict, *NAPA Bulletin*, 32: 12–22.

Messer, E. and Cohen, M. J. (2004) *Breaking the links between conflict and hunger in Africa*, 2020 vision briefs 10, International Food Policy Research Institute (IFPRI), Washington D.C.

Messer, E. and Cohen, M. J. (2007) Conflict, Food Insecurity and Globalisation. *Food, Culture and Society* 10(2): 297–315.

Miguel, E. (2007) Poverty and Violence: An Overview of Recent Research and Implications for Foreign Aid. In Brainard, L. and Chollet, D. (eds) *Too Poor for Peace? Global Poverty, Conflict and Security in the 21st Century*, Brookings Institution Press, Washington D.C.: 50–59.

Miguel, E., Satyanath, S. and Sergenti, E. (2004) Economic Shocks and Civil Conflict: an Instrumental Variables Approach, *Journal of Political Economy*, 114(4): 725–753.

Nel, P. and Righarts, M. (2008) Natural Disasters and the Risk of Violent Civil Conflict, *International Studies Quarterly*, 52(1): 159–185.

Nellemann, C., MacDevette, M., Manders, T., Eickhout, B., Svihus, B., Prins, A.G., Kaltenborn, B.P. (eds) (2009) *The Environmental Food Crisis – The Environment's Role in Averting Future Food Crises*, A UNEP rapid response assessment, United Nations Environment Programme, New York.

Njiru, B.N. (2012) Climate Change, Resource Competition, and Conflict amongst Pastoral Communities in Kenya, *Climate Change, Human Security and Violent Conflict*, 8: 513–527.

Nordås, R. and Gleditsch, N.P. (2007) Climate change and conflict, *Political Geography*, 26: 627–638.

O'Grada, C. (2009) *Famine: A Short History*, Princeton University Press, Princeton, New Jersey.

Ogola, T. and Sawe, J. (2013) The Origins of the Food Crisis: The Case of East Africa. In Scherrer, C. and Saha, D. (eds) *The Food Crisis: Implications for Labor*, Rainer Hampp Verlag, Munich.

Oniang'o, R. (2009) *Food and Nutrition Emergencies in East Africa. Political, Economic and Environmental Associations*, International Food Policy Research Institute Discussion Paper 00909.

Peters, P.E. (2004) Inequality and social conflict over land in Africa, *Journal of Agrarian Change*, 4(3): 269–314.

Pike, I.L., Straight, B., Oesterle, M., Hilton, C. and Lanyasunya, A. (2010) Documenting the health consequences of endemic warfare in three pastoralist communities of northern Kenya: a conceptual framework, *Social Science and Medicine*, 70(1): 45–52.

Porter, G., Hampshire, K., Kyei, P., Adjaloo, M., Rapoo, G. and Kilpatrick, K. (2008) Linkages between Livelihood Opportunities and Refugee–Host Relations: Learning from the Experiences of Liberian Camp-based Refugees in Ghana, *Journal of Refugee Studies*, 21(2): 230–252.

Pottier, J. (1999) *The Social Dynamics of Food Security*, Polity Press, Cambridge.

Raleigh, C. and Urdal, H. (2007) Climate change, environmental degradation and armed conflict, *Political Geography*, 26: 674–694.

Ratip, M. (2011) African Lessons for the International Criminal Court: 'Give us Food. You are our King, but if you don't feed us properly we will get rid of you', *Studies in Ethnicity and Nationalism*, 11(1): 143–148.

Richards, P. (1996) *Fighting for the Rain Forest: War, Youth, and Resources in Sierra Leone*, James Currey, Oxford.

Rossi, L., Hoerz, T., Thouvenot, V., Pastore, G. and Michael, M. (2006) *Public Health Nutrition*, 9(5): 551–556.

Rowhani, P., Degomme, O., Guha-Sapir, D. and Lambin, E.F. (2011) Malnutrition and conflict in East Africa: the impacts of resource variability on human security, *Climatic Change*, 105 (1–2): 207–222.

Scanlan, S.J., Jenkins, J.C. and Peterson, L. (2010) The Scarcity Fallacy, *Contexts*, 9(1): 34–39.

Scheffran, J., Brzoska, M., Brauch, H.G., Link, P.M. and Schilling, J. (eds) (2012) *Climate Change, Human Security and Violent Conflict. Challenges for Societal Stability*, Springer-Verlag, Heidelberg.

Schomerus, M. and Allen, T. (2010) *Southern Sudan at Odds with Itself: Dynamics of Conflict and Predicaments of Peace*, Development Studies Institute, London School of Economics, London.

Sen, A. (1981) *Poverty and Famines. An Essay on Entitlement and Deprivation*, Oxford University Press, Oxford.

Sikod, F. (2008) Conflicts and Implications for Poverty and Food Security Policies in Africa. In Nhema, A. and Tiyambe Zeleza P. (eds) *The Roots of African Conflicts*, James Currey, Oxford: 199–213.

Slim, H. (2007) *Killing Civilians: Method, Morality and Madness in War*, Hurst and Co., London.

Slim, H. and Mancini-Griffoli, D. (2008) *Interpreting Violence: Anti-civilian thinking and practice and how to argue against it more effectively*, Centre for Humanitarian Dialogue, Geneva.

Teodosijević, S.B. (2003) *Armed Conflicts and Food Security*. ESA Working Paper No. 03–11. Food and Agriculture Organization, Rome.

Terefe, H.A. (2012) *People in Crises: Tackling the Root Causes of Famine in the Horn of Africa*, Norwegian Agricultural Economics Research Institute, Oslo.

United Nations Development Programme (2013) Helping 6 million Iraqis vulnerable to food insecurity. Published at: http://www.iq.undp.org/content/iraq/en/home/presscenter/pressreleases/2013/06/05/helping-6-million-iraqis-vulnerable-to-food-insecurity/. Accessed on 22nd March 2014.

United Nations High Commissioner for Refugees (2013a) *Displacement. The New Global Challenge. Global Trends 2012*. UNHCR, Geneva. Published at: http://unhcr. org/globaltrendsjune2013/UNHCR%20GLOBAL%20TRENDS%202012_V05. pdf. Accessed on 4th March 2014.

United Nations High Commissioner for Refugees (2013b) *Number of Syrian refugees tops two million mark with more on the way*. UNHCR, Geneva. Published at: http:// www.unhcr.org/522495669.html. Accessed on 3rd September 2013.

United Nations High Commissioner for Refugees (2014) *Syria Regional Refugee Response Inter-agency Information Sharing Portal*. Published at: http://data.unhcr. org/syrianrefugees/regional.php. Accessed on 16th March 2014.

United Nations News Centre (2014) South Sudan: UN, partners appeal for $1.27 billion as humanitarian crisis deepens. Published at: https://www.un.org/apps/news//story. asp?NewsID=47075&Cr=south+sudan&Cr1#.UyYpWDmaT7I. Accessed on 11th March 2014.

UNICEF (2014) South Sudan Humanitarian Situation Report #13 – Reporting Period 4–10 March 2014. Published at: http://reliefweb.int/sites/reliefweb.int/files/resources/ UNICEF%20South%20Sudan%20SitRep%20No%20%2013%2C%2011%20 March%202014%20%281%29.pdf. Accessed on 13th March 2014.

Verwimp, P. (2012) Food Security, Violent Conflict and Human Development: Causes and Consequences, UNDP Working Paper, New York: 2012–2016.

World Food Programme (2013) WFP Working To Bring Urgently-Needed Food To Northern Mali As Food Security Worsens: 16th April 2013. Published at: http://www. wfp.org/news/news-release/wfp-working-bring-urgently-needed-food-northern-mali-food-security-worsens. Accessed on 27th April 2013.

World Food Programme (2014a) Afghanistan Overview. Published at: http://www.wfp. org/countries/afghanistan/food-security. Accessed on 22nd March 2014.

World Food Programme (2014b) Syria conflict enters fourth year as some food reaches previously inaccessible areas. Published at: http://www.wfp.org/news/news-release/ syria-conflict-enters-fourth-year-some-food-reaches-previously-inaccessible-areas. Accessed on 12th March 2014.

Young, H. (2007) Looking beyond food aid to livelihoods, protection and partnerships: strategies for WFP in the Darfur states, *Disasters*, 31, Suppl.1: S40–S56.

Young, H., Borrel, A., Holland, D. and Salama, P. (2004) Public nutrition in complex emergencies, *Lancet*, 364: 1899–1909.

# CHAPTER 1
## 'TRY TO IMAGINE, WE DIDN'T EVEN HAVE SALT TO COOK WITH!': FOOD AND WAR IN SIERRA LEONE

*Susan Shepler*

In early 2001, I was talking with people in the village of Rogbom,[1] a village about ten miles outside Freetown, the capital of Sierra Leone. Although the war was still officially ongoing, things had been calm in the area for some time. My purpose was to try to understand the events of less than two years before, when all of the children old enough to fight had been abducted and the village had been occupied for several months by rebels retreating from their attack on the capital on 6th January 1999. After a few weeks in Rogbom, I had already gathered abduction stories from some of the children, and one particularly horrifying story of torture from the village headman. I also knew that in the neighbouring village, in one bloody day, eight people had been lined up and shot; and I had stood under the coconut tree where these murders had taken place. As often happened to me in these situations, once people knew that I was there to hear their stories, they came around one by one and shared their own, in some way trying to communicate to an outsider what they had lived through. One woman whose son had been abducted told me:

> When the rebels took over our village, life was very hard. They made us work for them. We were totally cut off from the market. Try to imagine, we didn't even have salt to cook with!

It seemed strange to me that she would include in the same narrative the atrocities she and the rest of the village had experienced and the seemingly small inconvenience of eating food without salt. I wondered, why was salt so important to her story?

This chapter explores the central material and symbolic role of food, both during and after the war. I investigate how, in post-conflict Sierra Leone, food becomes central to narratives about the war and wartime experience. I tie the centrality of food in war narratives to the cultural meaning of food with respect to sociality, reciprocity and political clientelism[2] by discussing first what the people ate, then what the rebels ate, and finally what the politicians ate. I also describe some of the changing practices of food, and what they tell us about the long-term impacts of the conflict. The focus on food is important because it allows us to foreground people's quotidian suffering instead of the spectacular violence we hear so much about. The point is to use food as a lens through which to view the everyday experience of the war.

I heard a great many stories from people I met while doing fieldwork in Sierra Leone at the tail end of the war (1999–2001).[3] My research was on rehabilitation and reintegration of child soldiers, and it took me to 'Interim Care Centres' around the country and to a number of communities to which former child soldiers were returning. I was a participant observer, fluent in the language from my time in the Peace Corps a decade earlier. In addition to former child soldiers, I talked with community members of all types as well as my old friends and colleagues about their war experiences. As an obvious outsider, I was always cognisant of the fact that my presence might be assumed to be connected to some official aid programme or other, so I always tried to make clear that I was a student gathering information for a degree and not connected to any humanitarian agency or government institution. Sometimes, I was told war stories not because I asked, but because people seemed to need someone to whom they could tell their stories. I draw on this well of stories here. It was not my intention to collect stories about food. It was only many years after this initial fieldwork that I started to think about why I so often heard narratives of suffering that centred on food, and came to see food as a revealing window on wartime experiences.

## Why Food?

Food studies begin with the premise that 'food practices are implicated in a complex field of relationships, expectations, and choices that are contested, negotiated, and often unequal' (Watson and Caldwell 2005: 1). Watson and Caldwell go on to argue that attention to the most mundane and intimate aspects of people's ordinary lives – in this case, how they relate to food – can help us understand the big issues of twenty-first-century politics: state formation and collapse, global flows and anti-global reactions, and new notions of identity and the rebirth of nationalism (among other topics) (2005: 2). Jon Holtzman (2009), in his book on food, memory and politics in Kenya claims that 'Food has the uncanny ability to tie the minutiae of everyday experience to broader cultural patterns, hegemonic structures and political-economic processes' (2009: 9). Food is material, but also symbolic, and literally everyday. Our experience of food is a physical, sensual, shared human experience. Food is embodied, mundane and often gendered in its preparation and consumption. It allows the physical reproduction of bodies, but is also part of social reproduction. The experience of food evokes recollection that is not simply cognitive but also emotional and physical.

There is a recently growing literature on food and culture, but work on food and war is still relatively rare. Indeed, in the review article on 'Anthropology of Food and Eating' (Mintz and Du Bois 2002: 105), the authors conclude that 'the role of war – and the roles of many kinds of social changes – has been relatively neglected in food studies. These are areas ripe for research'.[4] When theorists do think about food and war, it is in the context of food as an element of a human security framework (Pottier 1999; Richards 2002; Sikod 2008; Messer 2009). Some have talked about food shortages as a cause of conflict.[5] For example, Flynn states 'Nothing prompts civil unrest faster than the rising cost of staple foods' (2005: 2).[6] There is policy-relevant scholarship about food security and risk of conflict, and on how aid can affect food security, but this chapter is neither. From a more anthropological and phenomenological bent, this chapter is concerned with how food and stories about food can be a way to understand the personal experience of war.

## What the People Ate

To my knowledge there is no definitive text on Sierra Leonean foodways, as there are about Nigerian food for example (Okere 1983; Ikpe 1994). The general meal for Sierra Leoneans is rice with an oily, spicy sauce on top. Sometimes various greens are added (cassava leaves, sweet potato leaves, etc.) and usually ground peanuts are used as a thickener. People add what protein they can, with dried fish more prevalent along the coasts, and chicken, goat, pig, cow and the occasional 'bush meat' elsewhere (Figure 1.1). Cassava is also boiled or roasted, or prepared into *fufu* (a doughy, starchy base for sauce) or *gari* (grated and dried for ease of storage). Millet is cultivated in small quantities. Undoubtedly, the most important element of the Sierra Leonean diet, however, is rice. If a Sierra Leonean does not eat rice during the course of a day, even if he has eaten other little snacks, he will say he has not eaten.[7] The UK's Overseas Development Institute (2000) notes that rice was first cultivated in Africa 3,000 years ago, and that the first writings on rice in West Africa were from Leo Africanus who travelled through the region in the 1560s.

The first, and most obvious, effect of the war on people's experience of food was relative scarcity. People went hungry a lot of the time. When people could not afford to cook rice for their families, they would mix it with bulgur wheat, 'a gift from the people of the USA'. The resulting mixture was called 'combat'. It was not their usual food, and not something they generally enjoyed eating. In a way that is hard to understand for one who has not experienced war or great hunger, several informants explained to me that their hunger forced them to take dangerous decisions. A woman in the East End of Freetown told me 'during the invasion of January 1999, we never left our home. There

**Figure 1.1**   Boy selling monkeys as food. Copyright Susan Shepler.

was shooting everywhere. We only went out to try to find food'. Indeed, what emerges is the centrality of hunger to their experience of the war. In another example, a teacher friend from the Kono district in the East of the country told me how her father was killed in front of her, and she and her mother and smaller sister had to flee into the bush to survive. As above, with the story of the salt, her story was brought home through the details of the difficulty of eating while in the bush. She said:

> We lived on bananas and bush yams, whatever we could find in the bush. We didn't dare light a cooking fire for fear that the rebels might find us. Eventually we made it to Freetown and to safety. I will never forget how we suffered, and I don't really like to eat bananas now.

Food is descriptive. It is through the language of food that people could most powerfully, and yet humbly, describe their suffering. Holtzman (2006), in a review article entitled 'Food and Memory' asks 'what facets of food – or what configuration of its varying facets – render it a potent site for the construction of memory? Which kind of memories does food have the particular capacity to inscribe …?' (2006: 362). Food and memory are linked in interesting ways. In *Remembrance of Repasts*, Sutton (2001) observes that his informants on the Greek island of Kalymnos frequently remember far-off events through food. Indeed, his work's biggest contribution is a demonstration of how the sensuality of food causes it to be a particularly intense and compelling medium for memory. The experience of food evokes recollection, which is not simply cognitive but also emotional and physical. I am interested in comparing the memory practice of testimony in front of the Truth and Reconciliation Commission, for example, with the memory practice of my friend turning away from bananas in the marketplace. Of these two, formal testimony is extraordinary and happens only once, while memories based in food are inescapable and happen every day.

## What the Rebels Ate

Sierra Leone was a poor country even before the war, and though no longer the very worst, at 177 out of 186 it still ranks close to the bottom of the most recent United Nations Development Programme's (UNDP) Human Development Index (United Nations Development Programme 2013), above only a handful of other African countries. During the war, rebels looted from civilians in rural settings what they had been denied as marginalised youth: vehicles, radios, clothes, metal window frames and so on. They also wanted more and better food than they had known, so they looted cows, goats and other food stocks, mainly rice and palm oil. One young former rebel, around eighteen at the time we met, while telling me about the difficulty of his reintegration process also revealed how rebels ate during the war:

> When we were in the bush, we ate meat every day. Now, here in the Centre,[8] we have to eat combat (half bulgur, half rice) with very little meat in the sauce. Before, I used to command people like this to cook for me, now I have to be patient.

The rebels of the Revolutionary United Front (RUF) initially claimed that they were bringing a revolution. Many informants told me that they agreed at the beginning of the war that a change was needed, but that the rebels lost public support when they took it too far and were too violent against the people. I heard from various informants that often, to demonstrate that they were on the side of the civilians, when the rebels killed a cow (slaughtering it not in the usual way, but using the tools at hand, shooting it with an AK 47) they would share the meat with people in the town or village where they were staying. Or when they broke open some rich person's rice store, they would sometimes call surrounding people to come and share in the bounty. This was meant to win people over to their side, but most people told me they were not fooled. The rebels were too unpredictable to trust, though people certainly enjoyed the food when it came.

## What the Politicians Ate

It goes without saying that wealthy people in Sierra Leone eat more and better quality food than poor people. More important to our discussion is that food and overeating are common symbols of corruption and patrimonialism gone astray. To describe all kinds of petty corruption, people will say, 'he ate the money'. Big men – known for their big bellies – 'eat' the nation's resources. A famous song by the young Sierra Leonean musician, Emerson,[9] entitled 'Borboh Belleh' (literally 'Belly Boy') draws on that symbolism to talk about the corruption of big men or politicians. He says, 'Borboh Belleh you're greedy. Haven't you filled up your belly enough? Do you feel that Sierra Leone is a farm to encourage all kinds of thieves? Wrong!'

As in Bayart's (2009) and Geschiere's (1997) writings on, respectively, 'the politics of the belly' and 'the eating of the state' in contemporary Cameroon, Shaw (2002) also explains how her informants conceived of politics in terms of 'eating'. One of her informants stated that, 'Politicians and other big persons . . . consume the foreign aid intended for the poorest people of Sierra Leone, diverting it for the exclusive use of their own families. . . . "their families eat it" . . . thereby turning proper circulation into improper accumulation' (2002: 258).

## Changing Foodways

Studies of 'changing foodways' seem to be mainly about changes wrought by modernisation or globalisation. In the case of Sierra Leone, the changes were wrought by displacement and social rupture. In the sections that follow, I will give examples of elements of Sierra Leonean food culture that were affected by the war and by the post-war period. Again, it is my hope that each of these small stories will contribute to a more grounded understanding of everyday life before and after the war.

A friend in Makeni, the capital of the Northern Province and home to the Temne ethnic group, told me about the changes that happened during rebel occupation:

> First they killed all our cows, then our goats, then they ate all the dogs. As you know, the Mende people (of the south) were many among the rebels and after a while we mixed with them. We Temne don't eat frog, but the Mende people do. So, eventually, out of desperation, we started eating frog as well. People would prepare it and carry it around to the palm wine bars for people to eat. They started calling it 'water fowl.' The funny thing is, even though the war is over, people are still preparing it and eating it at the palm wine bars.

Many dietary changes introduced during wartime remained in the post-war period. Immediately after the war, things started to go back to normal, but that process meant some strange sights. For example, for the first time, people started carrying chickens from the city to the countryside (the normal route had always been to bring fresh chickens from the farm to the city). A number of times while riding on public transport, I heard people laughing about the chickens going up country. The same thing was true of the livestock. Having been almost completely depleted by the rebels, people were now buying cows from neighbouring Guinea and walking them into Sierra Leone. One positive aspect for meat eaters was the fact that the bushmeat (wild pigs, antelope and monkeys) had a chance to breed without being hunted for a number of years. Their populations increased dramatically during the war.

Finally, people returned to their villages after having been refugees or 'internally displaced persons' (IDPs) with new skills and new ideas about food preparation. Some of this came from being packed together in camps with people from different ethnic groups, with different recipes and different local ingredients (as in the frog story above). Some of it came from skills training programmes offered by some of the relief agencies. In a small village of about fifteen families where I did some of my fieldwork, the people were just returning after five years in an IDP camp near the capital (Figure 1.2). They had to rebuild their houses and clear brush to start new farms. The wife of the Headman had learned to bake bread while she was in the IDP camp, and made bread to sell to the community every morning, something that had never occurred in the community before the war.[10]

**Figure 1.2** Women using a Nigerian Peacekeeper's helmet in food preparation. Copyright Susan Shepler.

Another dietary innovation from abroad is *achieke* (or *attiéké* in Francophone countries). It is made from *gari* (the grated and dried cassava I mentioned before), which is soaked in oil and vinegar with fresh tomatoes and fish or a range of other toppings. The story is that *achieke* came from Côte d'Ivoire with West African Peacekeepers. When I was staying in Kenema in the East of Sierra Leone in 2009 I ate *achieke* several times at Obama Restaurant. Now it has spread all over Sierra Leone and, indeed, even Guinea and Liberia. As a new kind of fast food that is not rice it is surprisingly popular, and a decade after the war it looks like it is in the market to stay.

One could say that war and displacement have made Sierra Leonean food more cosmopolitan. With warnings of an impending world food shortage, people are again suffering from hunger. As the human security literature warns, this could lead to renewed violence in Sierra Leone and in other poor parts of Africa. Although I said this chapter was not concerned primarily with food and security, perhaps some of the flexibility in food preparation that came from the war can help alleviate some of that tension.

## Conclusions

This chapter has engaged disparate themes relevant to post-war Sierra Leone, connected mainly by the fact that each theme is examined through the prism of food. Though the themes are perhaps somewhat disconnected, by using food as a way to address them all, I have connected memory practices, corruption and cultural transformation in ways not otherwise possible. In addition to sharing some stories of people's everyday experiences of war through the lens of food, I present two conclusions, perhaps more accurately described as areas available for further study.

First, memory is a practice, and the everyday practices of food preparation and eating can be powerful sites for the memory of war. I have discussed the presence of food in narratives of suffering, and pointed to ways that the everyday practice of food preparation and consumption can be sites for memory of the war. More precisely, I have drawn a connection to the bodily memory of discomfort. But I am not arguing that the everyday supersedes other loci of memory. Narratives of wartime experience use both material and symbolic registers. As Basu (2008) argues in his discussion of 'palimpsest memory' in Sierra Leone, 'the memoryscape is continually "overwritten", resulting in an accretion of forms ... constantly being excavated and reburied, mixing up the layers, exposing unexpected juxtapositions, and generating unanticipated interactions' (2008: 254). Memory of the war happens at multiple levels all at once. In a way I am privileging the everyday because it is so often ignored, even though memories of the war are a combination of spectacular and mundane events (e.g., 'I remember the day the rebels attacked our village, but I also remember the daily boredom and hunger of hiding in the bush for months afterwards'). Memorialisation practices, transitional justice and all forms of reconciliation after conflict, must take all these levels into account.

Second, war has changed the foodways of Sierra Leone, and this may bring a new culinary flexibility and be an enduring cultural shift. The new flexibility in use of ingredients and new knowledge about methods of food preparation will help Sierra Leone feed itself if food becomes scarce. This is one way of addressing the human security issue of food shortages as a cause of conflict. Changing foodways is just one aspect of how everyday practice has changed after the war. I believe there is a greater cosmopolitanism in many areas of culture and social life. Many of these changes may help Sierra Leone face the challenges ahead.

Changing foodways are obviously about changes in the way people prepare and eat real food, but also about the symbolic, in that they may also be changing elements of ethnic and national identity related to food choice. Ferme (2001) suggests that in decades to come the impact of war will be found in everyday practice, much as the impact of pre-colonial violence exists in the everyday present: 'The everyday objects, words and places of war will find their way into narratives and social relations, in a manner analogous to those of slavery and violence left behind by a buried past' (2001: 228). In the collection of essays entitled *Ethnography in Unstable Places: Everyday Lives in Contexts of Dramatic Political Change*, Carol Greenhouse (2002) points us towards the importance of everyday creativity in the face of war, noting 'the determined momentum of improvisation even in previously unimaginable circumstances makes meaning itself a mode of social action and not merely a reaction' (2002: 3). Finally, I want to argue that it is in the everyday improvisation (What shall we eat? How shall we live?) that post-war reconstruction takes place; not in government spon-sored truth and reconciliation commissions, for example, but in everyday choices and creations.

## Acknowledgements

This chapter is based on Shepler, S. (2011) The Real and Symbolic Importance of Food in War: Hunger Pains and Big Men's Bellies in Sierra Leone, *Africa Today*, 58 (2): 43–56. Field research from 1999 to 2001 was supported by a Rocca Scholarship in Advanced African Studies at the University of California, Berkeley. A follow up research trip was funded by an American University Faculty Research Grant in 2007. Thanks to Aisha Fofana Ibrahim, Wusu Kargbo, and Raymond June for fruitful discussions on this topic. Thanks also for useful comments from participants in the conference of the International Commission on the Anthropology of Food and Nutrition, held in Leiden in August 2011 entitled 'Food in Zones of Conflict'.

## Notes

1  A pseudonym to protect the identities of my informants. I write more about what happened to that village and those children in Shepler (2005).
2  Clientelism is a political system at the heart of which is an asymmetrical relationship between patrons and clients. The post-colonial African state has been understood by many scholars as essentially neo-patrimonial or clientelist in character.
3  There are now several excellent book length explorations of the war, how it started and how it was carried out. See in particular Richards 1996; Abdullah 2004; Gberie 2005; Keen 2005.
4  An interesting exception is Powles (2002), who presents the story of a Zambian refugee, all of whose stories are tied up with what food was available at each stage of her displacement.
5  Neighbouring Liberia's Truth and Reconciliation Commission goes back to the event they call 'the rice riots' when people protested a hefty increase in the price of rice.
6  Flynn's work is also notable for focusing on the lack of food, and strategies for getting by when food is hard to come by, but also on foodways in an African urban setting, whereas most focus on the rural production of food.
7  This is true all along the Upper Guinea Coast. See Joanna Davidson's work on the importance of rice to identity in the region (Davidson 2010).
8  An Interim Care Centre for former child combatants and other separated children, a stop on the way to eventual reintegration.
9  See Shepler (2010) for more on Emerson and other young musicians in post-war Sierra Leone.
10 Other innovations made this American researcher happy. While the UN Peacekeeping troops were stationed in the country, they received food from a central UN purchasing office. The soldiers were primarily from Africa (Kenya, Zambia, and later from Bangladesh). They were not interested in corn flakes, canned peas, or jam and would trade their food with local women for fresh local produce whenever possible. This food would find its way onto the black market and into the stomach of the American anthropologist for an occasional break from rice.

## References

Abdullah, I. (2004) Bush Path to Destruction: The Origin and Character of the Revolutionary United Front (RUF/SL). In Abdullah, I. (ed.) *Between Democracy and Terror: The Sierra Leone Civil War*, CODESRIA, Dakar: 41–65.
Basu, P. (2008) Palimpsest Memoryscapes: Materializing and Mediating War and Peace in Sierra Leone. In Jong, I., de and Rowlands, M. (eds) *Reclaiming Heritage: Alternative Imaginaries of Memory in West Africa*, Left Coast Press, Walnut Creek, California: 231–259.
Bayart, J.-F. (2009) *The State in Africa: The Politics of the Belly* (second edition), Polity Press, Cambridge.
Davidson, J. (2010) "Sacred Rice: Identity, Encounter, and Development on the Upper Guinea Coast." Paper presented at *The Upper Guinea Coast in Transnational*

*Perspective*, Max Planck Institute for Social Anthropology. Halle/Saale, Germany. 9–11 December, 2010.

Ferme, M. (2001) *The Underneath of Things: Violence, History, and the Everyday in Sierra Leone*, University of California Press, Berkeley.

Flynn, K.C. (2005) *Food, Culture, and Survival in an African City*, Palgrave Macmillan, New York.

Gberie, L. (2005) *A Dirty War in West Africa: The RUF and the Destruction of Sierra Leone*, Indiana University Press, Bloomington, Indiana.

Geschiere, P. (1997) *The Modernity of Witchcraft: Politics and the Occult in Postcolonial Africa*, University of Virginia Press, Richmond, Virginia.

Greenhouse, C.J. (2002) Introduction: Altered States, Altered Lives. In Greenhouse, C.J., Mertz, E. and Warren, K.B. (eds) *Ethnography in Unstable Places: Everyday Lives in Contexts of Dramatic Political Change*, Duke University Press, Durham and London: 1–36.

Holtzman, J.D. (2006) Food and Memory, *Annual Review of Anthropology*, 35(1): 361–378.

Holtzman, J.D. (2009) *Uncertain Tastes: Memory, Ambivalence, and the Politics of Eating in Samburu, Northern Kenya*, University of California Press, Berkeley.

Ikpe, E.B. (1994) *Food and Society in Nigeria: A History of Food Customs, Food Economy and Cultural Change 1900–1989*, Steiner, Stuttgart.

Keen, D. (2005) *Conflict & Collusion in Sierra Leone*, James Currey, Oxford.

Messer, E. (2009) Rising Food Prices, Social Mobilizations, and Violence: Conceptual Issues in Understanding and Responding to the Connections Linking Hunger and Conflict, *National Association for the Practice of Anthropology Bulletin*, 32(1): 12–22.

Mintz, S.W. and Du Bois, C.M. (2002) The Anthropology of Food and Eating, *Annual Review of Anthropology*, 31(1): 99–119.

Okere, L.C. (1983) *The Anthropology of Food in Rural Igboland, Nigeria: Socioeconomic and Cultural Aspects of Food and Food Habit in Rural Igboland*, University Press of America, Lanham.

Overseas Development Institute (2000) *The History of Rice in West Africa*. Published at http://www.odi.org.uk/publications/3170-rice-production-west-africa. Accessed on 20th March 2014.

Pottier, J. (1999) *Anthropology of Food: The Social Dynamics of Food Security*, Polity Press, Cambridge.

Powles, J. (2002) Refugee Voices: Home and Homelessness: The Life History of Susanna Mwana-uta, an Angolan Refugee, *Journal of Refugee Studies*, 15(1): 81–101.

Richards, P. (1996) *Fighting for the Rain Forest: War, Youth, and Resources in Sierra Leone*, James Currey, Oxford.

Richards, P. (2002) Youth, Food and Peace: A Reflection on Some African Security Issues at the Millennium. In Zack-Williams, T., Frost D. and Thomson, A. (eds) *Africa in Crisis: New Challenges and Possibilities*. Pluto Press, London: 29–39.

Shaw, R. (2002) *Memories of the Slave Trade: Ritual and the Historical Imagination in Sierra Leone*, University of Chicago Press, Chicago.

Shepler, S. (2005) *Conflicted Childhoods: Fighting Over Child Soldiers in Sierra Leone*, PhD Thesis in the department of Social and Cultural Studies in Education, University of California, Berkeley.

Shepler, S. (2010) Youth music and politics in post-war Sierra Leone, *The Journal of Modern African Studies*, 48 (4): 627–642.

Shepler, S. (2011) The Real and Symbolic Importance of Food in War: Hunger Pains and Big Men's Bellies in Sierra Leone, *Africa Today*, 58 (2): 43–56.

Sikod, F. (2008) Conflicts & Implications for Poverty & Food Security Policies in Africa, In Alfred Nhema and Paul Tiyambe Zeleza (eds) *The Roots of African Conflicts: The Causes & Costs*, James Currey, Oxford: 199–213.

Sutton, D. E. (2001) *Remembrance of Repasts: An Anthropology of Food and Memory*, Berg, Oxford and New York.

United Nations Development Programme (2013) *Human Development Report 2013, The Rise of the South: Human Progress in a Diverse World*, United Nations Development Programme, New York.

Watson, J.L. and Caldwell, M.L. (2005) Introduction. In Watson, J.L. and Caldwell, M.L (eds) *The Cultural Politics of Food and Eating: A Reader*, Blackwell Publishing, Malden, MA and Oxford, UK: 1–10.

# CHAPTER 2
## LANDMINES, CLUSTER BOMBS AND FOOD INSECURITY IN AFRICA

*Bukola Adeyemi Oyeniyi and Akinyinka Akinyoade*

## Introduction

This chapter examines the nexus between the use of landmines, cluster bombs and related ordnance and food insecurity in contemporary Africa. The chapter demonstrates that landmines, cluster bombs or cluster munitions used by combatants and rebels in Africa's civil wars and conflicts are currently stimulating crop losses and crop misses, as farmers and herders find it difficult to access farmlands and fields many years after peace has been restored in most 'countries-in-conflict'. Unfortunately for these countries, post-conflict reconstruction, most especially land allocation to refugees and displaced persons, has usually been too slow to be effective. The emerging situation, made complex by the impact of conflict-related trauma, diseases (including HIV/AIDS) and general impoverishment, threatens food production in 'countries-in-conflict' and 'countries-out-of-conflict'. As recent developments in the Democratic Republic of Congo (DRC) and Rwanda suggest, while conflicts and wars left deep-seated, long and short-term problems, such as death, destruction, displacement and disease in their wake, the need to feed large numbers of impoverished people places considerable strains on food resources in 'countries-with-relative-peace', which had earlier played hosts to refugees. Compounding these problems and frustrating post-conflict reconstruction is the need to debrief and reintegrate combatants, as well as the need to remove mines from the land. The ongoing food crisis in Somalia aptly illustrates what future awaits Africa, unless something drastic is done urgently.

Using representative examples drawn from countries suffering from conflict across Africa, this study, using oral interviews, documentary and archival records, finds that a silent war of food and nutritional insecurity is occurring in different parts of Africa. The consequences of food insecurity are devastating, as it leads to hunger and nutritional insecurity, which in turn leads to malnutrition and, in the absence of intervention, death. Either singly or collectively, stunting and death lead to reduced human capital, which causes a further slowdown in the pace of Africa's development.

In section two, cluster bombs and landmines are described and the current situation in Africa explained. In section three, we examine the deployment of cluster bombs, landmines, and other ordnance in Africa. This is followed, in section four, by an examination of how these munitions contribute to food insecurity. In the fifth section, we look at efforts by governments and non-governmental organisations (NGOs) to control such munitions, given their impacts on human lives. The sixth section looks at how African nations compared to others across the world have fared in ensuring food security by adhering to international treaties and regulations. The chapter concludes with some suggested recommendations.

## Anti-Personnel Ordnances and the African Condition

A cluster bomb is an explosive device that contains a cluster of between two and two thousand smaller bombs or bomblets. When these are released or ejected from the main bomb, they rain down on wide areas such as an entire field, a garden, a playing field, or trees, waterways, cities, markets, etc. (Human Rights Watch 2003). Cluster bombs are either air-dropped or ground-propelled to enhance their effectiveness (Integrated Regional Information Network 2006). They were used during the Second World War and in Lebanon during the Civil War; and more recently in the DRC and Rwanda. An important characteristic of this weapon is the ability to stay undetected and unexploded for many years. So, in Lebanon, as in other places where they have been used, millions of unexploded cluster bombs adorn the land; waiting for their unsuspecting victims.

Landmines are weight-triggered explosive devices that are intended to damage human and non-human targets by means of either a blast, or fragment impact, or both. They have had a longer usage than cluster bombs, having first been used by the Chinese Song Dynasty against the Mongols in 1277 AD (Needham 1954). In contrast, cluster bombs, although first manufactured by the US, Russia and Italy, were first used in warfare by Germany during the Second World War (Integrated Regional Information Network 2006). Although cluster bombs also aim at killing enemies, their peculiar capability includes their ability to target specific things, like vehicles, tanks, electricity supply and chemical or biological weapons, etc. (Amos 2011).

It must be emphasised that there are different types of cluster bombs and landmines, whose capabilities vary. In terms of design, most cluster bombs are either designed to conceal themselves when dropped or to disguise their purpose by looking like toys, footballs, leaflets, beer bottles, etc., in order to deceive and, sometimes, even to attract human targets. Thus, what might pass as a child's football or a doll could actually be an incendiary, an anti-personnel, an anti-armoured fighting vehicle, an anti-electrical installation or an anti-runway bomb, or perhaps a dispenser of a landmine or of a chemical or biological weapon. Landmines and cluster bomblets are weight-triggered explosives, except that cluster bombs differ from landmines in certain key respects. Although there are different methods for using cluster bombs, they are usually dropped from aeroplanes. Where low-altitude flying is involved, they can be fitted with small parachutes, which slow their descent in order to allow the aircraft dispensing them to leave the area before any explosion (Integrated Regional Information Network 2006). Depending on their design, upon touching the ground, cluster bomblets either explode or lie buried under the soil, lying dormant until any weight triggers them into action (Human Rights Watch 2003). Where they are designed to stay dormant, cluster bomb-lets often remain buried for many years under the soil, in tree branches and under dead leaves, etc., undetected and yet without any loss in lethality.

Currently, cluster bombs are produced by 34 countries globally, and used actively in at least 23 countries. In strict military terms, cluster bombs and landmines are called Anti-Personnel Ordnances (APOs) (Wiebe and Peachey 1997). However different countries called them by different names. For instance, the US military once called them 'steel rain', 'firecracker' or 'popcorn' shells (Kennedy and Kincheloe 1993).

Africa is bedevilled by wars and conflicts, corruption and political insta-bility, as well as an iniquitous land tenure system. These factors underwrite conflicts and wars, where APOs are used. In fact, African countries could be divided into 'countries-in-conflict', 'countries-out-of-conflict', and 'countries-with-relative-peace'. Countries-in-conflict are countries where overt conflict is taking place either between the state and rebel groups or between one rebel group and another. Notable examples include the DRC, Congo-Brazzaville, the Central African Republic, Somalia, South Sudan and Sudan (Food and Agriculture Organization 2004; Oyeniyi 2010). The term, countries-out-of-conflict, describes any country that emerged from overt conflict in the last five years such as Liberia, Rwanda, and Sierra Leone. The term, countries-with-relative-peace, describes any country where no overt conflict of any kind exists, or has existed in the last five years. Although intergroup conflicts and insurgent-group crises, such as those mounted by Niger-Delta militants and Boko Haram, exist in Nigeria, Nigeria has not experienced any civil war, except between 1967 and 1970. From this conceptualisation, it is clear that to the extent that no civil war or external aggression currently threatens Nigeria, it qualifies as a country-with-relative-peace. This categorisation is for analytical purposes and should not be construed to meaning that Nigeria has peace in absolute terms. Of the three classifications, it is only in countries-with-relative-peace that problems associated with APOs are not currently a significant issue.

## APO Usage in Africa

Any study of food insecurity in Africa, especially given Africa's dense conflict landscape, must take into consideration the three categorisations above. In countries-in-conflict, food insecurity is occasioned by wars and conflicts, the associated displacement and dislocation of people, which have, in general, a detrimental effect on food production. For instance, following the resumption of the Angolan war in 1998, over four million Angolans, mostly women and children, fled their homes and resettled elsewhere in the country (Oyeniyi 2007). Seventy percent of these people – malnourished, sick, and/or wounded – remained in transit in different parts of Angola, where they were considered as 'non-indigene' and therefore unable to access farmland or engage in any productive work. The fact that fifty percent of rural households in Angola are headed by women, and some by children, with (almost) no income (Graca 2004) means that more than fifty percent of the rural population is cut off from (food) production activities. While this does not apply to the entire country, studies by Care International reveal that female-headed households are on the increase in Angola and that these families are without 'productive assets, such as access to fertile land, seeds, tools, credits, and livestock, as well as sufficient labour from within the household to fully participate in the cultivation cycle' (Food and Agriculture Organization 2004: 5). Similar scenarios abound in other countries-in-conflict across Africa.

Paradoxically, countries-out-of-conflict, even after agreements have been reached and new governments formed, do not fare any better. Many months after peace deals have been concluded and new governments formed in both Rwanda and the DRC, citizens have had to cope with thousands of unexploded APOs. This new war, the war of APOs, although precipitated by combatants and rebels in previous wars, now targets everybody – rebels, government and the entire population. The war of APOs, as the following examples make clear, differs in scope and content from all conventional wars. It targets not just the enemy, but also those who deployed the ordnance in the first place. The war's unintended consequences are not just death and destruction in peacetime, but also the associated inability to access fields and farmland, a situation that is now precipitating food insecurity in the affected African countries. The enormity of the problem has led the International Committee of the Red Cross and other human rights groups to campaign for a total ban on cluster bombs and landmines, especially in populated areas (International Committee of the Red Cross 2010).

Hassan, a victim, sat quietly in his father's compound when a bomblet dropped at his feet. Before he could escape, it exploded and Hassan found himself clutching onto his spilled intestines. Although Hassan survived, 'I lost my hearing', he said.[1] Hardy, an eleven-year-old victim, was, according to his mother, in the shop when a bomblet fell from the rooftop. Ignorant of what it was, Hardy stepped on it. The impact of the explosion rammed him into the wall. Hardy's uncle, who attempted to save him, also stepped on another one; both died instantly.[2] Andres, a farmer, lost three toes to cluster bombs while returning from the Church. Andres's fate now hangs in the balance, as doctors warned that if the toes do not heal as expected, then Andres's leg may have to be amputated to save his life.[3]

In most countries-out-of-conflict, especially where evidence of APOs' use abounds, thousands of combatants and civilians have either been killed or maimed by APOs in peacetime. Even if the total number of victims may never be known, we know that large tracts of land remain uncultivated because of, or for fear of, APOs.

In some cases, rebel groups and governmental agents have openly admitted to APO usage either in their respective countries or in neighbouring ones. South Africa's Ministry of Foreign Affairs admitted that it manufactured and used APOs in 2005, although the ministry refused to disclose location(s) of use. In other countries, it is difficult to determine who deployed APOs. Gadhafi-led Libya explicitly denied using APOs despite incontrovertible evidence that it did. Regardless of acceptance and denial, UN Mine Action claimed that cluster bombs and landmines are littered everywhere in Rwanda and the DRC (Wiebe and Peachey 1997). The Food and Agriculture Organization (FAO) suspected that APOs were also used in Mozambique, Angola, Congo-Brazzaville, Sierra Leone, Madagascar, the Central African Republic, Liberia, Somalia, Guinea, Angola, Cape Verde, Ethiopia, Eritrea, Kenya and Burundi, a claim corroborated by the African Union (Food and Agriculture Organization 2004). In Rwanda alone, over 50,000 square kilometres of land remained uncultivated during the past fifteen years due to the presence of APOs. In Angola, more than one million square kilometres have remained uncultivated. Farran, cited in Wiebe and Peachey (1997), maintained that these large tracts of land may remain uncultivated for the next two decades, as it will take up to thirty years to clear mines from Rwanda alone. She has since warned farmers in affected countries to steer clear of their fields until they are successfully cleared of mines and cluster bombs.

As shown in Table 2.1, APOs have been used by both African governments and non-African countries, most especially France, in not less than fourteen African countries. In some cases, governments have been found guilty, while in some others, rebel groups have used APOs, as the case of Hutus and Tutsis in the DRC illustrates. In the case of Eritrea, the Djibouti government perpetually denies ever using APOs against its own people, despite widespread evidence in the country. Not only did Nigeria use APOs during the 1967–1970 civil war, the Nigerian government was also accused of using APOs in its military intervention in Sierra Leone in 1997. The case of Libya differs from that of Nigeria only by degree. Under Gadhafi, Libya was not only accused of using APOs within Libya, but also during its face-off with Chad between 1986 and 1987. Except South Africa, no other African country seems to have the capacity for making APOs.

**Table 2.1**   African countries with proven usage of APOs.

| S/N | Countries | APO Deployer | Location of Use |
|---|---|---|---|
| 1 | Angola | Unknown | In different locations. |
| 2 | Chad | Unknown, France and Libya. | Various locations in Chad between 1986 and 1987. |
| 3 | DR Congo | Hutus and Tutsis | Kasu, Katelwa and Kabalo villages in the DRC. |
| 4 | Eritrea | Eritrea (although it denies it). | Ayder School and neighbourhood, Mekele in Ethiopia. |
| 5 | Ethiopia | Eritrea | Asmara Airport, Gash-Barka, Melhadega (1998–2004) |
| 5 | Libya | Libya | Libya (1986–1987, and ongoing); Chad (1986–1987). |
| 6 | Mauritania | Morocco | Near Western Sahara and across borders. |
| 7 | Morocco | Morocco | Polisaro Front in Western Sahara, Akka, Guelta, Zemmour, Hausa, Messeid, Bu-Crag and Mauritania (1975–1998). |
| 8 | Nigeria | Nigeria | Sierra Leone (ECOMOG intervention in 1997). |
| 9 | Sierra Leone | Nigeria, Sierra Leone | Eastern Town of Kenema against ECOMOG and insurgent groups. |
| 10 | South Africa | South Africa | Unknown location, but South Africa Ministry of Foreign Affairs admitted in 2005 that they manufactured and used APOs. |
| 11 | Sudan | Sudan | Southern Sudan (1996–1999). |
| 12 | Uganda | Uganda | Gulu, in the North. |
| 13 | Zambia | Zambia | Chikumbi and Shang'ombo. |

Source: Human Rights Watch (2011).

In the case of the DRC, another dimension to the problems associated with APOs relates to the inability of the International Institute of Tropical Agriculture (IITA) to distribute high-yielding and mosaic-resistant cassava varieties and other agricultural support systems. The Institute claimed that 'a new strain of disease has added to the problem, and other pests and diseases have also compounded the situation. Reduced cassava harvests have dramatically increased the market price of leaves and roots, so that many people can no longer afford what was their main calorie source. This has been further exacerbated by problems with inter-regional food movement because of civil unrest' (International Institute of Tropical Agriculture 2005: 1).

Not only was cultivation of cassava, the DRC's main staple food, stopped during the war, but it was also discontinued after the war (Abele *et al.* 2007). Pest invasion, especially of locusts, is also exacerbating the problem in Burundi, Ivory Coast, Rwanda, Niger and Togo. During the long period it will take for de-mining activities to be completed, what are the food production prospects for these countries?

Besides wars and conflicts, other factors that threaten food insecurity include armed robbery, destruction of market systems, and insecurity on roads and major highways, with their attendant effects on commercial transportation in rural communities. When wars and conflicts protract, crop misses (inability to plant as and when due) and crop losses (inability to harvest as and when due) occur. Where conflicts involve governments and rebel groups, war-related killings and displacements increase; APOs recognise no combatants, no enemy, no region, no climate, no age, no gender and no nation.

## Food Insecurity in Africa

By October 2011, media reports showed that acute food insecurity plagued Somalia. As this section shows, Somalia may not be the only African country on the verge of collapse due to food insecurity. Angola, Burundi, the Central African Republic, Côte d'Ivoire, the DRC, Eritrea, Guinea, Liberia, Mali, Congo-Brazzaville, Sierra Leone, South Sudan, Sudan and Uganda are all experiencing acute food insecurity due to problems associated with refugees' return, conflicts and displacement. Others, such as Cape Verde, Chad, Ethiopia, Kenya, Lesotho, Madagascar, Mauritania, Mozambique, Niger, Swaziland, Tanzania and Zimbabwe are also facing food insecurity because of severe drought and other environmental factors (CARE 2004).

From the above, where pest invasion, drought, and acute weather conditions are not driving food insecurity; wars and conflicts with their associated displacement and refugee crisis intertwined with cases of unexploded APOs are. The United Nations Development Program (UNDP) estimated that in 1998, as many as 1.2 million APOs lay in Somali fields (CARE 2004). This, coupled with widespread loss of livestock and other income sources, has caused the disintegration of Somalia during the past few years. In Eritrea, Ethiopia, South Sudan and Sudan, similarly, serious food shortages persist with as many as two-thirds of these countries' populations facing severe food crises because fields are inaccessible due to APOs, successive poor rains and drought. In Burundi, the Central African Republic, the DRC and Rwanda, war-related displacements, drought, and unexploded APOs constitute a great challenge to food production. In Southern Africa, land problems coupled with widespread shortages of key inputs such as seeds, fertilizer, fuel and farm power underwrite food insecurity.

## Institutional Response to APO Use

The first international initiative to ban cluster bombs, known as the Oslo Process, was launched in February 2007 (United Nations Organization 2008). The Government of Norway spearheaded it. Although the Oslo Process began early in 2007, it was not until December 2008 that the legal instrument came into effect. The Oslo Process gave the United Nations the head start to institute the Convention on Cluster Munitions (CCM), which prohibits the use, transfer and stockpiling of cluster bombs or any type of explosive weapon that scatters sub-munitions or bomblets over an area (United Nations Organization 2008, CARE 2004). The convention was adopted on 30 May 2008 in Dublin, and opened for signature on 3 December 2008 in Oslo (United Nations Organization 2008). There is also the 1997 Convention on the Prohibition of the Use, Stockpiling, Production and Transfer of Anti-Personnel Mines and on their Destruction (the Mine Ban Treaty, MBT), which also aimed at ending the suffering and casualties caused by APOs (International Committee of the Red Cross 1997). Many other legal frameworks have since followed these initial efforts. According to these legal instruments, APOs serve as significant barriers to development. Concerted efforts have since been mounted not just against their usage, but also against their production. So far, sixty states have ratified the CCM, while fifty more have signed but not ratified it. Although the 1997 MBT was open for signature from 3rd December 1997, it did not come into force until 1st March 1999; 158 state parties and 38 non-state parties have signed and ratified the MBT (International Committee of the Red Cross 1997).

As shown by United Nations Mine Action (2010), the majority of countries in Africa have signed the two treaties, CCM and MBT, but only a handful have ratified and adopted what was agreed. In addition, as part of the two treaties, the United Nations, its agencies and other regional organisations have also put in place interventions on stockpiling, usage and destruction of APOs. Yet, across the world countries that have destroyed or are destroying their stockpiles of APOs are relatively few, while those still stockpiling them are many.

The majority of African countries are not even complying on openness about and the destruction of their stockpiles. Prior to Gadhafi's removal from power, Libya, like Somalia, Algeria, Eritrea, Egypt, Ethiopia, Morocco, Sudan and Zimbabwe, not only used and stockpiled APOs, but also refused to destroy their holdings. Given the large number of African countries involved in continuing to accumulate and use APOs, one can argue that African leaders are not concerned about the impact of APOs on their countries' populations. Despite this, de-mining activities, which UN Mine Action claimed would last for about thirty years per country, are currently ongoing in fourteen African states.

To forestall a Somali-type food crisis across Africa, a speedy de-mining process must be considered in the affected countries. However, a particular constraint is that, while it costs a little above one US dollar to make a bomblet, to demine one bomblet costs between 30 US dollars and 200 US dollars (Landmine Action 2005; Human Rights Watch 2011). Given the parlous state of most African economies, as Table 2.2 overleaf shows, it is clear that Africa cannot de-mine its fields without assistance. While there is no shortage of de-mining assistance, evidence across Africa shows that this comes with extra costs. Currently, allocation of de-mined lands appears to favour politicians and foreign business partners rather than local farmers and herders. As seen in Somalia and Sudan, these foreign partners prefer to cultivate sunflower and other alternative energy crops to the food crops, which these African countries urgently need. Owing to this, allocation of de-mined land in these countries is enmeshed in further conflict, as farmers and herders tend to offer resistance to agents of the state as regards land allocation.

Simple analysis of total national budgets, as against de-mining costs, shows that African countries have little or no alternative to assisted de-mining operations. Table 2.2 shows the cost of de-mining against the 2009 national budget in a few African nations. In this table, column one shows the country concerned, column two shows the total number of people affected by APOs relative to the national population, column three shows the number of provinces or regions affected by APOs relative to total provinces in that country and column four shows the total land mass cleared and released for use relative to the land mass affected by APOs.

It is clear from Table 2.2 that many of the affected countries cannot de-mine their lands without assistance. Unless urgent assistance is provided, a country like Angola risks a Somali-type food crisis, as cost of de-mining far outstrips its national budget. Mozambique's external funding to the National Programme for Agricultural Development (PROAGRI) common fund is US$43 million and US$41 million in 2008 and 2009 respectively (Cabral 2009), while the cost of de-mining for these two years (funded by external bodies) represents about one-quarter of total international contributions to the agricultural sector common fund. For the countries examined, from 2005 to 2009 the cost of de-mining is very high relative to total land area cleared. These costs also vary tremendously, from as little as US$57,000 per one square kilometre of land cleared in Ethiopia to more than US$6 million for the same land area in Sudan for the same five-year period. Similar situations are occurring in Burundi, the DRC, Eritrea and Somalia.

Another issue of importance in this discourse on APOs deals with life-time treatment of surviving victims. In Angola, the life-time treatment of a surviving victim costs an average of US$5,000 (Ayisi 1998). If this is considered as a given for other affected countries, Africa may also not be able to care for victims.

**Table 2.2** Cost of de-mining activities versus national budget in selected African countries.

| Country affected | Population affected | Provinces affected out of number of provinces in country | Land km² cleared and released out of km² affected | Cost of clearing (2005–2009) | Cost of clearance per km² | National budget (2009) |
|---|---|---|---|---|---|---|
| Angola | 2.4m. or 17% | 18 of 18 | 36 of 252 | $225,236,205 | $893,794 | $23,282,490,860 |
| DR Congo | N.A. | 4 | Most Parts | $31,858,571 | N.A. | $1,832,723,298 |
| Ethiopia | 1.5% | 9 of 9 | 313 of 597 | $34,478,863 | $57,084 | $5,508,474,576 |
| Eritrea | 11.50% | N.A. | 34 | N.A. | N.A. | $245,528,455 |
| Mozambique | N.A. | 6 provinces | 12 of 31.7 | $37,273,649 | $1,175,825 | $1,751,028,807 |
| Somalia | Undefined | Undefined | N.A. | $9,349,609 | N.A. | N. A. |
| Sudan | 76% | Most Parts | 55 | $347,848,143 | $6,324,511 | $9,000,000,000 |

Sources: (a) Europa Publications (2011); (b) Human Rights Watch (2011).

N.A. means that the data are not available.

## Conclusion

Baynham (1994: 25–26) predicted that though landmines 'were conceived as local defensive weapons to disrupt advancing armies'; mines have become a 'strategic weapon to empty territory, to close food distribution networks, immobilise large tracts of agricultural land, raising the costs of reconstruction and development'. Current situations in fourteen African countries are confirming this prediction.

External intervention notwithstanding, the exceedingly high cost of demining and the slow pace of the process shows that Africa cannot de-mine its fields. Somali-type food crises loom large on the horizon for these fourteen countries, especially as none is able to meet the demand for safe land. Furthermore, the safe land allocated so far is not devoted to food production. Even if this situation is altered, these fourteen countries remain endangered, as food insecurity easily slips into nutritional insecurity and then chronic malnutrition.

To remove all mines from Africa's fields and ensure food security, technological innovations capable of reducing the financial resources involved in de-mining operations and also reducing the number of years involved, at least by a half, are urgently required. Equally, new APO monitoring systems need to be developed to ensure APOs are not used any more in Africa. In addition, less secrecy, especially in relation to the use of munitions, which could stay unnoticed and undetected for years, should be incorporated into disarmament, demobilisation and reintegration (DDR) programmes in Africa. Ongoing economic recession in the developed economies, however, portends that foreign aid to Africa is likely to decrease. More than ever before, nations of the world should insist on a total ban on the manufacture and use of APOs. For the attainment of any (if not all) of the above, what is needed is political will.

## Notes

1  Hassan, 25 years old, oral interview at Kampala, Uganda on 25th August 2009.
2  Marian, 45 years old, oral interview at Entebbe, Uganda on 25th August 2009.
3  Andres, 32 years old, oral interview at Entebbe, Uganda on 25th August 2009.

## References

Abele, S., Twine, E. and Legg C. (2007) *Food Security in Eastern Africa and the Great Lakes*, USAID, New York.

Amos, V. (2011) *UN Humanitarian, Development and Human Rights Chiefs Call on States Not to Undermine the International Ban on Cluster Bombs*, UN Press Release, 23 November 2011.

Ayisi, R.A. (1998) Landmines Inflict Heavy Costs on Africa, *Africa Recovery*, 11(3): 22.

Baynham, S. (1994) Landmines in Africa: Indiscriminate Warfare, *Africa Insight*, 24 (4): 25–26.

Cabral, L. (2009) *Sector Budget Support in Practice: Desk Study Agriculture Sector in Mozambique*, Overseas Development Institute and Mokoro (UK).

CARE (2004) *CARE USA: Humanitarian Demining Initiatives 1999–2000*, cited in World Vision Cambodia (2011), *Integrating Demining with Development: The Way Forward*, Domrei Research and Consulting, Cambodia: 124.

Europa Publications (ed.) (2011) *Europa Regional Survey of the World (2010): Africa South of the Sahara*, Routledge, New York: 234.

Food and Agriculture Organization (FAO) cited in International Food Policy Research Institute (2004), *Mitigating, Preventing, and Ending Conflicts in Africa*, IFPRI, Washington, DC: 70–74.

Graca, M. (2004) Mitigating, Preventing, and Ending Conflicts in Africa in International Food Policy Research Institute, *Assuring Food and Nutrition Security in Africa by 2020: Prioritizing Actions, Strengthening Actors, and Facilitating Partnerships*, IFPRI, Washington, DC: 70–74.

Human Rights Watch (2003) *New International Law on Explosive Remnants of War*, 28 November: 17.

Human Rights Watch (2011) *Cluster Munitions and the Convention on Conventional Weapons: Myths and Realities*. Published at: http://www.hrw.org/news/2011/03/28/cluster-munitions-and-convention-conventional-weapons. Accessed on 22nd April 2012.

Human Rights Watch (2011), International Campaign to Ban Landmines, *Landmines & Cluster Munitions, Country Profiles 2010*. Published at: http://www.the-monitor.org. Accessed on 2nd April 2012.

Integrated Regional Information Network Films (2006), *Field of Fire: Cluster Bombs in Lebanon*. Published at: http://www.irinnews.org/Report.aspx?Reportid=84384. Accessed on 22nd April 2012.

International Committee of the Red Cross (1997) International Humanitarian Law – Treaties & Documents: *Convention on the Prohibition of the Use, Stockpiling, Production and Transfer of Anti-Personnel Mines and on their Destruction*, International Humanitarian Law, ICRC, Geneva: 5.

International Committee of the Red Cross (2010) *The Convention on Cluster Munitions*, ICRS, Vienna, Austria: 12.

International Institute of Tropical Agriculture (2005) IITA Reviews Cassava Work in DRC, *The Bulletin*, 180927, June 2005.

Kennedy, D. and Kincheloe, W. (1993) Steel Rain: Submunitions, *US Army Journal*, January 1993.

Landmine Action (2005) *Explosive remnants of war and mines other than anti-personnel mines: Global survey 2003 –2004*. Published at: http://www.landmineaction.org/resources/UKWGLM.pdf. Accessed on 22nd April 2012.

Needham, Joseph (1954) *Science and Civilisation in China: Introductory Orientations*, Cambridge University Press, Cambridge, UK.

Oyeniyi, B.A. (2007) Peoples Without Homes: Displacement and Security Situation in Africa. In Falola, T. and Afolabi, N. (eds) *The Human Cost of African Migration*, Routledge, New York: 303.

Oyeniyi, B.A. (2010) Resources Management and Africa's Wars and Conflicts. In Uche N., Agwuele, A. and Akinwumi, O. (eds) *Multidisciplinary Perspectives on Overcoming the African Predicament*, MediaTeam IT Publishers, Germany: 127–153.

United Nations Mine Action (2010), *The United Nations Mine Action Service Annual Report 2010*. Published at: http://reliefweb.int/sites/reliefweb.int/files/resources/2010%20UNMAS%20Annual%20Report%20Final.pdf. Accessed on 22nd April 2012.

United Nations Organization (2008), *Convention on Cluster Munitions*, UNDP/BCPR, Geneva: 6.

Wiebe, V. and Peachey, T. (1997) *Drop Today, Kill Tomorrow: Cluster Munitions as Inhumane and Indiscriminate Weapons*, Mennonite Central Committee, USA: 19.

# CHAPTER 3
## SPECIAL NUTRITIONAL NEEDS IN REFUGEE CAMPS:
## A CROSS-DISCIPLINARY APPROACH

*Jeya Henry and Helen Macbeth*

### Introduction

Conflict due to international, civil or tribal war, ethnic or religious persecution or other oppression is the most common reason why people flee from their homes and become refugees. A refugee is defined as a person who, by reason of real or imagined danger from such conflict, has left their home country or country of their nationality and is unwilling or unable to return, although any definition of the term 'refugee' is debated (see Black 2001). According to the office of the United Nations High Commissioner for Refugees (UNHCR), at the end of 2012 the number of people forcibly displaced worldwide had reached 45.2 million and of these 10.5 million were under the mandate of the UNHCR (www.unhcr.org/about us/key-facts-and-figures.html). At the time that figure broke down into a global total of 15.4 million refugees, 28.8 million internally displaced persons and a further 840,000 waiting to be given refugee status (www.unhcr.org.uk/about-us/key-facts-and-figures. html). Whereas refugee populations fell during the 1990s and early 2000s, the number of refugees has recently been rising again, and the number of forcibly displaced persons in 2012 was the highest figure since 1994 (United Nations High Commissioner for Refugees 2013).

There has been a massive escalation of those fleeing the civil war in Syria in 2013. For example, the report of the UNHCR of February 2014 refers to more than 2.4 million Syrian refugees now residing in neighbouring countries, including 932,000 in Lebanon, 613,000 in Turkey, 574,000 in Jordan, 223,000 in Iraq and 134,000 in Egypt (www.unhcr.org/53072f4f6.html). The refugee situation in parts of Sub-Saharan Africa has reached crisis proportions, particularly in the Sahel, where tens of thousands have fled the conflicts in Mali and the Central African Republic during 2013. The situation in Darfur has also deteriorated considerably in the past two years, creating new flows of refugees into Chad. The internal conflict in South Sudan, which started in late 2013, has led to people moving across its borders into Kenya, Ethiopia, Uganda and north into Sudan. Many other refugee situations exist around the world. The challenges faced by international agencies in managing refugee populations are compounded by the fact that 46 percent of refugees now recorded are under eighteen years of age (www.unhcr.org.uk/about-us/key-facts-and-figures.html).

The feeding and care of refugees is a major undertaking of several United Nations (UN) agencies, which provide food, clothing and shelter, most frequently but not always, in camps. Such camps for refugees may be within or near a zone of conflict, but are not necessarily so. Usually they are over some political border, generally in another nation state. While legally the welfare of refugees is the responsibility of each host nation's government (Lorenzo 2007), the reality is that the majority of refugee camps worldwide are in marginal areas where host governments themselves have few funds and the camps depend on the international community for resourcing. Four fifths (80 percent) of the world's refugees are now hosted in developing countries (www.unhcr.org.uk/about-us/key-facts-and-figures.htm).

The Office of the UNHCR was established in December 1950 by the UN General Assembly. The agency is mandated 'to lead and co-ordinate international action to protect refugees and resolve refugee problems worldwide. Its primary purpose is to safeguard the rights and well-being of refugees. It strives to ensure that everyone can exercise the right to seek asylum and find safe refuge in another state, with the option to return home voluntarily, integrate locally or to resettle in a third country. It also has a mandate to help stateless people' (www.unhcr.org/pages/49c3646c2.html). However, it is recognised that multiple UN and other national and non-governmental agencies, in addition to the UNHCR, work to improve the health and nutrition of refugees. Finances regularly fall short of requirements. In some situations, the refugees are able to disperse into the host populations (Harrell-Bond 2000), but this essay concerns the nutritional sustenance of those living in the abnormal circumstances of the refugee camps. Too frequently individuals and families may stay in a refugee camp for a considerable period of time (Toole *et al.* 1988).

As there are geographic differences in the foods available in different economic and ecological situations, there is also geographic, ecological and economic diversity in the areas around refugee camps, which, for one reason or another, affects what food supplies reach the camps. This may be due to local availability or scarcity, locally peaceful conditions or conflict, or local diversion of the foods to private sales or use. As a consequence there is geographic diversity in the nutritional deficiencies and diseases, and Schofield and Mason (1996) argued that refugee rations should be calculated according to each specific context. Nevertheless, acute malnutrition and micronutrient deficiencies are common in most refugee camps (e.g., Seaman and Rivers 1989; Moren *et al.* 1990; Toole 1992; Mears and Young 1998; Mason 2002) especially in those in Africa and parts of Asia. For example, Kemmer *et al.* (2003) showed that iron deficiency was unacceptably high in refugee children from Burma; Malfait *et al.* (1993) identified niacin deficiency in Mozambican refugees in Malawi; Seal *et al.* (2005) demonstrated iron and vitamin A deficiency in long-term refugees in African camps, while as recently as 2010 Khatib *et al.* (2010) showed vitamin A deficiency, iron deficiency and anaemia in Iraqi refugees in a border camp in eastern Jordan.

In general, wherever they are, rations for refugee camps tend to be cereal-based and insufficient in both quality and quantity. In the majority of cases, a refugee diet is based on a cereal, some pulses, vegetable oil and some salt and sugar (Henry and Seaman 1992). Confined to a camp, refugees are rarely able to supplement their rations nutritionally by obtaining work or money to buy more food. Cultivation is seldom possible. Hence, refugees must survive on only these rations, which are insufficient, leading to outbreaks of diseases such as scurvy, pellagra, beri beri and vitamin A deficiency, as exemplified above. Harrell-Bond *et al.* (1989) drew attention to the importance of fortifying the rations for refugees, and Henry (1995) further defended the case for this.

## Refugee Rations

Refugee rations, particularly in developing countries, are usually composed of food aid commodities. Twenty years ago, Tomkins and Henry (1992) described a typical daily refugee ration as made up of 400–500 g of cereal, 10–20 g of oil and a small quantity of beans or lentils (30–40 g) and maybe 5 g of sugar. Although there was some variation in these rations, they were, and too often still are, more or less deficient in a range of essential nutrients, including vitamin A, vitamin C, some B vitamins, iron and zinc.

Table 3.1 shows the average vitamin and iron content of a typical refugee ration in 1992 and compares it with an average pet food in a developed nation. The refugee ration was not only deplete of vitamin C and A, it was also low in riboflavin, niacin, and iron.

In this example, the only vitamin provided for the refugees at any physiologically acceptable level was thiamine, and even that would have been inadequate if the cereals were milled inappropriately or there was too long a delay in delivery. By contrast, the pet food was not only balanced but also had an excellent micronutrient composition.

Demonstrating this comparison with pet food in a developed nation made the point about refugee nutrition dramatically two decades ago, and, although attention has been given to improving the situation, inadequacies remain. The resulting ill health from vitamin deficiencies within a camp population living on refugee rations has been reported and observed in other studies (e.g., Toole and Waldman 1997; Mason 2002). Experimental studies of dietary

**Table 3.1**   Comparison of vitamin and iron content in refugee rations[a] and pet food[b]

| Food Item | Quantity (g) | Thiamine (mg) | Riboflavin (mg) | Niacin (mg) | Folic acid (µg) | Vitamin C (mg) | Vitamin A (µg) | Iron (mg) |
|---|---|---|---|---|---|---|---|---|
| *Refugee ration* | | | | | | | | |
| Wheat flour | 400 | 1.28 | 0.08 | 8.0 | 40 | 0 | 0 | 6.8 |
| Kidney beans | 30 | 0.16 | 0.05 | 1.6 | 39 | 0 | 0 | 2.0 |
| Vegetable oil | 20 | 0 | 0 | 0 | 0 | 0 | 0 | 0 |
| Sugar | 5 | 0 | 0 | 0 | 0 | 0 | 0 | 0 |
| Total | 455 | 1.44 | 0.13 | 9.6 | 79 | 0 | 0 | 8.8 |
| *Pet food*[c] | 455 | 1.07 | 0.62 | 22.5 | 52 | 0 | 1090 | 44 |
| *RNI*[d] | | 1.1 | 1.3 | 17 | 200 | 40 | 700 | 14.8 |

[a]Based on food consumption tables; [b]typical analytical values; [c]comparable quantity (on a dry weight basis; [d]reference nutrient intake per day (values for adults 19–50 years). Dietary reference values for food, energy, and nutrients for the UK (Report on Health and Social Subjects no. 41, HM Stationery Office, London, 1991).

Source: Tomkins and Henry (1992).

deprivations in otherwise healthy adults have also been carried out, but the ill-effects of micronutrient deficiencies would occur far more swiftly in refugees who tend already to be in a very poor nutritional state before reaching any camp.

## Protein-Energy Malnutrition in Children

Many of the studies about malnutrition in refugee camps refer to adults. However, a particular problem afflicts children; even when rations are available, their access to food may be limited (Godfrey 1986). In addition to micronutrient deficiencies, many children are underweight in refugee camps due to poor access to food. The term protein-energy malnutrition (PEM) was first introduced in relation to children, because children's protein-energy requirements are relatively higher than those for adults. Olwedo *et al.* (2008) showed a high prevalence of PEM in children in refugee camps in northern Uganda. As mentioned below, public attention from the outside world may be directed towards the children with PEM, especially in extreme emergency situations, but quite often children are resident in refugee camps for a considerable period of time and yet far less attention is paid to malnutrition amongst them.

Indeed, in urgent emergency feeding programmes, protein-energy supplementation generally should be the first priority, but for longer-term residents in refugee camps micronutrient deficiencies as well as protein-energy deficiency cause health problems. Yet, it tends to be primarily the sickest children with severe PEM who are shown in television news reports of drastic hunger in zones of conflict. There are two extreme conditions of PEM: kwashiorkor and marasmus. In the early 1930s, Cicely Williams, the first professional paediatrician to be appointed to the British Colonial Medical Service, introduced the term 'kwashiorkor'. Kwashiorkor in the Ga language of Ghana means 'the disease of the displaced child', which referred to the child displaced from the breast when the next sibling was born, but can equally well refer to the refugee child. Marasmus is a condition of severe muscle and fat wasting. For either of these diseases, remedial action is urgent. However, for longer-term residence in refugee camps, it is important also to consider micronutrient deficiencies as these too cause health problems – and can be fatal (LaMont-Gregory *et al.* 1995).

## World Health Organization Guidelines

The World Health Organization (WHO) has developed guidelines for managing severe malnutrition (1999). These guidelines, which, with some adaptation to local conditions, have been used to reduce case fatality rates, state:

Management of the child with severe malnutrition is divided into three phases. These are:

- *Initial treatment*: life-threatening problems are identified and treated in a hospital or a residential care facility, specific deficiencies are corrected, metabolic abnormalities are reversed and feeding is begun.
- *Rehabilitation*: intensive feeding is given to recover most of the lost weight, emotional and physical stimulation are increased, the mother or carer is trained to continue care at home, and preparations are made for discharge of the child.
- *Follow-up*: after discharge, the child and the child's family are followed up to prevent relapse and assure the continued physical, mental and emotional development of the child (World Health Organization 1999: 2).

Much of the early feeding regimes used in the second phase were based on liquid-based beverages made from skimmed milk powder, sugar, oil and water, but increasingly the response has been to fortify the foods with micronutrients

(Young 2004). Therefore, the preferred response of the agencies concerned with providing food for refugee camps has been to use such fortified foods. There have been several studies of the effects of fortifying foods to boost nutritional benefits. For example, Bilukha *et al.* (2011) investigated the effectiveness of adding micronutrient powder into the feed of infants, while van den Briel *et al.* (2007) summarised results from Afghanistan, Angola and Zambia and pointed out that much of the food delivered by the World Food Programme (WFP) was now fortified with iron, vitamin A and other micronutrients before being shipped. However, the authors provide several reasons why it would be preferable to mill and fortify the food as close as possible to the recipients rather than before being shipped. In the following year, Seal *et al.* (2008) studied the effects of providing vitamin-fortified maize, while in 2012 Tappis *et al.* concluded that the increase in supplementary feeding programmes in camps in Kenya and Tanzania had succeeded in preventing severe malnutrition and recommended that such programmes continue.

Some high energy, high protein drinks are now available to be used to supplement nutrition in refugee camps, but most of these come in powdered form, to be mixed with local water. The lack of potable water and the microbial proliferation likely in the marginal places where refugees are frequently encamped can result in contamination by the vectors of waterborne diseases, leading to diarrhoea, especially serious in already malnourished subjects and so negating the theoretical benefits of such supplements. Cronin *et al.* (2008) undertook a study of water and sanitation in refugee camps and found that in many camps the standard of water cleanliness was acceptable but not in all. The health significance of poor standards of hygiene thus becomes relevant to the value of any nutritional supplement to be mixed with the local water. Another problem of dried foods is that they are easily taken to local markets to be sold on rather than used for the purposes for which they were donated. However, Shepler (personal communication) explained that private onward sales of aid foods were not limited to dried foods.

## Ready to Use Therapeutic Food (RUTF)

To overcome this problem some products called 'ready to use therapeutic foods' (RUTF) were developed as alternatives to liquid-based therapies. RUTFs are energy dense vitamin/mineral enriched foods that were originally designed to treat severe acute malnutrition. They require no cooking, water or fuel for heating. This has been an area of research for a number of years.

The idea of developing local, low cost RUTFs, rich in protein, energy-dense and suitable for feeding to young children and other vulnerable groups, arose in the early 1950s (Waterlow 2006). The simplest recipe for a RUTF is one which has only two ingredients, for example a cereal or root crop mixed with a legume. However, other foods must be added to this basic mix in order to prepare a multimix that is nutritionally suitable for the treatment of acute malnutrition (Collins and Henry 2004). A nutritionally suitable multimix for RUTF has four basic ingredients:

1. A staple (carbohydrate rich) as the main ingredient – preferably a cereal.
2. A protein supplement from a plant or animal food – beans, groundnuts, milk, meat, chicken, fish, eggs, etc. To be practical such foods must be low-cost, and this requirement has pushed development towards legumes and oilseed as these are cheaper than products containing milk or other animal products.
3. A vitamin and mineral supplement – a vegetable and/or fruit.
4. An energy supplement – fat, oil or sugar to increase the energy concentration of the mix.

In addition, an ideal RUTF formulation must have the following attributes:

- Good nutritional quality (i.e., protein, energy and micronutrient content)
- Long shelf life
- Highly palatable with a good taste
- A consistency and texture suitable for feeding to children
- Require no additional processing prior to feeding
- Amino acid complementation for maximum protein quality
- Product stability
- Ingredients should be easily available in developing countries

Technologically, RUTFs possess a number of advantages over other foods, making them an excellent food product for local production since they have a low water activity ($A_w$), which makes them microbiologically safe. Unlike products such as high energy biscuits, RUTFs do not require protection against damage during transport. Even if they are contaminated (e.g., by children's dirty fingers), microbes cannot grow in such low $A_w$, making RUTFs a 'safe' product. The product can also be stored at ambient temperatures without the need for refrigeration, and the three to four month shelf-life at tropical temperatures is sufficient for RUTFs to be delivered to likely places of need (Henry 1990; Collins and Henry 2004).

An RUTF is eaten directly without cooking, or the need to use water, or be diluted with potentially contaminated water. Each packet has a standard amount of food. Moreover, most children can feed themselves from the package requiring little or no help from their mothers. Provided peanuts or other oil rich legumes are available, the manufacturing process for RUTFs uses simple technology, and requires a relatively low investment in equipment and facilities. The inherent microbiological safety also means that the level of control needed during processing and distribution is less rigorous than for many other protein-rich foods. Local RUTF production also offers the opportunity to stimulate agricultural production and widens the benefits to farmers in surrounding communities.

## Product Development

In recent research numerous cereal, legume and oilseed mixtures were evaluated by Henry and his team (Collins and Henry 2004) on the basis of the above criteria. In particular, efforts were made to combine the various cereal, legume and oilseed mixtures to maximise the protein quality, attempting to offset any essential amino acid deficiencies in one ingredient by combining it with another ingredient that was high in that particular amino acid. This process led to a list of thirteen products that had reasonable theoretical properties. Following numerous product development trials, the list was reduced to three potential alternatives. The foods were prepared from roasted or processed ingredients with total exclusion of water. They had low dietary bulk, low potential for bacterial contamination and were ready to eat without cooking. Similarly, the commodities chosen had the most appropriate energy density and high biological value of protein. Moreover, the proposed foods had an optimal physical characteristic of being soft in consistency, easy to swallow and suitable for infant feeding. An example of a suitable recipe is given below.

## Rice–Sesame RUTF

Ingredients used are roasted rice flour, roasted sesame seed paste, Soyamin 90, sunflower oil, icing sugar, vitamin and mineral premix. The quantities of these ingredients are listed in Table 3.2. Table 3.3 provides an analysis of Rice–Sesame RUTF, and Table 3.4 shows the mineral analysis.

**Table 3.2**   Quantities of ingredients for the Rice–Sesame RUTF as quantities (%).

| Ingredients | Quantities (%) |
| --- | --- |
| Roasted rice flour | 20.0% |
| Soyamin90 | 8.0% |
| Roasted sesame seeds paste | 29.0% |
| Sunflower oil | 19.4% |
| Icing sugar | 22.0% |
| Premix | 1.6% |
| **Total** | **100.0%** |

**Table 3.3**  Nutritional composition of Rice–Sesame RUTF per 100 g and percentage contribution to energy.

| Nutrients | Data |
|---|---|
| Energy* | 551 kcal |
| Energy | 2307 kJ |
| Protein | 13.8 g |
| Carbohydrate** | 43 g |
| Fat | 36 g |
| Ash | 4.3 g |
| Moisture | 2.9 g |

\* The energy has been calculated using Atwater factors.
\*\* Carbohydrate is by difference assuming protein to be nitrogen (N) times 6.25.

**Table 3.4**  Mineral analysis for Rice–Sesame RUTF.

| Mineral | mg/kg |
|---|---|
| Copper (Cu) | 2.1 |
| Zinc (Zn) | 10.9 |
| Calcium (Ca) | 338.1 |
| Sodium (Na) | 256.5 |
| Magnesium (Mg) | 118.4 |
| Iron (Fe) | 5.6 |

Note: The water activity of Rice–Sesame RUTF is 0.290.

## Future Developments

As mentioned, these new RUTFs can be eaten uncooked and have a low water content. This makes them suitable vehicles to deliver not only vitamins/antioxidants, but also probiotics and prebiotics.

The future challenge is to develop RUTFs using locally available staple cereals and legumes. This will enable low cost development of high energy-protein products with long shelf-life in localities at or close to where they are needed and will be used. This initiative will have a great impact on the treatment and management of malnutrition in the refugee camps in less developed countries.

## Conclusion

The need for experts from different disciplines to cooperate on topics of common interest is demonstrated throughout this volume and in this example.

These formulations reflect research by specialist nutritionists working in a laboratory. Such laboratory-based studies need to be translated into what is appropriate in practice. Cross-disciplinary cooperation is necessary in order to add value to the work, through studies such as acceptability trials (Mears and Young 1998), local agricultural and production feasibility studies and research into the economic, social and political outcomes of any projects which finance local production of the ingredients of the most appropriate formulation for any given area. These are relevant issues for those involved in the provision of food for refugee camps. Local production of such foods will not only provide easier access and less time for deterioration, but, due to its lower cost, have wider appeal, with hopefully beneficial effects on the economy of the locality in which the camp is situated. These broader questions cannot be answered adequately in a nutrition laboratory, nor solely by the organisations running the refugee camps. In our view the questions to be answered would benefit from a holistic approach involving experts drawn from different disciplines interested in applied human science. To us, the study of humanity concerns many disciplines and sciences, all interested in understanding the human condition. So, in concordance with the ideals of the International Commission on the Anthropology of Food and Nutrition (ICAF) and of this volume, this topic about how to improve the nutritional status of refugees in camps exemplifies well the need for analysis by different specialists and cross-disciplinary cooperation and discussion.

## References

Bilukha, O., Howard, C., Wilkinson, C., Bamrah, S. and Husain, F. (2011) Effect of multi-micronutrient home fortification on anaemia and growth in Bhutanese refugee children, *Food and Nutrition Bulletin*, 32(3): 264–276.

Black. R. (2001) Fifty years of refugee studies: from theory to policy, *The International Migration Review*, 35(1): 57–78.

Collins, S. and Henry, C.J.K. (2004) Alternative RUTF, *Field Exchange Supplement*, 2: 35–39.

Cronin, A.A., Srestha, D., Cornier, N., Abdulla, F., Ezard, N. and Aramburu, C. (2008) A review of water and sanitation production in refugee camps in association with selected health and nutrition indicators – the need for integrated service provision, *Journal of Water and Health*, 6(1): 1–13.

Godfrey, N. (1986) Supplementary feeding in refugee populations, *Health Policy Plan*, 1(4): 283–298.

Harrell-Bond, B. (2000) Are refugee camps good for children? *UNHCR Working Paper*, No. 29.

Harrell-Bond, B.E., Henry, C.J.K. and Wilson, K. (1989) Fortification of foods for refugees, *Lancet*, 333(8651): 1392.

Henry, C.J.K. (1990) Refugees: nutritional management. In *Encyclopaedia of Human Nutrition*, Academic Press, London: 1685–1689.

Henry, C.J.K. (1995) Improving food rations for refugees: a case for food fortification, *Postgraduate Doctor: Middle East Edition*, 18(3): 84–89.

Henry, C.J.K. and Seaman, J. (1992) Micronutrient fortification of refugee rations to prevent nutritional deficiencies in refugee diets, *Journal of Refugee Studies*, 5: 359–368.

Kemmer, T.M., Bovil, M.E., Kongscomboon, W., Hansch, S.J., Geisler, K.L., Cheney, C., Shell-Duncan, B.K. and Drewnowski, A. (2003) Iron deficiency is unacceptably high in refugee children from Burma, *Journal of Nutrition*, 20(3): 248–260.

Khatib, I.M., Sammah, S.M. and Zghol, F.M. (2010) Nutritional interventions in refugee camps on Jordan's eastern border: assessment of status of vulnerable groups, *Eastern Mediterranean Health Journal*, 16(2): 187–193.

LaMont-Gregory, E., Henry, C.J.K. and Ryan, T.J. (1995) Evidence-based humanitarian relief interventions, *Lancet*, 346(8970): 312–313.

Lorenzo, M. de (2007) Global: the accountability gap in refugee protection, *Pambazuka News*, issue 30. Published at: http://pambazuka.org/en/category/refugees/41773. Accessed on 25th February 2014.

Malfait, P., Moren, A., Dillon, J.C., Brodel, A., Begboyian, G., Etchegorry, M.G., Malenga, G. and Hakewell, P. (1993) An outbreak of pellagra related to changes in dietary niacin among Mozambican refugees in Malawi, *International Journal of Epidemiology*, 22: 504–511.

Mason, J.B. (2002) Lessons on nutrition of displaced people, *Journal of Nutrition*, 132(7): 2096S–2103S.

Mears, C. with Young, H. (1998) *Acceptability and Use of Cereal-based Foods on Refugee Camps: case studies from Nepal, Ethiopia and Tanzania*, Oxfam Working Paper, Oxford.

Moren, A. Lemoult, D. and Brodel, A. (1990) Pellagra in Mozambican Refugees, *Lancet*, 335: 1403–1404.

Olwedo, M.A., Mwcrozi, E., Bachou, H. and Orach, C.G. (2008) Factors associated with malnutrition among children in internally displaced person's camps, northern Uganda, *African Health Sciences*, 8(4): 244–252.

Schofield, E.C. and Mason, J.B. (1996) Setting and evaluating the energy content of emergency rations, *Disasters*, 20(3): 248–260.

Seal, A.J., Creeke, P.I., Mirghani, Z., Abdalla, F., McBurney, R.P. Pratt, L.S., Brookes, D., Ruth, L.J. and Marchand, E. (2005) Iron and vitamin A deficiency in long-term African refugees, *Journal of Nutrition*, 135(4): 808–813.

Seal, A., Kafwembe, E., Kassim, I.A., Hong, M., Wesley, A., Wood, J., Abdulla, F. and van den Briel, T. (2008) Maize meal fortification is associated with improved vitamin A and iron status in adolescents and reduced childhood anaemia in a food-aid dependent refugee population, *Public Health Nutrition*, 11(7): 720–728.

Seaman, J. and Rivers, J.P. (1989) Scurvy and Anaemia in Refugees, *Lancet*, 333(8648): 1204.

Tappis, H., Doocy, S., Haskew, C., Wilkinson, C., Oman, A. and Spiegel, P. (2012) United Nations High Commissioner for Refugees feeding program performance in Kenya and Tanzania: a retrospective analysis of routine Health Information System data, *Food and Nutrition Bulletin*, 33(2): 150–160.

Tomkins, A. and Henry, C.J.K. (1992) Comparison of nutrient composition of refugee rations and pet foods, *Lancet*, 340(8815): 357–368.

Toole, M.J. (1992) Micronutrient deficiencies in refugees, *Lancet*, 339: 1214–1216.

Toole, M.J. and Waldman, R.J. (1997) The public health aspects of complex emergencies and refugee situations, *Annual Review of Public Health*, 18: 283–312.

Toole, M.J., Nieberg, P. and Waldman, R.J. (1988) The association between inadequate rations, undernutrition prevalence, and mortality in refugee camps: Case studies of refugee populations in eastern Thailand, 1979–1980, and eastern Sudan, 1984–1985, *Journal of Tropical Pediatrics*, 34(5): 218–224.

United Nations High Commissioner for Refugees (2013) *Global Trends 2012. Displacement: the New 21st Century Challenge*, UNHCR, Geneva. Published at http://www.unhcr.org/51bacb0f9.html: 5. Accessed on 26th February 2014.

van den Briel, T., Cheung, E., Zewari, J. and Khan, R. (2007) Fortifying food in the field to boost nutrition: case studies from Afghanistan, Angloa and Zambia, *Food and Nutrition Bulletin*, 28(3), 353–364.

Waterlow, J.C. (ed.) (2006) *Protein Energy Malnutrition*, Smith-Gordon, London.

World Health Organization (1999) *Management of Severe Malnutrition: A manual for physicians and other senior health workers*, World Health Organization (WHO), Geneva.

Young, H. (2004) Public nutrition in complex emergencies, *Lancet*, 365: 1899–1090.

# CHAPTER 4
## PATTERNS OF HOUSEHOLD FOOD CONSUMPTION IN CONFLICT AFFECTED HOUSEHOLDS IN TRINCOMALEE, SRI LANKA

..........................................................................................................................

*Rebecca Kent*

### Introduction

In order for village level project interventions to improve household food security it is necessary to understand the nature of the problem. To put it simply: who is hungry, when and why? These questions were posed by an international non-governmental organisation (NGO) in Sri Lanka in 2001 as it sought to move its food security activities from relief to rehabilitation and development during a period of improved security and sustained ceasefire during the Sri Lankan conflict. Eighteen years of conflict and the accompanying destruction of civil war had contributed to high levels of malnutrition and protracted periods of food shortage in Trincomalee District, Sri Lanka (Reinhard and Kramer 1999). In this context the NGO, Action Contre la Faim (ACF), sought to identify programme activities that would be most effective in improving the food security of beneficiaries. The research took place between October 2001 and January 2002.

During the conflict, irrigation systems had been neglected as a result of outmigration from conflict-affected areas and the limited ability of state agencies to access areas for maintenance. This had led to a deterioration of reservoirs (known as 'tanks') and a backlog of repairs to bunds, sluice gates and irrigation channels. The rehabilitation of this infrastructure was an obvious priority for post-conflict development programmes, with potential to improve food production and incomes. However, the capacity of such interventions to address the food insecurity of the poorest households was not clear.

The study reported here was undertaken to increase programme staff's understanding of who was most vulnerable, when, and why, in order to improve targeting of project activities. In addition, it was hoped that it would address the question of whether tank rehabilitation was an appropriate intervention to benefit food insecure households.

A range of factors that affect household food security could be linked to the conflict, including damaged irrigation infrastructure, reduced access to markets, restricted use of natural resources, and high incidence of disability and widowhood. In rural communities in Trincomalee District, livelihoods had become adapted to these constraints and the occasional opportunities created by the conflict. Understanding these responses was central to developing an understanding of the nature of food insecurity in the district.

## Study Site and Methods

At the time of the study, Trincomalee District comprised areas controlled by the government of Sri Lanka and areas held by the Liberation Tigers of Tamil Elam (LTTE), so-called 'uncleared' areas. To ensure that these very different contexts were represented, the five villages selected for study comprised three 'cleared' villages (two Singhalese, one Muslim) and two 'uncleared' (Tamil) villages. To capture a range of conditions facing rural households, villages were selected to include those with different levels of access to paddy land and food security status, using data collected from a prior assessment (Integrated Food Security Programme 2001). Table 4.1 shows the characteristics of the five selected villages. Villages ranged in size from nineteen to over two hundred households. In all villages paddy labour formed an important component of livelihood strategies but they varied in levels of access to paddy land and to natural resources for activities such as fishing, firewood collection and hunting.

Fieldwork was carried out in November and December 2001 using semi-structured household interviews as the principal data collection method. Households for interview were selected using a food security ranking exercise (a modified wealth ranking exercise) in which a small number of informants in each village were asked to sort households according to their food security situation ('whether families had enough to eat'). Households for interview were then randomly selected from each of the food security groups to ensure that the range of food security situations found in that village was represented. In total 68 household interviews were carried out. Focus group discussions were also held in each village on topics that emerged during the food security ranking exercise and household interviews.

The household interviews combined the basic principles of Household Economy Analysis (HEA) (Seaman *et al.* 2000) with a food security calendar (Freudenberger 1999). Interviews were conducted by drawing up a food intake calendar and discussing it with respondents; in most cases all members of the household took part. The woman of the household was first asked to identify periods of different levels of food security over the previous year (for

**Table 4.1** Characteristics of study villages and patterns of rice shortages.

| Ethnicity | Security status | Size | Access to paddy land | Income sources (other) |
|---|---|---|---|---|
| 1 Muslim | Cleared | 59 hh | Medium – Close to large irrigated area. One third of families estimated to cultivate their own rice. | Paddy labour, firewood, fishing, brick making, sand excavation, home gardening |
| 2 Singhalese | Cleared (border area) | 19 hh | High – All households have access to paddy land but small tank means only one rice crop per year. | Paddy labour, home guard |
| 3 Singhalese | Cleared | 110 hh | Medium – Between one third and one half of households are estimated to cultivate their own rice | Paddy labour, hunting, honey, brick making, mat weaving |
| 4 Tamil | Uncleared | 210 hh | Medium – Damage to nearest tank means that area of irrigated paddy is small and only 10% of households are producing irrigated rice. Upland maize cultivation is widely practiced. | Paddy labour, firewood, fishing, honey, maize, leaf collecting, begging |
| 5 Tamil | Uncleared | 125 hh | Low – Very few paddy cultivators, limited access to land. | Paddy labour, firewood, fishing, honey, labour for onion harvest |

example 'in which months can you eat until you are full?' or 'in which months is it hardest to feed your family?') and to describe the typical composition of meals and the sources of foods consumed during these periods. This information was represented visually on a large sheet of paper. This was followed by drawing an income and expenditure calendar to ascertain the sources and variations in household income over the year. The collation of data on various themes on a single calendar allowed cross checking of 'typical' meals for a given period with their sources (e.g., whether from own production, bought or given), levels of food expenditure and reported incomes. This method relies on households remembering food consumption patterns over a year and is subject to the well-known limitations of recall methods. However, in this study the aim was not to derive detailed nutritional assessments of household food intake but rather to identify the origins of food shortfalls and arrive at an improved qualitative understanding of the problems facing households in order to support the development of relevant programmes.

## Analysis

For each village the data from the household interviews were summarised and then households were classified according to their reported food consumption patterns. In total, six food security scenarios were identified across the five villages. Not all types were found in every village; in some villages no households were interviewed that fell into the highest food security category and in others a strong seasonal pattern was not identified.

In villages where seasonal patterns of food shortage were described, household food security was judged primarily on the length of the 'good' food security period described in the household calendar. In villages where seasonal patterns were not pronounced, other indicators of relative food security were used to differentiate households, for example: the daily quantity of rice cooked per consumption unit; the quality and number of accompaniments; the type of breakfast foods taken; and the consumption of more expensive items (milk, potatoes, dal, meat). The six food security scenarios identified were as follows:

1. **Good food security** – Households that can meet household food needs all year round and have enough to make more expensive food purchases such as milk and meat. They do not change their diet in response to seasonal changes in income.
2. **Adequate food security** – Households who are coping well – they can meet household food needs all year round. This means they can eat three times a day – they take some food at breakfast, and two further meals. Consumption levels of rice are good. Variety in diet seems good.
3. **Seasonal nutritional deficiency** – Households who manage for most of the year to provide food needs (eating 2–3 times a day, varied diet), however this intake is not secure – they experience periods when they are unable to sustain this level of food variety and quality.
4. **Chronic nutritional deficiency** – Households who are managing for most of the year to provide calorific needs (eating 2–3 times a day) but whose reported food intake appears inadequate in terms of variety and quality.
5. **Seasonal food deficiency** – Households who are unable to meet basic needs for part of the year. They are unable to meet desired rice consumption (two rice meals per day) all year round, and reduce rice intake to one meal per day for one month or more.
6. **Chronic food deficiency** – Households who fail to provide basic needs

for most of the year. They are in a more or less permanent struggle to meet rice needs (only one rice meal per day).

## Characteristics of Food Secure Households

Households in category 1 'good food security' were found in the two government-held Singhalese villages. These households had a member in the army or home guard (civilians paid a monthly stipend to provide security services in border villages) and were thus able to secure a regular income. This finding highlights the importance of home guard payments to achieve higher levels of food security in some households, particularly in those areas where other income opportunities were low, and suggested that some households may face difficulties when these payments are withdrawn.

In the Muslim and Tamil villages households classed as having 'adequate food security' were those who were able to engage in a variety of income generating activities across the year and were able to secure rice stores from household production or from payment in kind for agricultural labour. These households were placed in a lower food security category than those found in the Singhalese villages because of the lower quality of the reported accompaniments to the rice and the absence of more expensive food purchases.

## Characteristics of Food Insecure Households

Households that fell into category 6, 'chronic food deficiency', were found in four of the study villages. These households were consuming one rice meal or less per day for more than eight months of the year.

Households in this group were notably similar across villages and usually comprised female-headed households and households with elderly or disabled members. The disadvantaged circumstances of many of these households were a direct result of the conflict. Such households faced constant difficulty earning sufficient income to meet food needs. In addition to the shortage of labour faced by female-headed or disabled households, young widowed and separated women were reported to lack the confidence to engage in income earning activities outside the home.

A variation from this trend was found in the large Singhalese village. In this village, the elderly and female-headed households interviewed did not constitute the most insecure food security group due to income from mat weaving and the support they received from family members. In this village the lowest food security group was comprised mainly of households of remarried women and their children. The interview team suspected alcohol abuse by husbands and reported that these women were living in poor conditions with few possessions.

These findings suggest that the most food insecure are those households unable to earn sufficient income through existing labouring opportunities. In these circumstances increased paddy production through tank rehabilitation is unlikely to have a direct impact on household food security. If programme activities based on increasing household incomes are proposed they need to be appropriate to this group. For households suffering from the impacts of alcoholism another approach is required.

## Seasonal Food Insecurity

The northeast of Sri Lanka experiences two agricultural seasons coinciding with the northeast monsoon, *Maha*, from September to January and the short rains, *Yala*, between June and August. Previous studies have reported that food shortages are experienced by both farmers and labourers in the months preceding harvests (see Eide *et al.* 1986). In the study a strong seasonal pattern of rice consumption was widely reported in only two of the study villages (the Muslim village and the small Singhalese village). Within these villages length of the good food security period served as a useful indicator of relative food security.

In the Muslim village two thirds of the households interviewed experienced food shortages lasting more than three months in which they were limited to one meal per day. This occurred most often in November, December and January, which is the period when rice stored from the *Yala* harvest is finished and, because this is the height of the monsoon, opportunities for fishing, firewood collection or brickmaking are reduced.

The 'good' food security period in this village followed the *Maha* harvest in February. Although most households did not produce rice themselves, field work was paid in paddy and accounted for the bulk of rice procurement for many households and was stored for between three and ten months.

The second village where a seasonal pattern in food security was readily described was the small border Singhalese village. Although all households had access to paddy land this was irrigated from a small tank only capable of supporting one crop in the main *Maha* season. In this village, aside from home guard salaries and one shop, no non-agricultural income sources were described. This can be explained by the relative isolation of this village and its location in a border area which limited possible livelihood activities due to security concerns (for example, hunting or firewood collection, travel for paddy labour). Thus opportunities for income earning were low and food shortfalls occurred in September and October when most households had finished rice stored from the harvest. This situation was eased in November when land preparation work became available.

These examples demonstrate the importance of non-farm-based income earning opportunities to increase households' ability to sustain themselves between harvests. However, in the isolated Singhalese village, tank rehabilitation to allow double cropping may be a potentially useful strategy to supplement household rice stores.

In the remaining three villages a food security gradient according to the duration of the 'good food period' was not found, hence the number of months that a household could consume two or more rice meals a day did not serve as a useful indicator of relative food security. In general in the two Tamil villages households were more likely to describe a steady (if poor) intake for most of the year (what we categorised as 'chronic nutritional deficiency'). Where seasonal reductions in food intake were described, this was for one to three months.

A consideration of the reasons for this difference in seasonal patterns brings us back to our original question about the role of paddy production in household food security. In the first Tamil village, despite limited access to irrigated land, two thirds of households interviewed reported taking rice meals twice per day for at least ten months of the year. The remaining households largely had the opposite experience – unable to provide rice twice a day for more than two months of the year. In this village the low availability of income earning opportunities between November and January was linked to the period of rice shortage. This is illustrated in Figure 4.1, which shows the variation in potential income from different activities over the year. It can be seen that

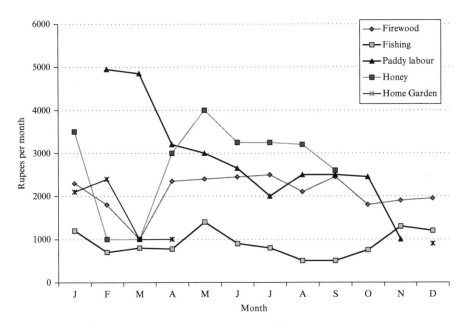

**Figure 4.1**   Average monthly incomes derived from livelihood activities for participating households (Tamil village with land).

incomes from paddy labour and honey collection fall off sharply from October onwards. There is also a small decline in income from firewood collection during this period (October–December). In these circumstances non-paddy related income opportunities are needed to help households bridge the gap.

## Household Rice Provision

An unexpected feature of the Tamil villages, given the limited availability of land for paddy production, was the reported high levels of rice consumption and storage. In contrast to other villages, all the interviewed households that were producing paddy reported storing rice for twelve months of the year. In addition, harvest labour in these areas was paid in kind which meant that labouring households also acquired significant rice stores.

This observation with regard to storage and selling patterns may have been a consequence of restrictions on the movement of people and goods between LTTE and government held areas, since this has the effect of reducing the marketability of all agricultural produce, including rice. Other studies have highlighted the impact of these restrictions on farmers' decisions to sell rice (Korf et al. 2001), and this in turn may impact the patterns of household rice procurement. In the 'cleared' villages, paddy labour was more often paid in cash, whereas in the 'uncleared' areas payment was largely in kind. This may account in part for the observed 'rice security' in households in 'uncleared' areas even where food security was low (as suggested by low dietary diversity). Table 4.2 shows the number of households interviewed in each village that had rice stores, their source, and the average number of months they lasted. This summary suggests that access to paddy land does not predict households' ability to store rice. In fact the lowest levels of rice storage were found in the large Singhalese village, where access to paddy land was good but less than half of interviewed houses had their own rice stores. Here paddy wages were mainly received in cash and therefore households did not maintain rice stores from this work. Rice received as payment was more often the source of stored rice than rice from own production in areas where this is the principle payment method for paddy work.

The lack of variability reported in household diets in the two Tamil villages, even during 'good food security' periods, suggests that interventions which improve household incomes alone may have little likelihood of impact on food security in the short term. Certainly dietary diversity for many households appeared to be very poor even where rice intake and incomes were high. In these circumstances, increased rice production through tank rehabilitation is unlikely to be sufficient for improving food security and reducing malnutrition. Infrastructure repair needs to be coupled with interventions geared to improving nutritional knowledge and access to more diverse foods, in addition to issues related to health, sanitation and care.

**Table 4.2**   Patterns of rice storage in interviewed households.

| Village | Number of households interviewed | Number of households with rice stores | Average number of months with rice stores | Sources of stored rice (in order of importance) |
|---|---|---|---|---|
| 1. Muslim | 11 | 10 (90%) | 6.5 | 1. Payment in kind<br>2. Own production<br>3. Pickings (from threshing floor) |
| 2. Small Singhalese | 9 | 7 (78%) | 6.0 | 1. Own production<br>2. Lease payment |
| 3. Large Singhalese | 15 | 7 (45%) | 8.5 | 1. Own production<br>2. Lease payment<br>3. Gift<br>4. Pickings |
| 4. Tamil village with land | 16 | 15 (94%) | 8.5 | 1. Payment in kind<br>2. Own production<br>3. Pickings<br>4. Gift |
| 5. Tamil village without land | 17 | 12 (70%) | 5.0 | 1. Payment in kind<br>2. Pickings<br>3. Own production |

## Conclusions

The purpose of the study was to improve understanding of who was most vulnerable, when, and why, in order to improve targeting of project activities. The study showed that households containing widowed, elderly or disabled persons were particularly vulnerable to chronic food insecurity, and those intending to intervene need to recognise that these households have limited ability to benefit from traditional income earning opportunities. The study also highlighted the problems facing younger remarried widows and their children.

Seasonal food insecurity was a particular problem for households in villages where income opportunities were affected by the monsoon and where paddy cultivation was limited to one crop per year. The months during which food shortages were most common varied slightly between villages depending on the agricultural calendar and the type of livelihood activities pursued (for example, fishing, brick making and firewood collection are reduced during the monsoon). In 'uncleared' areas, seasonal variation in rice consumption was less pronounced than expected due to household rice stores. However, in some cases a consistently poor dietary diversity pointed to chronic nutritional insecurity despite good availability of rice. These different scenarios illustrate how the potential impacts of infrastructure rehabilitation will depend on the circumstances of each particular village.

Inadequate access to food is one of the underlying causes of malnutrition. Maternal child care, sanitation and access to health care are also critical (UNICEF 1990). Communities in the 'uncleared' areas in Trincomalee suffer from poor housing, damaged infrastructure and inadequate basic health services. In these villages access to a more varied diet is also limited by poor market access.

## Effects of Conflict on Food Security Patterns

In rural areas livelihoods are shaped by patterns of resource availability (land, forests, water) and access to markets, which can vary from village to village even in relatively small geographic areas, such as Trincomalee District of Sri Lanka. The effect of the conflict was to lay upon this patchwork of livelihood strategies an additional layer of constraints and opportunities that further differentiate the livelihoods and food intake patterns of households between villages.

These opportunities were particularly shaped by the status of a village as 'cleared' or 'uncleared', since this affected the movement of goods and people and the activities of government agencies. This has an impact on farmers' decisions to produce crops and their decisions to sell. It also affected the population's access to a wider range of purchased foodstuffs. In border areas, the fear of moving outside the village reduced the ability of households to make use of natural resources (such as the collection of honey or firewood), whilst in other villages the availability of arms had increased opportunities for hunting.

The movement of people due to the conflict has had impacts on claims on property and land-use decisions, including investment and maintenance. This may have influenced decisions to invest in irrigated land and led to greater emphasis on upland cultivation in some areas.

The payment of home guard salaries to some households helps smooth variation in household income and is important in areas where other opportunities are low. The most food secure households in cleared areas were those receiving a home guard salary. Some have suggested that these payments also reduced incentives to seek other livelihood activities (Korf *et al.* 2001).

Finally, widowhood and disability are clear consequences of the conflict which have devastating impacts on some households' ability to secure food and income. Remarriage and alcohol abuse are also important secondary effects which impact on both food availability and the care of mothers and children.

# References

Eide, W.B., Holmboe-Ottesen, G., Oshaug, A., Wandel, M., and Perera, D. (1986) *Introducing Nutritional Considerations into Rural Development Programs with a Focus on Agriculture, Report no.3 A Case Study: Nutritional Evaluation of Kirama Oya Basin Development Scheme in Hambantota, Sri Lanka*, Institute of Nutrition Research, University of Oslo.

Freudenberger, K. (1999) *Rapid Rural Appraisal (RRA) and Participatory Rural Appraisal (PRA): A Manual for CRS Field Workers and Partners*, Catholic Relief Services (CRS), Baltimore.

Integrated Food Security Programme (2001) *Trincomalee District Poverty Profile: Village Data Sheets*, Technical Paper 10, Integrated Food Security Programme, Trincomalee. Published at: http://www.ifsp-srilanka.org/html/tp10_village_data_sheets_2000.html.

Korf, B., Flämig, T., Schenk, C., Ziebell, M. and Ziegler, J. (2001) *Conflict – Threat of Opportunity? Land use and Coping Strategies of War-Affected Communities in Trincomalee, Sri Lanka*, SLE – Centre for Advanced Training in Rural Development, Berlin.

Reinhard, I. and Kramer, D. (1999) *Baseline Survey on Health and Nutrition*, Working Paper 24, Integrated Food Security Programme, Trincomalee. Published at: http://www.ifsp-srilanka.org/wp-24-baseline-survey.pdf.

Seaman, J., Clark, P., Boudreau, T. and Holt, J. (2000) *The Household Economy Approach: a resource manual for practitioners*, Save the Children, London.

UNICEF (1990) *Strategy for Improved Nutrition of Children and Women in Developing Countries*, UNICEF Policy Review Paper, UNICEF, New York.

# CHAPTER 5
## ENGAGING RELIGION IN THE QUEST FOR SUSTAINABLE FOOD SECURITY IN ZONES OF CONFLICT IN SUB-SAHARAN AFRICA

*Lucy Kimaro*

### Introduction

The World Food Summit of 1996 defined food security as existing 'when all people at all times have access to sufficient, safe, nutritious food to maintain a healthy and active life' (Food and Agriculture Organization 2008:1). Natural disasters and conflicts represent the two major threats to food security.

In 2012, approximately 870 million people around the world were estimated to be chronically undernourished (Food and Agriculture Organization 2012: 1). Conflict is a significant cause of undernourishment, since it hinders the production, distribution and consumption of food. This is particularly the case in Sub-Saharan Africa, a region which is highly food insecure. A report by the African Union (2009) indicates that between 1990 and 2005, Africa accounted for about half of the world's conflicts.

Food security is built on three pillars:

- Firstly, food availability, the existence of sufficient quantities of food on a consistent basis.
- Secondly, food access, which requires having sufficient resources to obtain appropriate foods for a nutritious diet.
- Thirdly, food use, which involves access to appropriate knowledge of basic nutrition and care, as well as adequate water and sanitation.

Conflict results in social disorganisation, inaccessibility of markets and substantial job losses, increasing food insecurity in both rural and urban areas (Cohen and Andersen 1999). According to a report from the Women's United Nations Report Network (WUNRN) (2009), conflict is also the major cause of poor healthcare, often through the destruction of health facilities like clinics, health centres and hospitals, as well as the increased medical load due to injuries incurred in conflict. Physical and economic access to food that not only meets people's nutritional needs but also their food preferences is crucial, yet its provision presents a big challenge in conflict zones (Gichure 2002: 165).

This chapter examines the current involvement of religious organisations in ameliorating suffering in zones of conflict, drawing on interviews with informants from Rwanda, the Democratic Republic of Congo (DRC), Sudan and South Sudan. It focuses on the moral role religious organisations play in promoting peace and fostering dialogue between warring factions, and also argues that women have a special role in engendering sustainable food security in conflict zones of Sub-Saharan Africa.

## Religion and the Quest for Sustainable Food Security in Zones of Conflict

Ethnographic literature is full of examples of the role that belief systems and religious personnel play in conflict resolution and in ensuring the sustainability of food security in conflict zones (e.g., Sundkler 1961; West 1975; Wanjohi 1997; Uwazie et al. 1999; Bujo 2001). Traditional societal values, passed on through the socialisation of children, have a suppressive effect on the level of conflict. However, the widespread nature of conflict in contemporary Sub-Saharan Africa indicates that genuine African traditional religion is not being adhered to in many areas and that traditional methods for conflict resolutions are not as effective as they once were.

As the efficacy of indigenous religions in Sub-Saharan Africa has declined, many international religious organisations are now involved in ensuring sustainable food security in conflict zones in Sub-Saharan Africa. As well as distributing food, the services provided by these religious organisations[1] include improving water supplies, raising awareness and lobbying governments and the United Nations (UN) with specific policy proposals. They encourage reconciliation through dialogue and sponsor women in self-help projects, which assist them in procuring food for their families (c.f. Danielle 2001: 16). Religious organisations also offer conflict mitigation training, while furthermore encouraging governments to increase their commitment to humanitarian assistance and dialogue for peace (Vassall-Adams 1994).

Christian religious institutions advocate peace through encouraging nonviolent solutions and sponsoring activities, such as playing sport (Melady 1974). In Rwanda, the Catholic Church has set up a national committee composed of both Hutu and Tutsi clergy and lay leaders to organise debates, workshops and seminars, leading to reconciliation, so enabling people to work together and produce sufficient food (Vassall-Adams 1994; Ellis 2007).

According to Jacobsen *et al.* (2001), forgiveness is an important strategy in creating peace, from which sustainable food security can be encouraged.

At the interfaith Action for Peace summit in South Africa in 2005, different religious groups, including representatives of traditional African religions and Bahai, Buddhist, Christian, Hindu, Islamic and Rastafari faiths, focused on peace-building mechanisms in Sub-Saharan Africa. Their emphasis was on the need for religious institutions to commit themselves to work for lasting peace in order to restore human dignity by helping Africans live decently. It was further observed that religious leaders have an important contribution to make, not only through their teachings, but also as a unifying force in society, encouraging their respective governments to adopt all-inclusive peace initiatives (Lutheran World Federation 2005). In the same way, Catholic bishops representing the nine Episcopal Regions of the Symposium of Episcopal Conferences of Africa and Madagascar (SECAM) in their meeting in 2009 urged all warring factions to stop all hostilities and destruction of human lives and property. They also asked neighbouring countries to get involved in promoting lasting peace and stability in the Great Lakes region (Carrera 2009).

Religious groups also encourage their supporters to help internally displaced persons (IDPs). A good example of this is from Rwanda during the war in 1994, when appeals by religious leaders helped those who were internally displaced. According to one informant interviewed for this chapter,[2] local churches mobilised their congregations in the area between the towns of Byumba and Kigali to collect whatever food they could and bring it to the parish for distribution to the many IDPs in need. Food collected included potatoes, maize, sorghum and beans. According to another informant,[3] in the town of Kabuga many people took refuge in local mosques that could accommodate only 200 people, but ended up accommodating 1,500. Likewise, the local Christian church with a similar capacity accommodated 2,000 people.

As well as promoting peace, religious leaders have an important moral role, condemning crimes committed by armed forces, such as the rape of women (Candiru 2007). This often leads to conflict between them and the warring factions, and they may ultimately be expelled from the areas where they are working. In Kabgaji Diocese in Rwanda in 1994, the Benedictine sisters of Sovu worked with the Catholic non-governmental organisation (NGO), Caritas International, to feed IDPs. Also, displaced people harvested fruit from the diocesan gardens and slaughtered cows and other animals belonging to the diocese, leading to religious leaders, including the local bishop, being targeted by militia groups.

In the case of South Sudan, an informant[4] reports that during the 1983–2005 Civil War, churches established a council to facilitate the distribution of food among IDPs and refugees. Christian organisations (including Caritas International, Missio Aachen from Germany, Manos Unidas of Spain, and others) also supported projects that helped to sustain food security, such as planting vegetables and buying animals. However, religious prejudice in areas of conflict can also affect the distribution of food. According to another informant, most Christian organisations that provided relief services for refugees and IDPs in South Sudan during the Civil War entrusted the task to Christian community leaders. The latter apparently would often not consider providing help to those who were Muslim or held animist beliefs, even though they were also affected by war.[5] In other areas of Sudan, however, Christian and Muslim leaders have worked together to promote peace[6] and it can be argued that the majority of Christian NGOs and organisations that provide relief services in war zones distribute aid to members of all religious groups without prejudice (Candiru 2007).

## Religion and Concern for Women and Children in Conflict Zones

In many traditional African societies, women have responsibilities for healing, for fostering the moral upbringing of children and for production of food. Thus women's roles in protecting life means that they are often recognised as more natural mediators than men, resolving social conflicts and promoting peace and harmony in society.

However, women are often a target for soldiers in conflict zones and prevented from fulfilling a mediatory role (this contradicts the observation by Mbiti 1988). In most African societies, women are viewed as 'life givers'; paradoxically, however, displaced women and children in conflict zones are usually the most marginalised groups, and are more vulnerable to violence and suffering (Cohen and Andersen 1999).

According to one Sudanese informant,[7] during the Civil War, soldiers from the Sudan People's Liberation Movement (SPLM) would often come at night to the individual's camp, looting food from the inhabitants and ordering women to cook food for them. They also forced women to harvest crops such as cassava, groundnuts and beans from their gardens for them, and transport the food to military camps. In this case, most women felt humiliated because some of these soldiers were very young, so the women felt that it was as if the soldiers were giving orders to their mothers. Furthermore, many women were raped and killed by the soldiers. In traditional belief systems in Africa, rape is regarded as a serious offence not only against the victim but against the whole society, including living and dead ancestors (Olupona 1991). The treatment of women in this way contradicts traditional African beliefs about the value and role of women in the family and society – turning women's bodies into battlefields – and is a clear indication that traditional values are no longer respected (Cohen and Andersen 1999).

In a study carried out in 2009 among women living in displacement camps in the DRC, Somalia and Uganda, more than seventy percent were reported to have been raped (Chibuye 2009). One report argues that rape and sexual violence against women and children have reached an epidemic level in Sub-Saharan African conflict zones (Lynn 2008). It has become a risk for women to harvest food even on their own farms, a situation which greatly hinders women's mobility and their ability to feed their families (c.f. Egan 1998). According to one informant from the DRC,[8] there have reportedly been many cases of women raped while working in their gardens, or when returning home from their fields. Other cases of rape, sexual violence and forced marriage have affected girls as young as twelve years old in some areas (Njenga 2008; Nsambu 2009). As well as causing psychological illness, this has made women vulnerable to contracting sexually transmitted infections (STIs). As military populations are two to five times more likely to be infected than civilians during such conflicts, the incidence of diseases like HIV/AIDS in the female population rises, further hindering their ability to engage fully in food production (Women's United Nations Report Network 2009).

In their preventive campaigns, religious groups try to create safe havens and help victims – especially women and children, who often need additional micronutrients beyond the nutritional rations provided by aid agencies (see also Henry and Macbeth this volume). A lack of iron is common. A study among Somali refugees showed that up to seventy percent of the women of reproductive age were anaemic (World Health Organization 2005), something which can be a serious problem in pregnant women. Malnutrition can cause the impairment of physical and mental functions and growth in children, causing stunting (Young 2000). Religious institutions help victims through the distribution of nutritional food (Bain 2007). They also sometimes help women to grow vegetables in refugee camps and thereby supplement the micronutrients missing in the food aid diet. In some areas they also help women to start small businesses, which enable them to provide better conditions for their families.

## Conclusion

The persistence of conflicts in Sub-Saharan Africa has contributed immensely to food insecurity in many areas (see also Oyeniyi and Akinyoade this volume). As observed in the discussion above, conflict often makes it impossible for victims to produce sufficient food for their needs. Traditional religious practices and associated methods of dispute resolution and reconciliation have broken down in many areas. International religious organisations have been in the forefront in providing the necessary help in terms of spiritual, economic and political support to the victims of conflict, thereby sustaining food security in the region. These organisations do not only provide food supplies to the victims, but they also support sufficient food production post-conflict with agricultural projects. This leads to self-reliance and ultimately food security. Religious leaders assist people to find ways to live in greater peace in zones of conflict, while advocating political stability and good governance to foster peace and enhance sustainable food security in Sub-Saharan Africa. Finally, religious groups have a particularly important role to play in helping the most marginalised groups in conflict zones, which are often displaced women and children.

## Notes

1  These include organisations such as African Muslim Agency, Caritas International, Catholic Relief Services, Jesuit Relief Services (JRS), Jesus Alive Ministries, Jewish Relief Services, Lutheran World Relief, Manos Unidas, Missio Aachen, Norwegian Church Aid and the Salvation Army, as well as traditional African religious institutions.
2  Third interviewee from Rwanda (2nd July 2012).
3  Second interviewee from Rwanda (7th June 2012).
4  Second interviewee from South Sudan (9th June 2012).
5  First Interviewee from Sudan (25th May 2012).
6  Second interviewee from Sudan (9th June 2012).
7  Second interviewee from South Sudan (9th June 2012).
8  First interviewee from the DRC (4th July 2012).

## References

African Union (2009) Towards Enhancing the Capacity of the African Union in Mediation, *ACCORD*, Addis Ababa, Ethiopia 15–16 October 2009. Published at: http://www.accord.org.za/downloads/reports/AU_Mediation.pdf. Accessed on 2nd May 2011.

Bain, C. (2007) Darfur: A Prison with No Walls, *The Tablet*, 9th June 2007.

Bujo, B. (2001) *Foundations of an African Ethic: Beyond the Universal Claims of Western Morality*, Pauline Publications, Nairobi.

Candiru, G. (2007) DRC Bishops Concerned over Violence, *Leadership: For Christian Leaders*, 463, August: 10.

Carrera, F. (2009) Burundi: SECAM Calls for Peace in the Great Lakes, *New People: The African Church Open to the World*, 120 (May–June): 6.

Chibuye, M. (2009) Poverty and Social Justice in the AMECEA Countries, *AFER*, 51(3): 242–260.

Cohen, M.J. and Andersen, P. (1999). Food Security and Conflict, *Social Research*, 66(1): 375–416.

Danielle, V. (ed.) (2001). *War has Changed Our Life, Not Our Spirit: Experiences of Forcibly Displaced Women*, Jesuit Refugee Service, Prati, Rome.

Egan L. (1998), Achieving Political rights – A First Step in Promoting Human Rights for All. Published at: http://www.trocaire.org/resources/tdr-article/achieving-political-rights-first-step-promoting-human-rights-all. Accessed on 23rd November 2011.

Ellis, S. (2007) *The Mask of Anarchy: The Destruction of Liberia and the Religious Dimension of an African Civil War*, New York University Press, New York.

Food and Agriculture Organization (2008) *An Introduction to the Basic Concepts of Food Security*. Published at: http://www.foodsec.org/docs/concepts_guide.pdf. Accessed on 6th June 2013.

Food and Agriculture Organization (2012) *The State of Food Insecurity in the World 2012*, Food and Agriculture Organization, Rome.

Gichure, P. (2002) Ensuring Sufficiency of Food in Africa. In Kanyandago, P. (ed.) *The Cries of the Poor in Africa: Questions and Responses for African Christianity*, Marianum Publishing, Kisubi, Uganda: 161–170.

Jacobsen, K., Lautze, S. and Osman A. (2001) The Sudan: The Unique Challenges of Displacement in Khartoum. In Vincent, M. and Sorensen, B.R. (eds) *Caught Between Borders: Response Strategies of Internally Displaced*, Pluto Press, London: 78–98.

Lutheran World Federation (2005) *Second Inter-Faith Action for Peace in Africa Summit: Collected IFAPA Documents and Reports*. Published at: http://www.lutheranworld.org/Special_Events/Peace_Summit/IFAPA-20050425.html. Accessed on 24th April 2012.

Lynn, J. (2008) Rape 'Epidemic' in Africa Conflict Zones – UNICEF. Published by Reuters at: http://in.reuters.com/article/2008/02/12/idINIndia-31908520080212. Accessed on 24th April 2012.

Mbiti, J. (1988) The Role of Women in African Traditional Religion, *Cahiers des Réligions Africaines*, 22: 69–82. Centre d'études des Religions Africaines, Université Louvain de Kinshasa, Kinshasa.

Melady, T.P. (1974) *Burundi: The Tragic Years: United States Ambassador to Burundi November 1969–June 1972*, Orbit Books, Maryknoll, New York.

Njenga, C. (2008) The forgotten victims, *New People*, 114: 12–14.

Nsambu, J. (2009) Why Africa Wallows in Conflict, *Leadership*, February 2009: 12–15.

Olupona, J. K. (1991) *African Traditional Religions in Contemporary Society*, Paragon House, St. Paul, Minnesota: 73–80.

Sundkler, B.G.M. (1961) *Bantu Prophets in South Africa*, Oxford University Press, London.

Uwazie, E.E., Albert, I.O. and Uzoigwe, G.N. (eds) (1999) *Inter-Ethnic and Religious Conflict Resolution in Nigeria*, Lexington, London.

Vassall-Adams, G. (1994) *Rwanda: An Agenda for International Action*, Oxfam, Oxford.

Wanjohi, G.J. (1997) *The Wisdom and Philosophy of the Gikuyu Proverbs: The Kihooto World-View*, Pauline Publications, Nairobi.

West, M.E. (1975) *Bishops and Prophets in a Black City: African Independent Churches in Soweto*, D. Phillip, Johannesburg and Cape Town.

World Health Organization (2005). Vitamin and Mineral Nutrition Information System (VMNIS). Published at: http://who.int/vmnis/anaemia/data/database/countries/som_ida.pdf. Accessed on 8th February 2011.

Women's United Nations Report Network (2009) *Our Bodies – Their Battleground: Gender-Based Violence in Conflict Zones*. Published at: http://www.wunrn.com/news/2009/10_09/10_12_09/101209_war.htm. Accessed on 4th May 2011.

Young, H. (2000) *Food Scarcity and Famine: Assessment and Response*, Oxfam Practical Health Guide No. 7, Oxfam, Oxford.

# CHAPTER 6
## LIVESTOCK PRODUCTION IN ZONES OF CONFLICT IN THE NORTHERN BORDER OF MEXICO

*Daria Deraga*

### Introduction

Drug wars and other related criminal activities along the northern border of Mexico have caused fear, unrest and abandonment of some livestock and other food production traditionally carried on in this zone. Cattle ranchers in the northern regions of Mexico, especially in the states of Sonora, Chihuahua and Coahuila, have historically been important suppliers of beef to the United States, as well as to the interior of Mexico. The importation of livestock into Mexico for breed improvement or the introduction of new breeds has also been an ongoing productive process. Ciudad Juarez has been one of the important crossing places for livestock and other products between Mexico and the United States, and is now the most affected.[1] Furthermore the Santa Teresa/Jerónimo installation at the New Mexico – Chihuahua border is well known for having efficient livestock import and export facilities, but is showing a decline in cattle passing through due to insecurity and other related factors.

In this chapter, I will try to address these problems and evaluate as far as possible the extent of the transformation of rural life in this extremely conflictive area. The main topics are the observed modification in livestock production, the insecurity or even closure of the northern border crossings for the movement of cattle and the migration of ranchers to other places. The border crossings are first described, and I outline the impact that insecurity has brought to cross-border transport of horses, as an example. I then go on to discuss the pressures that are brought to bear on individuals by those involved in drug cartels. In the final section of the chapter, I focus on the effects of declining livestock production rates on the socioeconomic situation in northern Mexico. Research is based on my personal knowledge of livestock production (Deraga 2008), observation and discussion with informants, and when possible, official government reports. In places, detailed information on moving horses is used to exemplify similar problems to the moving of cattle in this border region.

## The Border Crossings

There has been a very long tradition of cross-border transport of livestock between Mexico and the United States. Geographically, the main states for cattle crossings on the US–Mexican border are Arizona (US) with Sonora (Mexico), and New Mexico and Texas (US) with Chihuahua (Mexico) (Figure 6.1). The Mexican states of Coahuila and Durango use the facilities of the state of Chihuahua for movements to and from Texas or New Mexico.

On the Mexican side, the states of Sonora, Chihuahua and Coahuila are the most important cattle producing areas. Export–import is a thriving business; cattle that are destined for meat consumption are sold to the US, and a large number of breeding stock and young steers for fattening are exported from the US to Mexico. The state of Chihuahua is the largest cattle producer in the country, and the high quality meat from this area is distributed nationwide within Mexico, and large numbers of live cattle are exported to the US. On the US side, Texas is one of the most important cattle producing zones. Thus, the border crossings between Chihuahua and the states of Texas and New

**Figure 6.1**   Map of US–Mexican border states.

Mexico are crucially important for the economies of the regions on both sides of the border.

A brief example of the import practices of cattle moving from Mexico into the US at Santa Teresa, New Mexico has been described by Skaggs *et al.* (2004). This port is near El Paso, Texas, directly across the border from its Mexican counterpart, San Jerónimo. The cattle spend one to two days at the facilities of Santa Teresa, where they go through a veterinary visual and tactile inspection, and are sent through 60-foot-long vats of insecticide. The cattle then walk across the international border into the US where they are loaded on to trailers and transported to their final destinations.

The US government has been improving the facilities for the process of livestock coming and going across the international boundary between the US and Mexico; one example of this process is the Presidential Permit authorising the Greater Yuma Port Authority to construct, operate and maintain a livestock border crossing called the San Luis Livestock Crossing in the state of Arizona (United States Department of State 2007). This demonstrates the economic importance of the exchange of animals between the two countries. One of the important border crossings is between Ciudad Juarez, Chihuahua and El Paso, Texas, which has now unfortunately been virtually shut down due to the intensity of the ongoing drug wars in the area.

## Cross-Border Horse Transport

As a comparative example I shall use a case study involving horses travelling back and forth between Mexico and the US. (Although I use horses as an example, cattle go through similar processes.)

During 2010 the border crossing for horses at Ciudad Juarez was closed due to fighting between the Sinaloa and Gulf drug cartels over dominance and smuggling rights. The facilities consist of corrals and stables for keeping horses in quarantine until blood tests prove negative for the various contagious diseases that are controlled for at border crossings. There is a veterinarian service and office building on the grounds. This is normally an extremely busy place, and has direct contact with services on the other side of the border, such as veterinary care and transportation units for travel in the US. What is more, there are livestock brokers who organise the necessary paperwork for export and import of live animals.

Due to the closure of this facility, horses were instead sent to distant border crossings, being transported into California at the Tijuana (Mexico)–San Diego (US) border and onward to Kentucky for the World Equestrian Games that took place during that year. Many people lost money due to this situation. In the case of animals destined for food, to transport livestock such distances became economically impractical; the stress on the animals being transported for much longer periods than normal can cause weight loss and other health complications. Also, there is a much greater risk of encountering criminals who may hijack the transportation vehicles and steal the livestock. Trucks and trailers are sometimes stolen as well, along with the personal belongings of the drivers and other passengers. Theft of horses and cattle while being transported in northern Mexico now happens very frequently and is extremely serious. My informants have friends who have undergone this very traumatic experience while transporting horses.

Other informants stated that although the crossing at Ciudad Juárez was reopened in March 2011, the drivers and grooms who made the trip with horses stated that they had a private security escort accompanying them at all times. They were lodged in the office building at the holding area and told not to leave the building at all at night. It takes several days for livestock to be allowed to cross due to the tests undertaken. Needless to say, drivers and grooms were happy when they were finally able to cross into the US. It is a similar situation for cattle, which can also cross only with very strict security measures in place.

Furthermore, many of the ranches in this area are owned by people who specialise in Spanish and Friesian horses. In the last few years, as the drug wars have become more and more violent in these states, it has been observed that some of these ranchers have also become involved in these drug-related activities. It is very important to emphasise that there are many law-abiding citizens that have ranches dedicated to breeding, training and competing with the breed of Spanish horses known as PRE (*Pura Raza Español*). These people should not be confused with those operating in the criminal drug world, who also have a preference for this particular breed of horses. Yet, because of the involvement of the latter, in some areas of Mexico this breed has become associated in the public mind with those involved in drug-running. However, these criminals are a minority group and should not be regarded as representative of the majority of ranchers.

## Effects of Insecurity on Individuals

Bad experiences can cause a situation to be extrapolated in people's minds and become notorious. Purina is a well-known company which produces food for livestock in general and for pets such as dogs. A representative of this company sells grain mixtures for horses in the states of Sonora, Chihuahua and Nuevo Leon. The representative in question described an incident that occurred recently concerning the payment for grain that the Purina distribution store had sent for horses based at one of the more dubious ranches. The person in charge of the ranch only offered to pay half the total price, and proceeded to threaten the Purina delivery man with a gun. The delivery man was told that if he did not comply and leave – needless to say without his full payment – he would be shot on the spot. The man from Purina left without his payment, and obviously after that experience the company no longer sells in the area. During the interview, the individual informing me of this episode became very agitated and upset, a reflection of the level of trauma he had experienced, even though similar incidents had happened to other Purina workers as well.

The Purina factory in question is located in the city of Monterrey, in the state of Nuevo Leon, and the workers there are very much concerned with what has been happening. Production and sales for this area are dropping as jobs are being lost, and the company's purchasing power has been reduced to a low level. This has come about mainly due to the exodus of ranchers and livestock to other zones of Mexico, or the complete closure and selling-out of production installations, such as dairies and cattle pens. Many of the wealthier residents have shifted north to the US, taking up long-term residence there.

Meanwhile, the high levels of insecurity due to the drug wars mean that those who remain in northern Mexico go out only for reasons of necessity, and of course this affects their everyday consumer activity. As one woman told me, eating out at restaurants is out of the question for many local people due to the dangers they would be exposed to, even if they have armoured cars and bodyguards.

According to one informant, many cattle ranchers in the area have been kidnapped, and ransoms demanded for their release. Additionally, the theft of horses and cattle is on the rise. Due to this constant threat, some ranchers – especially the larger producing ones – have moved their cattle to the state of Veracruz, which is a safer zone. Others have sold all their livestock, and moved to other locations for their families' safety. Again it is the small family run units, raising dairy or beef cattle, which suffer since they have no economic opportunity of migrating to a different part of Mexico. However, there is little or no concrete information on these small family units due to the ongoing conflict in the zone, which has caused a distortion of news and data.

## Livestock Production and the Socioeconomic Situation in Northern Mexico

Fortunately there are many cattle ranches that maintain a successful production rate; it is possible that they have some sort of arrangement for protection from the drug cartels, because there are still a good number of animals crossing at different ports. The *Union Ganadera Regional de Chihuahua* (Regional Livestock Association of Chihuahua), the most important in the country, remains active at auctions, sales, expositions and so forth. Whilst the Association publicly criticises robbery, it makes no mention of any of the other forms of violence occurring in the area. Instead the association presents a very positive image. This could be a tactic to cover up bad publicity and to maintain consumer confidence as much as possible, which is understandable given the circumstances. Or, on the other hand, it could be that production losses in this zone are less than in other areas.

Recently there has been a further setback, as there has been a reduction of US and Mexican livestock inspectors being sent to work at some of the very important border crossings between the Mexican state of Chihuahua and the US states of New Mexico and Texas; because of the violence their personal safety cannot be guaranteed. This is another reason why there has been a decline of livestock passing through these ports.

In the state of Chihuahua, many families depend on work related to live-stock production. As the drug war crises continue, employment has become more and more difficult due to the relocation of livestock to safer regions of Mexico. This has led to reduced demand for ranch hands, cowboys and the like, which in the past was a steady way of life for many in this northern zone. Also affected are veterinarians, livestock brokers, animal transportation specialists and feed suppliers, among others.

I was unable to get official up-to-date statistics on the increase or decrease of production from Mexican sources. Most official data come from agricultural services on the US side of the border. These publications show that there has been a decline in cattle production; fewer cattle are being exported to the US but they do not mention the drop in meat destined for national consumption (c.f. United States Department of Agriculture 2010; New Mexico Border Authority 2011).

Mexican newspapers seem more interested in reporting the violence, such as the number of drug or gang-related assassinations or the capture or killing of a notorious drug lord, rather than the possible effect of all this on the production of food. So far the country's media have not commented on problems involving food production or the scarcity of livestock products. This may be due to poor or censored news reporting, or perhaps no real significant change is noticeable to those not directly involved in the situation.

The low media interest is exemplified by the lack of coverage on the murder of a high-ranking member of the Lala Dairy Company, founded in 1950 in Gomez Palacio, Durango (also in the northern zone). The Lala Dairy Company is now considered to be the largest in Latin America since it expanded into the United States in 2009, acquiring National Dairy and Farmland Dairies. Needless to say, the company has all the possible economic resources to ensure security one way or another for their installations, dairy workers, cows, and production transport units in the zone. However, just one informant from the area commented about the problems and the local conflict. I was told that when the murder of the businessman had been committed, the local population put the blame on criminals involved in the ongoing drug conflict. Yet according to this informant, after a rigorous police investigation had been conducted, the event turned out not to be related to drugs at all, but was due to a personal dispute which had been planned to take advantage of the ongoing criminal activities in the area as a cover for the crime.

Much better information comes directly from discussions with people involved in the livestock industry. Three different informants from Monterrey and Torreon, both cities located in the north, commented on how cattle ranching friends had been assaulted, and, due to these experiences, they had abandoned their ranches and moved their whole families to Houston, Texas. They also discussed the ongoing problems of cattle ranches being invaded by the criminal gangs, forcing out the owners. Often the military intervene to remove these illegal invaders. However, even after the owners have their ranches returned to them, this does not resolve the situation as it is often too risky to try to maintain a successful and sustainable cattle production operation. In addition, there is no real guarantee of safety for families or livestock; so, most of these ranchers prefer to abandon the area, and move on to other activities or relocate to a safer zone in Mexico or to the US. Consequently cattle production is on the decline. To meet national consumer demand, meat is increasingly being imported from the US, as this obviates the need for live animals to be transported through northern border crossings into Mexico. However, unfortunately for the consumer, the price of beef has gone up as a result.

## Conclusions

I have commented on the difficulties of carrying out research in this specific conflict zone, ranging from personal safety to accessing valid information. One main point I would like to stress is that under conflict situations, as in this case – and I might add in many other similar cases worldwide – it is extremely hard to document exact numbers, amounts in weights, or heads of livestock, to be able to calculate food increase or decrease. People in conflict areas who are involved and responsible for carrying out these tasks are continuously disrupted in their work due to the volatile, disruptive and very insecure environment. Animal health inspectors, for example, are restricted and cannot carry out proper documentation of the health and movement of cattle going back and forth across the US–Mexico border. This situation then makes it hard to obtain more exact numbers related to cattle production based on buying and selling between the two countries.

The issue of ethics also plays an important part in the approach adopted towards the research, particularly when the research is being conducted among people directly involved in the conflict in question. Jonathan Goodhand (2000) covers the problem and the importance of ethics related to research in war zones, pointing out that informants' names and positions must be carefully handled due to possible repercussions that could be directed towards these individuals when research results are published. In the case of the northern border of Mexico, several news reporters who lived and worked in the area and who spoke out by naming criminals along with their activities have been murdered. There exists an atmosphere of censorship, with those involved in the drug cartels controlling the media to a large extent.

People who want to survive and continue in their way of life as best as possible have set up defence mechanisms, such as keeping quiet, maintaining a low profile, and drawing as little attention to themselves as possible. This seems to work in this northern Mexico conflict zone among the cattle ranchers, because many are able to continue to produce successfully, although unfortunately not all.

My research work is founded on an anthropological perspective, and has been based mainly on observations – although, I might add, from a certain distance – and on discussions with people involved in livestock activities in this zone of conflict. Also, my experience and long-time involvement in the area of livestock production in Mexico has played a part in understanding the very difficult situation that has been described. I have tried to expose a topic that has not been discussed in Mexico. The response to my research has been very positive, and new contacts are now coming forward who wish to talk about what is going on, especially since they feel that their experiences are being set in an academic context. For these informants, academia seems to represent a safe world which stands apart from the realities of the violence going on around them.

## Note

1  The main criminal elements operating in Mexico are the following. 1. Drug Cartels – the Sinaloa and the Gulf cartels fighting over control of the northern border for smuggling drugs into the United States. 2. *Zetas* – a criminal gang of ex-military and police who joined forces with the drug lords. 3. *La Resistencia* – a new gang of outlaws who are taking advantage of the unrest and violence, but work separately from the other criminal affiliations.

## References

Deraga, D. (2008) *Sobre vacas y caballos en Jalisco. El saber especializado: un estudio en antropología cognitiva*, México Colección Científica, Serie Antropología, Instituto Nacional de Antropología e Historia, México.

Goodhand, J. (2000) Research in conflict zones: ethics and accountability, *Forced Migration Review*, Oxford Department of International Development, Oxford, 8 (Accountability): 12–14.

New Mexico Border Authority (2011) *Livestock Imports and Exports*. Published at: http://www.nmborder.com/livestock.html. Accessed on 7th May 2013.

Skaggs, R., Acuña, R.L., Torrell, A. and Southard, L. (2004) Live cattle exports from Mexico into the United States: where do the cattle come from and where do they go? *Choices: the Magazine of Food, Farm and Resource Issues*, 19(1): 25–29.

United States Department of Agriculture (USDA) (2010) *Mexico – Livestock and Products Annual 2010*, approved by Alan Mustard, prepared by Zaida San Juan and Daniel R. Williams II, Global Agriculture Information Network (GAIN) report number MX0064, 23rd September 2010.

United States Department of State (2007) Presidential Permit 07–02. *Authorizing the Greater Yuma Port Authority to construct, operate, and maintain a livestock border crossing called "San Luis Livestock Crossing" near San Luis, Arizona, at the international boundary between the United States and Mexico.* Published at: http://www.state.gov/documents/organization/99771.pdf. Accessed on 7th May 2013.

# CHAPTER 7
## THE LOGIC OF WAR AND WARTIME MEALS

*Nives Rittig Beljak and Bruno Beljak*

### Introduction

We shall start in a somewhat unusual way, with the conclusion. Although every war has its own peculiar logic, the 'how to' instruction manuals intended for people who are in the middle of wars are written on the basis of experiences of some past war that may have ended years earlier. All the instructions should emphasise this fact, even more so because every new war hides its basic riddle well – that is, the war's duration and intensity. Yet, these are important factors when considering how to deliver supplies to the military and civilians in a war that may end tomorrow or not for a long while; how to replenish supplies to besieged cities or when the war gets drawn out; how to ensure a steady supply of food and water; how to predict the intensity and manner of the enemy's actions.

This chapter discusses the experiences of the war in Croatia (see Figure 7.1 for a map of the area and places mentioned in the chapter), exemplifying conditions with particular reference to water, bread, preserves and livestock. The war began in 1991 and, with varying intensities, lasted for five years. In a short article it is difficult to present the whole character of the war and conflict in the Balkans (see Sundhaussen 1993; Allcock 2000; Jansen 2005). In order to understand the main conflict that led to this war one must understand that Yugoslavia in those days was multinational and multicultural. To make it easier to picture, there were six ethnic groups, four languages, three religious faiths and two official writing scripts. Different feelings of belonging had developed because of the variety in which ethnic groups had lived before Yugoslavia was formed after the Second World War. For example, past conflicts and crises were different for the Croatian and the Serbian populations, and different again for the Bosnians. Statistical surveys in the pre-war situation

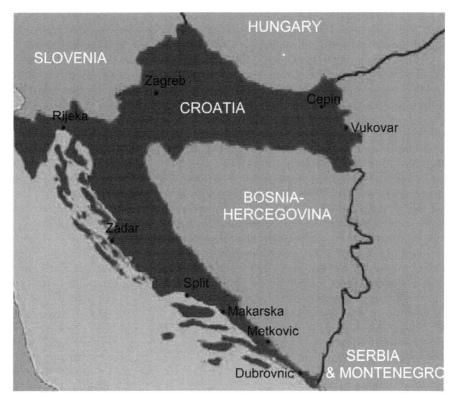

**Figure 7.1**   Map of Croatia.

in Yugoslavia show that only some of the population declared themselves to be Yugoslavs, especially those in mixed marriages. In 1971, 1.3 percent of the Yugoslav population declared themselves to be Yugoslavs. Nowadays this identity is problematic and causes numerous controversies (Jansen 2005).

## Breaking with Normal Everyday Life

The 'pre-war situation' is impossible to detect before a war's onset. In this pre-war period which is defined only in retrospect, preparations begin in accordance with the political climate of the country. In the case of the war in Croatia, one political side was calming the population down with soothing pacifist 'no-war' messages, while the other side was announcing all-out war and discussing possible war zones. News was reaching people through different channels: by word of mouth, from television, newspapers and weekly magazines, and through the most favourite medium – the radio – which gained in popularity because of its convenience. Radio was listened to especially during electricity cuts, or when people would run for safety and hide in shelters but managed to follow up-to-the-minute war news on their battery-powered portable sets.

An analysis of the press from the time just before the war shows that regular sections of newspapers, such as 'gardening', 'family care' or 'healthy cooking', were all turned towards war themes. The lack of certainty about the war – whether it was coming and, if so, how long it would last – was evident in the type of stories and food advice that news editors and reporters chose to run. Some advice resembled the type of perennial old-fashioned hints found in the Croatian, *Hundred Year Calendar*, and reference books for farmers and agriculture. In fact, some of the articles were most likely retrieved from such old sources. People could read about how to prepare dried beans for cooking a stew by wrapping them in a blanket to keep them warm before going to work, how the cool of a drawer well could replace the fridge and be used for food storage, how barley and wheat could be substituted for black coffee beans or how local wild plants could be used in macrobiotic cuisine. Similarly, Redžić (2010) wrote of the nutritional use of wild plants during the siege of Sarajevo in Bosnia and Herzegovina.

However, informal and formal headquarters for the distribution of food and management of public health during the war were established only after the situation had already become critical. Well-organised nation states maintain security protocols which set out procedures and rules for emergencies. The Republic of Croatia had nothing like that in 1991 for it was not an independent state. However, a small number of people did a great job, for example in containing animal diseases in war-affected areas during the war years, for such contagions pose a severe threat in times of war. The expert team dealing with this was mostly made up of veterinarians. Also notable in this work was the Crisis Headquarters of the Ministry of Health, which immediately started collecting medicine and medical supplies. The Ministry of Health and the Veterinary Service worked hard, and thanks to their efforts, infectious diseases did not spread. As in every war, some people showed outstanding initiative and bravery.[1] Nevertheless, they only began their activities after the war began.[2]

## What Were the Reasons for Delay?

At that time, only the Yugoslav People's Army (YPA) was professionally trained for emergencies and had the logistics capabilities and staff to deal with them. Aligned with the Serbian minority, the YPA left its army barracks in Croatia and moved to Serbia, which was at that time legally still one of the republics of the former Yugoslavia.

Until a Croatian army and police force were mobilised and consolidated, they were not able, especially on the front lines, to provide food and care (such as storing and rationing food, distributing pills for water purification and delivering bread) to civilians. With the strengthening of the Croatian military and its logistics capacity, proper rules of conduct in zones of conflict started to apply. Written instructions regarding these issues were then circulated throughout the armed forces, but the civil authorities dealing with the crisis needed more time to make decisions over the best courses of action. During the time of communism, the activities of humanitarian civil organisations had been discontinued. So, they had to be restored; even a network for the delivery of food had to be reconstructed. However, the Red Cross, United Nations protection forces, United Nations High Commission for Refugees (UNHCR), and Caritas (a Catholic humanitarian organisation) all remained active. Other connections with the world's humanitarian organisations were established quickly. Many of them opened their own centres in the capital of Croatia, Zagreb, which was not under direct threat.

## Ethnographic Reports

Here we provide a brief overview of everyday life during the war as reported by Croatian ethnologists who published two significant edited volumes during the war in order to report the situation to intellectuals around the world (Čale Feldman *et al.* 1993; Jambrešić Kirin and Povrzanović 1996).

During the 1990s, under the auspices of the Institute of Ethnology and Folklore Research in Zagreb, a research group investigated the ethnography of war. This group answered a need for cultural insight, investigating the causes and consequences of war in Croatia with straightforward research and a series of presentations, a 'Croatian ethnography of war'. The works published in this field of research became famous. Worthy of particular mention in this regard are the volumes, *Between Destruction and Deconstruction: The Preconditions of Croatian Ethnography of War* (Prica 1995); and especially *The Poetics of Resistance* (Prica *et al.* 1992). Two collections were published in English, *Fear, Death and Resistance. An Ethnography of War. Croatia 1991– 1992*, edited by Čale Feldman *et al.* (1993), and *War, Exile and Everyday Life*, edited by Jambrešić Kirin and Povrzanović (1996). They were well received in national and international anthropological publications. Both books reached the literature lists of foreign Slavic and anthropological studies.

From those first ethnological fieldwork studies, today's Croatian ethnologists can learn about different aspects of nutrition during the war, but they did not live through the experience of the war themselves; they did not suffer as their informants, who escaped from the front line, did. Although ethnologists could not identify directly with the informants, the refugee experience, memories and testimonials were nevertheless so full of emotion that they were often unable to combine academic distance with the reality of fieldwork.

Curiously enough, the stories about food did not pop up frequently in open interviews (c.f. the experience in Shepler's interviews, this volume). Although food is an essential everyday human need and without water people cannot live more than a few days, war topics, such as horror stories, destruction, death, isolation, hiding from snipers or political assessments were talked about more often. This is quite understandable: ethnologists were talking with refugees[3] who described themselves as 'angry and bitter people'; while in exile their basic existence was provided for. Reports about getting food and organising new war housing were discussed only when insisted upon. With time they realised that this report was necessary for the future. Survival skills were mostly involved with the distribution of food supply. Although these survival skills were part of the strategy of adaptation only in this war, only for one particular place, they belong to the 'history of survival skills'. Every report about survival skills will be crucial in the construction of common survival knowledge.

Our survey included besieged cities like Vukovar, Dubrovnic, Vinkovci; it was a complex story with many details, as refugees were not a homogeneous group. People did not believe that the war would begin, and when it did, they thought it would not last long. The summer before the war brought an unusual abundance of fruit, vegetables and grains. People shared what was left of their food provisions for winter with families and neighbours who ran out of their supplies. After the first bombs fell on Vukovar, people did not expect that they would have to spend months hiding in their cellars, so they just kept repairing the damage and moved the children to rooms in the back of the house.

The war was survived without psychological consequences by those who were able to accept the new reality and use all their creativity for their survival. War humour was the way to put grim reality aside.[4]

## Water, Water. . .

To exemplify conditions, we shall first describe some situations regarding water. Through necessity, the citizens of Vukovar came to realise the value of old and obscure wells. Water wells were frequently targeted by enemy forces, so the ones in the backyards of houses proved to be the most reliable. Eyewitnesses claim that there had been some very precise tip-offs about these, even about some well-secluded wells, so that they too were often hit. Going out to fetch water could mean risking one's life. Therefore, after they became aware of the enemy's habits, people fetched water early in the morning when enemy activity was at its lowest. This was also when all the other important activities, like delivering bread, giving blood for the hospital, etc., were carried out. Several witnesses commended the resourcefulness of a certain doctor who had filled the swimming pool in his garden with water in time. They took water from this for days, even when it turned completely green. People purified the water by using tablets or by boiling it. One informant reported:

We always had water reserves. Everything we could use to put water into was filled ... And it was taken from the well ... The location of the wells was a secret, to say nothing about the food, where a certain warehouse was located. They even shelled those wells, because there were tip-offs. The city centre itself did not have water, because the hospital used enormous amounts of it. (Testimony by V. Zlatko, 12th February 1992)

In the cities, people often had to wait for water in lines, where they were exposed to bombs and snipers, but water was indispensable and it did not even matter when it tasted of chlorine. The city of Dubrovnic had no power or water supply for 92 days. However, reports on the scarcity of water in Dubrovnic were not taken very seriously. This was because inhabitants could use old water cisterns for drawing water for cooking, and these were filled with fresh water by fire fighters with their cistern trucks. Every neighbourhood needed to build its own water supply plan. Radio Dubrovnic sent daily information regarding water supply locations, but people had to choose only the closest supplies because of the constant threat of bombing.

## Hunger and Bread

What would be the average quantity of bread in order for each citizen of Vukovar to get a daily ration of a quarter of a kilogram of bread? There would need to be about four thousand kilograms of bread baked for the 15,000 citizens of Vukovar, a city which before the war had a population of 45,000 inhabitants. When the city was under siege for days and there was no way provisions could be delivered into the city, people had to obtain them somehow. Where and how they baked bread, and whether they baked it at all, were secrets which were disclosed only after connection with the outside world was re-established. It was a city miles from other urban areas, under attack from enemy forces, with no electric power or water. How, indeed, did they bake bread? Did they eat it at all?

As in most of the accounts by the citizens of Vukovar, a reporter from radio Vukovar, while speculating on conditions in the besieged city, directly links hunger to lack of bread. The assessment of hunger is relative to the lifestyle that people were used to before the war. Hunger is caused by different sorts of shortages in different places: a citizen of Vukovar will experience and describe hunger differently from a modest fisherman from one of the islands in the Adriatic who is used to eating chard spread with olive oil. In areas where wheat is grown, such as the Vukovar region, to feel hunger almost stands for not having enough bread. Therefore, food that was lacking was exclusively replaced by flour-based meals. 'That's the way we were brought up', is what the people of Vukovar would say, in defence of their food habits, which is characteristic of the entire grain-growing region.

When we asked an experienced leader of the Vukovar refugees at a refugee reception centre in Zagreb which things he would provide for the citizens of Vukovar in times of war – if he had to do it again – he said to us straight away: water, yeast and flour (Rittig Beljak 1993).

> Yeast was the main problem. It was our number one problem. You couldn't make bread without it, and the bread you did make without yeast was, as they say, hard as shoe-leather. People would soak it in water or tea, and then eat it. When they had soup, they soaked the bread in it. That's why people asked to have liquid food, precisely because of that . . . When we did not bake, when there was no more yeast, you can't bake any more, then we would . . . My sister would knead some dough, and we had a wood-stove and we would bake small, something like, unleavened pastries. They were so hard, one couldn't . . . Then we would soak them a little, you soak them a bit, and then again it was all right. (Testimony by V. Zlatko, 12th February 1992)

Bread has a symbolic meaning because being without bread means to be hungry or to starve. The smell of fresh bread reminds one of 'home sweet home', a phrase that in a war situation sounds ironic because it was not one's warm cosy house but some dark and cold room in it from which you would often have to escape as soon as possible into the basement or shelter. Civil authorities in the major cities of Zadar, Dubrovnic, Vukovar and Vinkovci sought to ensure the continuous operation of bakeries. People in Vukovar discovered some old secret Yugoslav People's Army supplies that included stored yeast. In spite of that, there were periods of yeast shortages.

Taking into consideration the role of bread in nutrition, a shortage of bread is a big problem. Boxes containing yeast were airdropped for a while, which the defenders gathered and dragged into the city. After the roads were blocked, some basic commodities, including medicines and yeast, were dropped by air into the city, although the target was often missed.

> While we had the yeast, we used it. After that, we mostly baked unleavened bread, and only rarely was yeast replaced by substitutes (e.g., by sodium bicarbonate, by letting the dough grow stale, by adding hop preparations or red pepper preparations or by other old traditional methods). There often wasn't time enough to do it, especially in the Vukovar hospital, in whose crowded kitchen there were four hundred loaves of bread to be baked each day. (Testimony by Dr Juraj Njavro, a surgeon from Vukovar)

It is interesting that the young defenders of Vukovar, dug in near the Danube, came up with the idea of baking bread in live coals and in ashes, after remembering an educational series on the life of the Australian aborigines

and not, as might have been expected, by following any well-known, local tradition. There was an attempt to alleviate the problems with low-quality bread
('You cannot tell whether you're eating bread or your own teeth') by cooking
special meals. However, even at its best – with some eggs added – bread-mash
was considered to be the meal of the poor. The same amount of repulsion was
displayed for crisp bread and durable dried rolls.

## The Role of Other Foods

It has been shown that hunger is often aggravated by nervousness and anxiety.
Freshly cooked preserves helped because 1991 and 1992 were such abundant
fruit seasons, as did smoking: tea was used for smoking when there was no
tobacco. Smoking would decrease tension, and many non-smokers started
smoking during the war. The price of tobacco rose. In the shelters of Vukovar,
chess was played, not only as a way to pass the time. An older lady told the
story of inviting soldiers, who would come to wait in the shelter to play a game
of chess or two, because she was an excellent chess player. She would win a
cigarette for every game played. Tobacco was also a currency in war-torn
Sarajevo.

Hunger was more difficult to withstand and the need for food could not
be planned that well: in some houses and shelters there were fewer people
and in others several families together, so that perhaps twenty people had
to be fed. Food was fairly regularly distributed in public kitchens, hotels and
refugee camps behind the lines, but people were not happy because such
kitchens could not satisfy their tastes or traditional dietary habits, no matter
how modest these habits were. The people of Dubrovnic lived on grapes, figs,
olives and edible herbs that they would mix with potatoes. During moments
of calm, they would quickly pick herbs, fruit and vegetables in abandoned
gardens outside the city, which were not cultivated because it was not safe
to stay outside for too long. Such a diet resembled their everyday traditional
diet. Fishermen would risk their lives in their fishing boats and in speedboats
when venturing out to the open sea or islands close by, where fish were
abundant.[5]

People in rural areas that were not directly affected by warfare, but were
surrounded by enemy troops, had to think hard about how to survive on their
own. Their primary task was to cultivate their fields irrespective of the threat
of bombing. They fixed their old watermills where it was possible. Cattle feed
had to be provided, even more than before because the residents of destroyed
neighbouring villages entrusted their animals to them. The Croatian army
tried to help by sanitising hundreds of thousands of carcasses, taking care of
wandering and ill cattle, implementing comprehensive pest control procedures, disinfection and disinfestations of areas ravaged by war. That certainly
contributed to the favourable epidemiological situation in Croatia. Rescuing

a large part of the livestock allowed a faster recovery of cattle breeding after the war. The veterinary services acted autonomously, continually educated their experts in the field, and equipped peacetime mobile teams for emergency situations. We should remind ourselves that there is little time-lag between disasters that threaten animals and disasters that will affect the human population. If there is no effective response during that short time, people's suffering is also inevitable.

The inhabitants of Vukovar were fond of pork crackling, their favourite delicacy. Frozen crackling would melt when taken out of their freezers because of the long power cuts. So, to preserve the pork, they would prepare it by first roasting it well and then dipping it into pork fat – a process that was used prior to the advent of refrigeration.

'We were not receiving packets from the sky', complained some in the villages behind the lines. Relief packages were only airdropped into besieged areas and when convoys with food were not allowed to pass. Only basic provisions were dropped: flour, salt, sugar, oil, soap, detergent. Packages that arrived by roads were 'luxurious', containing such items as pasta, rice, chickpeas, baby nappies, toothpaste, powdered milk, canned meat, beans and pudding – and even popcorn and coconut, which just confused the displaced people, who were not that familiar with such exotic foods and did not have microwave ovens. War victims – users of these packages – were new both to hunger and also to foods that were different from their traditional foods. Chickpeas, for example, were foreign to people from Vukovar but much liked by Dalmatians. War sufferers from Vukovar were used to food made from white flour but could not prepare it because of constant shelling.[6]

## Conclusions

From the earliest history of wars, hunger has been used as a weapon – with the aim of bringing surrender or withdrawal of the enemy. This war was not an exception, as the dramatic headlines from the press testify. The ingenious recipes which people remember today reveal that starvation was less of an issue than how to ease the monotonous everyday diet. Women used to mix herbs for homemade 'Vegeta' (a popular brand of food seasoning) and made 'Eurocrem' (like Nutella, a hazelnut and chocolate spread) for kids. They baked war-cakes without eggs, and if they were able to raise chickens they would make homemade mayonnaise from eggs and horseradish. They recall how helpful information was from television shows, such as those on the Discovery Channel. For Christmas, they prepared delicious cabbage and meat rolls (*sarma*) from canned beef from Denmark. Local chemists gave helpful tips on how to bake bread in a pressure cooker, or how to make brandy out of rice, and engineers taught people how to charge car batteries in ancient watermills or by using a bicycle, or how to extend battery life.

As a part of the structural violence of war, we must not forget hunger, monotonous diet, foods on charity lists, limited mobility and loss of dignity – although insisting on dignity was quickly seen as pointless, and the majority of people found out that there was no shame in asking for food from those who had it. All people received the same amount and quality of food and more food was not given as a reward or for some accomplishment. There were, though, some unconscionable hoarders who incessantly stored food, as if another Thirty Years War was beginning. The code of ethics was frequently forgotten.

And finally, we hope that you will never have to go through these kinds of experiences during your professional lives.

## Notes

1  Special thanks for suggestions made by Dr.Vet.Med. Zlatko Čulig, author of a war manual referring to veterinary sanitation. Other experts and civilian associations published short 'how to do' manuals during the war. Booklets with written instructions were more useful than the Internet (which anyway was only in its infancy at the time) because of long power cuts.
2  For example, advice to psychologists who were dealing with war trauma: Krizmanić (1993); Krizmanić *et al.* (1994).
3  Refugees – usually a group of people or individuals that arrived in Zagreb in waves when their survival in war territory became critical.
4  The jokes about the couple Mujo and Haso adopted their themes to the war situation. For more examples see Povrzanović (1993).
5  A special contribution to the ethnography of war is the dissertation of the author, Maja Povrzanović (1997) concerning the fear experienced by ordinary people in the whirlwind of the war in Dubrovnic.
6  1.5 million missiles sized over 100mm were fired on Vukovar and 5 million projectiles under 100 mm (*Jutarnji list*, 8th November 2006).

## References

Allcock, J.B. (2000) *Explaining Yugoslavia*, C. Hurst, London.
Čale Feldman, L., Prica, I. and Senjković, R. (eds) (1993) *Fear, Death, and Resistance, An Ethnography of War, Croatia 1991–1992*, Institute of Ethnology and Folklore Research, Zagreb.
Jambrešić Kirin, R. and Povrzanović, M. (1996) *War, Exile, Everyday Life, Cultural Perspectives*, Institute of Ethnology and Folklore Research, MH, X press, Zagreb.
Jansen, S. (2005) *Antinacionalizam. Etnografija otpora u Beogradu i Zagrebu*, Biblioteka XX vek/152, Ivan Čolović (ed.), Beograd.
Krizmanić, M. (1993) *Ublažavanje i uklanjanje psiholoških posljedica rata*, Filozofski fakultet, Odsjek za psihologiju, Zagreb.
Krizmanić, M., Fučkar, G., Havelka, M. and Kolesarić, V. (eds) (1994), *Psihološka pomoć ratnim stradalnicima*, Dobrobit, Zagreb.

Povrzanović, M. (1993) Culture and Fear: Everyday Life in Wartime (Routine). In Čale Feldman, L., Prica, I. and Senjković R. (eds) *Fear, Death and Resistance. An Ethnography of War, Croatia 1991–1992*, Institute of Ethnology and Folklore Research, Zagreb: 148–149.

Povrzanović, M. (1997) *Kultura i strah: ratna svakodnevica u Hrvatskoj 1991–92*, doktorska disertacija, Zagreb: Filozofski fakultet, Sveučilište u Zagrebu. (*Culture and Fear: war in everyday life in Croatia 1991/92*, doctoral thesis, University of Zagreb).

Prica, I. (1995) Between Destruction and Deconstruction: The Preconditions of Croatian Ethnography of War, *Collegium Antropologium*, 19(1): 7–16.

Prica, I., Senjković, R. and Čale Feldman, L. (1992) The Poetics of Resistance, *Narodna umjetnost*, 29(1): 45–105.

Redžič, S. (2010) Use of wild and semi-wild edible plants in nutrition and survival of people in 1430 days of siege of Sarajevo during the war in Bosnia and Herzegovina (1992–1995), *Collegium antropologicum*, 34(2): 551–570.

Rittig Beljak, N. (1993) War lunch. In Čale Feldman, L., Prica, I. and Senjković, R. (eds) *Fear, Death and Resistance. An Ethnography of War: Croatia 1991–1992*, Institute of Ethnology and Folklore Research, Zagreb: 163–177.

Sundhaussen, H.(1993) *Experiment Jugoslawien. Von der Staatsgründung bis zum Staatszerfall 1918–1991*, Meyers Forum 10, Mannheim.

# CHAPTER 8
## NUTRITION, FOOD RATIONING AND HOME PRODUCTION IN THE UK DURING THE SECOND WORLD WAR

*Helen Lightowler and Helen Macbeth*

## Introduction

Several chapters in this volume discuss the disruption of food supply as a weapon in war. This chapter is about a nation's defence of the nutrition of its population during disruption of its previous food supply due to enemy action. It is commonly held that the British population across all socioeconomic levels had a healthier diet during the Second World War than either before or after the conflict. This chapter will explore the evidence for this assertion, and, if true, how it was achieved.

The British Isles are surrounded by seas which throughout history have been a protection against easy invasion. Furthermore, Britain had developed its empire on the basis of a strong navy and a large merchant fleet. This led to increasing importation of the nation's food using maritime routes both from the colonies and from elsewhere, including from other European countries. The Ministry of Food (1946: 7) publication, *How Britain was Fed in Wartime*, states, 'In the years before 1939 the United Kingdom depended on imports for considerably more than half her supplies of food'. This booklet goes on to provide statistics on these imports and their sources.

During the First World War, German submarines had attacked transatlantic shipping. Meanwhile the British Navy had blockaded German ports. In both cases these were deliberate acts of war, in which the aim and the effect was disruption of the importation of food and other necessities. As discussed by Rusca (this volume), food scarcity and famine in Germany at the end of the First World War remained strong in the memories of the German public during the interwar period.

Conditions during the First World War were also remembered in Britain because, according to the Ministry of Labour Retail Price Index (Mitchell and Deane 1962), prices, including food, had risen dramatically, and serious undernutrition of sectors of the population had resulted. So, in 1936 a 'Food (Defence Plans) Department' of the Board of Trade had been set up in case of emergency, and early in September 1939 this became the 'Ministry of Food' (MoF). It was recognised how much of the country's cereals, fats, meats and sugar were imported, and by the time that war was declared and the MoF officially formed, plans had already been discussed for the control of buying and distributing essential foods around the UK. Meetings continued between national and local government members and the relevant producers and traders throughout the 1940s (Ministry of Food 1946).

With war and the speed of German military successes in Europe, the foreseen shortages of food became a reality within a few months, and the government's proposed controls were put into effect. The objective of the MoF and the Ministry of Agriculture was to make the UK self-sufficient with enough food to provide the population with adequate nutrition and 'to ensure equal shares of the more important scarce foods to all consumers' (Ministry of Food 1946: 42), while also arranging some communal meal facilities and special provision for groups with particular nutritional needs. There were several aspects to this task and they all had to be planned: there was how to rationalise food imports with scarce shipping; there was how to produce more food within Britain; there was the control of distribution at regional and at personal levels; and there was the calculation of what was adequate nutrition for the population, bearing in mind individual variables, like age, occupation and health status.

This chapter will discuss how solutions to these aspects of the problem were planned and carried out and how the nutrition of the population was affected. It will provide supporting evidence for a period of relatively healthy nutrition for the British population as a whole during the Second World War.

## Food Supply

### Imports

For the first few months of the Second World War, food imports into Britain were maintained, but German forces continued occupying European countries that had exported food to the UK and were increasingly destroying ships carrying foods and animal feeds by sea to Britain. From June 1940 when Italy joined the war on Germany's side, the Mediterranean became dangerous for merchant shipping. Also, many British merchant ships and even trawlers were taken over by the navy, so that supplies of meat and fish were concurrently reduced for the population. By late 1941, Japanese successes in southeast

Asia, the Pacific and the Indian Ocean further reduced imports from that part of the world (Ministry of Food 1946).

Despite continued losses at sea, merchant shipping still brought food across the Atlantic and by spring 1940 the MoF had become 'the sole importer of . . . cereals, oilseeds, oils and fats, meat, bacon, dairy products, sugar, rice, starch, dried fruits, tea, coffee and cocoa' (Ministry of Food 1946: 25) and controlled their distribution. This enabled the MoF not only to make bulk purchasing contracts, but also to promote the technologies for condensing, canning and drying foods in order to rationalise space on scarce ships. 'Canned meat and fish, bacon, cheese, dried egg, condensed and dried milk were imported from the United States and Canada' (Ministry of Food 1946: 11). As the hard wheats of North America were more suitable than British wheat for bread making, by 1944 83 percent of wheat came from Canada (Williams *et al.* 2012) and it was estimated that 56 percent of all calories consumed by the British public were still imported.

## Home Production

Nevertheless to compensate for the reduction in imported foods, increasing home production of food became a government priority (Hollingsworth 1983). Farmers had to liaise with both the Ministry of Agriculture and the MoF. Owing to agricultural depression in the 1930s, a proportion of agricultural land in Britain had become uncultivated (Williams *et al.* 2012). This was ploughed up for crops. One crop that was increased was sugar beet, to replace the import of cane sugar. There was a move to reduce animal husbandry, with the exception of dairy herds, so that animal feed did not compete with human food and in order to increase land for crops. However, overall there was little reduction in pigs and poultry, as schemes to collect scraps, waste and swill to feed them were devised and more silage destined for animal feed was created from a variety of vegetation. Engineers worked to devise improved agricultural machines, renovate old machines and improvise equipment. Despite the pressure for military, naval, aeroplane and munitions production, other factories worked hard to produce agricultural machinery. As Williams *et al.* (2012: 2) point out: 'By the end of 1942, the Minister of Agriculture boasted "We have the most highly mechanised agriculture in the world".'

## Increase in Labour

The Women's Land Army was mobilised to increase the agricultural labour force. They worked in the fields, and not only drove, but learned how to maintain, agricultural machinery; other women were mobilised into the factories. Women entering occupations in which they had generally not worked before played a significant part not only in replacing male labour but in increasing labour as needed in wartime. Also, farm working holiday camps were set up for adults and children to help in harvesting crops.

An important, but hard to quantify, increase in labour for food production was by individuals in their home environments and in their 'spare' time. People began to raise chickens and rabbits at home, and there were 7,000 'pig clubs', whereby neighbours got together to raise a pig, even in the cities (Williams *et al.* 2012). Food scraps and waste were saved and either given to home-raised animals or gathered at community level. Harrison (n.d.) estimated that allot-ments contributed 'some 1.3 million tonnes of food from 1.4 million plots' (http://www.allotment-garden.org/allotment/Allotment-History.php). The government promoted the 'Dig for Victory' (Figure 8.1) campaign and public parks, railway embankments, road verges and gardens were dug up and cul-tivated for food. In Hansard (1943) is a House of Commons discussion of an incident highlighting competing wartime demands: railings from allotments in Ilkley were removed under the direction of the Ministry of Supply for metal

**Figure 8.1**   'Dig for Victory' poster. Copyright Imperial War Museum PST0200.

collection, after which moorland sheep had invaded the allotments and eaten plants destined for human food. The railings were reinstated.

## Distribution, Rationing and Public Information

### Dispersal and Transport

There was also Ministry control of all foods whether imported or produced in UK and it was prohibited to sell most foods except to the MoF; farm animals could only be slaughtered at specified collection centres; all milk went to the Milk Marketing Board, etc. Dispersal of foods around the country was also rationalised because of the limitation of all transport. Dispersal from ports was swift because of risk from bombing, and from most warehouses to avoid spoilage. Transport schemes were devised which pooled resources and divided delivery areas into sectors. Retail deliveries, which before the war had involved rival retailers covering similar routes, were rationalised and consumers had to register with one retailer; for example, those delivering milk were each given one specific route (Ministry of Food 1946).

For many foods, brand names were replaced by national names in plainer packaging and the ingredients standardised and generally economised. Furthermore, research went into how much one could reduce packaging, looking at issues such as how thin packaging could be, what material could replace tin, the use of synthetic rubber and the creation of recycling schemes.

### Rationing

In preparation for war, personal ration books had been printed and stored in 1938. Within the month that war was declared (September 1939), registration of all individuals for their identity cards and ration books was carried out (Charman 2009); there was a requirement in November 1939 for individuals to register with retailers for certain rationed foods, so that the MoF could effect a system of appropriate distribution (Ministry of Food 1946). Rationing began in January 1940, with meat, bacon and sugar the first items rationed. Holding a ration book became a necessity but despite negative articles in some newspapers (Charman 2009), it is said that most people felt that rationing was 'fair'. This feeling was enhanced as the Royal Family was included in the rationing scheme. Registering with retailers, however, caused problems for those regularly on the move, whether 'traveller' folk or travelling salesmen.

Several foods were never rationed during the war, for example bread (although that was rationed in the immediate post-war period), potatoes, coffee, vegetables, fruit (other than citrus fruits) and fish. Being unrationed did not necessarily mean availability. Different food items were rationed in different ways, for example, most were rationed by weight or quantity, while the meat ration was monetary, i.e., one shilling and two pence of meat a week (Ministry of Food 1946; www.birmingham.gov.uk; www.livingmemory. org.uk). This variant, of price rather than quantity, enabled people to get a greater quantity of cheaper cuts of meat and offal if they chose. Stephen and Sieber (1994) state that the general rise in fat consumption during the twentieth century was temporarily reversed during the Second World War. British life no doubt included queues, grumbling, and accusations about some retailers and a lack of diversity in the food, but the system worked to share scarce food resources throughout the population.

The full details of rationing schemes for individuals and how these progressed through the five years of war and thereafter in the post-war period are beyond the scope of this chapter but they can be found in Appendix D of the Ministry of Food (1946) booklet.

## Off the Ration

The government required factories with more than 250 workers to have canteens, and food beyond the ration was distributed through these. In 1939, 1,500 factories had canteens but by 1945 18,500 had (www.birmingham.gov. uk). Local authorities were encouraged to set up restaurants for workers in towns to provide nutritious, simple and inexpensive meals. The first of these 'British Restaurants' was established in London in 1940 (Ministry of Food 1946) and others followed in other cities. There was a 'Rural Pie' scheme to provide meat pies and sandwiches, delivered to agricultural workers by volunteers, and there were school meals. Eating at any restaurant remained off rations throughout the war. There were the 'Queen's Messengers', an emergency feeding scheme that provided food to victims of air raids. Finally, those who could do so supplemented their rations with wild foods, and a state-imposed rationalisation of game shooting was set up (Martin 2011).

## Education, Publicity and Propaganda

The MoF made a point of getting food information and advice out to people in several popular ways. On weekdays, the BBC broadcast 'The Kitchen Front' on the radio and a collection of 122 of those BBC wartime recipes, selected by the Ministry of Food, was published under the same title (Bruce 1942). In a recent study, Barker and Burridge (2013) showed how MoF dietary information was regularly featured in British women's magazines of the 1940s, advocating relevant nutritional advice, and suggesting that it was the housewife's duty to the war effort to provide nutritional food. Marguerite Patten[1] was part of a team that went out to hospitals, canteens, organisations and marketplaces

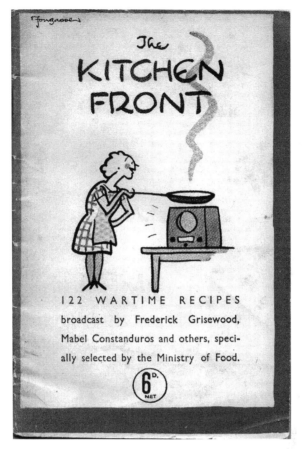

**Figure 8.2**  *'The Kitchen Front'* booklet.

to advise people about food and cooking under wartime conditions (Moss 2010). There were posters, of which much remembered are those of 'Dr. Carrot' and 'Potato Pete'. Both vegetables were used in 'Woolton Pie', an all-vegetable 'pie' topped by mashed potato. When people went to the cinema there were minute-long light-hearted films giving useful food advice (Moss 2010). Also, people shared recipes such as for a 'butterless, milkless, eggless cake' (handwritten recipe).

## The Holistic Approach

In twentieth-century Britain, as elsewhere, there had been increasing specialisation, and so diversification, in occupations, businesses, industries, academic disciplines and government departments. So, it was important to the innovative organisation needed to procure sufficient nutrition for the whole population that two individuals, both with varied backgrounds, came to be responsible for so much of the planning. These two understood and fostered a holistic approach to the complex problems.

The first is Lord Woolton, who had a background that had combined business success, social concern and several government advisory positions. He had previously witnessed the effects of malnutrition on health and understood that nutritional requirements must be fundamental to the complex planning required, so that even the poor should have a basically healthy diet throughout the war. As well as overseeing efficient organisation of procurement and distribution on a huge scale, in national and regional offices around Britain, he required the collection of relevant statistics and was a good and trusted communicator (Charman 2010).

The second, Jack Drummond, had a university background in research into the biochemical study of nutrition, but he also had a broad interest across all topics concerning food and nutrition. This was a period when McCarrison (1953) was one of the first to promote the need to apply scientific nutritional knowledge to public health. With Wilbraham, Drummond had published *The Englishman's Food* (Drummond and Wilbraham 1939), a survey across five-hundred years of dietary habits. Although seconded to the MoF to be Chief Advisor on Food Contamination, he wrote two memoranda relevant to the broader view needed (Hollingsworth and Wright 1954), one in 1939 on coordinating all perspectives of food research, and one in January 1940 on the food situation right across the whole UK (Dennehy *et al.* 1940). In February 1940 Drummond was appointed as Scientific Adviser to the MoF. This brought to the MoF his nutritional expertise, his view on applying scientific information to public health and his broad-ranging understanding of the British diet, together with an exceptional ability to communicate scientific information to non-science colleagues (Hollingsworth and Wright 1954).

It would seem that the combined broad-ranging skills and pursuit of the holistic approach of these two dedicated men, in cooperation with Henry Dale, Lord Horder and others, played an important part in ensuring the positive nutritional state of the UK general population by the end of the Second World War. These nutritional perspectives are now considered.

## Nutrition

The experience of malnutrition (in particular undernutrition) and poor health during the First World War was remembered in 1939, but twenty one years had elapsed since the end of the First World War, during which scientific understanding about the energy and nutrient content of foods and the nutritional requirements of different individuals had increased greatly. So, memory plus knowledge underpinned the MoF decisions about the management and rationing of essential foods, discussed above, and the first comprehensive nutrition policy (Darke 1979), resulting in a national policy for food rationing. The aim of this policy was to 'maintain the minimum nutrient intake for the population compatible with health' (Huxley *et al.* 2000: 247).

The wartime changes to the supply of food tended to lead to a diet that was dull and lacked palatability, and as such people tended not to eat sufficiently to meet their energy requirements. In order to help ensure an adequate supply of energy and protein, attention was given to increasing the UK supplies of milk, cheese, fish, grain products (including for bread), potatoes and other vegetables compared to supplies before the war (Hollingsworth 1983). However, with the reduction in meat, eggs, oils and fats, sugar and imported fruits there were inevitably changes in the nutritional composition of the diet, which could have consequences for some micronutrients, in particular vitamin A, vitamin C, thiamine and calcium.

## Enrichment of Foods

One of the key aims of the MoF nutrition policy was to maintain an adequate energy supply. The energy value of the food supplies in 1946 was 96 percent of supplies before the Second World War (Hollingsworth 1983). Fat and vitamin A were the only nutrients that were in short supply – 86 percent and 95 percent of supplies before the war, respectively – while the supply of many nutrients showed an improvement. To ensure that people were meeting their daily nutrient requirements, the enrichment of certain foods with vitamins and minerals was introduced in 1941 (Fisher 1977). The main food source to be fortified was flour and, as a consequence, bread. Flour was enriched with calcium carbonate, thiamine, niacin and iron. Margarine was fortified with vitamin A and vitamin D; enriching margarine with vitamin D helped to ensure that the calcium added to flour and bread would be better absorbed. In addition, the fortification of margarine made it nutritionally interchangeable with butter, thus helping to maintain adequate energy and nutrient supplies to the total population.

Other foods that were enriched included infant dried milk which was fortified with vitamin D. In addition, orange juice and cod liver oil were made available to pregnant women and children up to the age of five years (Hollingsworth 1979).

Furthermore, prior to the Second World War, the extraction rate of flour had fallen to below seventy percent, resulting in a white bread of reduced nutritive value. However, due to supply reasons rather than nutritional reasons, the extraction rate of flour was raised to seventy-five percent in 1941 and eighty-five percent in 1942 to make the wheat go further. This not only provided extra flour per ton of wheat but also produced bread with an improved nutritive value, notably with B-vitamins, iron and fibre (Magee 1946; Fisher 1977;

Hollingsworth 1983). Furthermore, as bread was not rationed until 1946, the energy demands of people, and in particular the increased energy demands of workers in heavy industry, were largely met.

## Rationing Constraints

When rationing was introduced in January 1940, there were four different categories of ration books: RB1 for adults, RB2 for young children, RB3 for travellers and RB4 for older children (Ministry of Food 1946; Fisher 1977). Two important aims of the rationing policy were to maintain an adequate supply of energy and to ensure that this supply was distributed according to physiological requirements. Basic foodstuffs were rationed more or less equally among the population. These basic foods included bacon, fats (butter, margarine, cooking fats), cheese, eggs, tea, sugar, preserves and sweets, and carcass meat with children under five years old getting 'more milk, eggs, cheese and less meat and fats than adults'. Also, vegetarians were able to obtain more cheese instead of meat. In order to maintain flexibility to meet energy needs, bread, flour and potatoes were not rationed and this was preserved for as long as possible (Hollingsworth 1979, 1983). However, bread was later rationed for two years in 1946, and potatoes were sold under a 'special control system' from 1947 to 1948 (Darke 1979; Hollingsworth 1983).

As well as the rationing of basic foodstuffs, special schemes were devised to help maintain the health of the total population. These included encouraging people to consume more green and root vegetables and therefore to grow more vegetables, fruits and potatoes (Fisher 1977), for example in gardens and allotments as mentioned above. Although fruits, especially imported citrus fruits, were an important source of vitamin C before the war, the restriction on imports of fruits meant that other sources of vitamin C had to be obtained (Magee 1946). Thus, potatoes and vegetables became the main source of vitamin C and people were encouraged to produce the maximum amount of potatoes and vegetables. Moreover, an increase in the production of potatoes also helped to meet the energy demands of the population.

Special nutritional adjustments were also achieved through the off-ration school meal, factory canteen and rural pie schemes mentioned above (Hollingsworth 1979, 1983). Individuals undertaking heavy work could obtain extra food from their work canteen or from community feeding centres. Other classes of heavy workers (for example agricultural labourers and miners) were given an extra ration of cheese if they could not access food from community feeding centres (Magee 1946). In addition, a number of special measures were taken to safeguard the nutritional status of pregnant and lactating women, infants and children. These measures included the development of a national milk scheme (see below) and a vitamin scheme. The vitamin scheme included supplements of welfare orange juice and cod liver oil for pregnant and lactating women and children up to the age of five years. In addition, a priority supply of eggs was available for pregnant women and children aged six months to two years (Darke 1979). School meals helped the nutritional needs of children aged five to fourteen years. These meals drew on special rations, in particular a larger meat ration than for industrial canteens (Hollingsworth 1983).

## Milk and the National Milk Scheme

Britain was a milk-producing country and the highly nutritive value of milk had been clearly demonstrated between the two world wars (Magee 1946). In particular, the importance of milk with regards to intakes of energy, protein, calcium and riboflavin was recognised. Before the Second World War, milk consumption was 0.41 of a pint (233 ml) per day, but the consumption of milk increased during the war up to 0.66 of a pint (375 ml), although this was still below the 0.88 of a pint (500 ml) considered desirable from a health point of view (Magee 1946).

Priority schemes for supplies of milk were devised. These included a reduced price or free milk for children under five years of age and pregnant women, and priority supplies of milk at home for children aged between five and eighteen year and lactating women. A national milk scheme was introduced in 1940 (Darke 1979), whereby one pint of milk per day was available at a reduced price for pregnant and lactating women and those with children under five. For bottle-fed children, one tin of 'National Dried Milk' per week could be claimed (Darke 1979). The national milk scheme was also expanded to include a national milk cocoa drink, which was made available to adolescents (age fourteen to eighteen years) who worked in the factories and to youth clubs (Darke 1979; Hollingsworth 1983).

Although the Oxford Nutrition Survey established by Hugh Sinclair carried out surveys of the British population throughout the war, generating copious data and some analysis, almost none of the results were ever published.[2] However, one set of Oxford Nutrition Survey data on the nutritional status of pregnant and lactating women, a sub-group of the population considered to be at risk of malnutrition, has more recently been reviewed and the conclusions published (Huxley et al. 2000). In 1942, prior to the food supplementation schemes, the Oxford Nutrition Survey found deficiencies in a number of nutrients (Figure 8.3). In particular, of the pregnant women studied in 1942, deficiencies were found in the haemoglobin status (48 percent of women), protein status (25 percent of women), vitamin A status (63 percent of women), and vitamin C status (78 percent of women). However, by 1944 the addition of food supplements to the diets of pregnant women, as presented in Figure 8.3, showed a positive effect on reducing vitamin A, vitamin C and riboflavin deficiencies, but the proportion of women within the normal range for haemo-

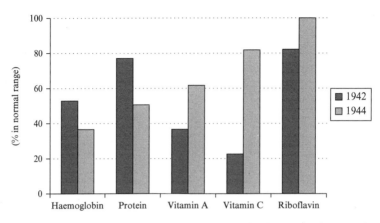

**Figure 8.3**  Percentage of pregnant women within the normal range for biochemical measures of iron, protein, vitamin A, vitamin C and riboflavin (data from Huxley *et al.* 2000).

globin and protein levels had reduced (Huxley *et al.* 2000). Meanwhile the rates of stillbirths, neonatal and infant deaths and maternal mortality all decreased (Darke 1979).

## Nutrients Available for Consumption

Data on the nutrients available for consumption give an indication of the nutritional value of the diet during the war, but do not necessarily give accurate information on the amount actually consumed by the population. However, because of the war propaganda against waste, it can be assumed that food wastage during the Second World War would have been less than in the pre-war years.

The diet as a whole was nutritionally more balanced than during pre-war years. Although protein intakes were adequate during the war, the protein quality of the diets caused some concern as increases in milk and cereal protein and a decrease in animal protein were observed (Magee 1946). The amount of animal protein available for consumption was below the pre-war requirement, although the amount available for children and pregnant and lactating women was deemed adequate (Hollingsworth 1983).

Fat intake was reduced but it is interesting to note that the percentage of energy from fat during the war years (33 percent) was similar to the percentage that is now recommended for health (Department of Health 1991). With this reduction in fat intake came a reduction in energy intake overall. In addition, other foods which were available during the war may have been rendered 'less palatable' with this reduction and restriction of fat (Hollingsworth

1983). The amounts of micronutrients available for consumption were generally adequate. In particular, calcium (due to the increase in milk consumption) and thiamine (after the higher flour extraction rate) were increased (Magee 1946).

Whereas the worst year nutritionally for food consumption during the Second World War was 1941 (Magee 1946), the nutrition policy, increase in knowledge and various schemes devised seem to have helped to ensure that the actual diet and nutrients available in 1941 were not very different from in the pre-war years, and were distributed more evenly across the population.

## Conclusion

At the end of the Second World War, the nutrition policy programme was deemed highly successful and the nutritional status of the population improved – the health of the nation was deemed to be better in 1945 than in 1939 (Darke 1979). Improvements in all measurements of health, such as growth in children and reduction in infant and maternal mortality, were seen. The success of this nutrition policy may be attributed in part to the adequate supply of energy that was maintained throughout the war. In addition, the distribution of food supplies according to physiological requirements and the scientific approach to nutritionally balanced foods available all contributed to this success.

Further support for this conclusion is provided by comparison with the nutrition in Germany and other European countries at the end of the Second World War. Several British nutritionists, for example, Sinclair, McCance and Drummond, were seconded to study the nutritional state of people in these countries as access became available from 1944 onwards, and were shocked by what they found. Sinclair, wrote from Germany (cited in Ewin 2001: 167) that the German diet was 'now almost entirely bread and potatoes ... with very little bread and almost no potatoes ... Add to that the difficulties of cooking (no fuel, no utensils)'. Conditions in Holland were particularly bad in the last year of the war (Burger *et al.* 1948). Mouré (2010) concluded that the French rationing system was poorly organised, while Theien (2009) writes of good cooperation of the public to rationing in Norway and suggests that the avoidance of famine in Oslo was due to the rationing. The League of Nations (1946: 4) describes the rationing systems in different countries and concludes that 'the British system remained throughout the war more elastic than the German system and better adjusted to individual needs'.

Two contemporary perspectives arise: first, the health benefits or detriments of the Second World War's food policies are long as well as short term. While those, who were born or young under the circumstances of those policies, continue to live and die, Neugebeuer *et al.* (1999) have pointed out that their lifelong health experience can be tracked allowing epidemiological studies related to early nutrition. Such studies exist.

Secondly, as this chapter concludes that the Second World War's food policies in the UK were beneficial, can this information be useful in current or future situations of economic stress? Could such government-controlled nutrition policies be valuable again?

## Notes

1  Marguerite Patten was a subsequently famous cookery writer and broadcaster.
2  The original intentions of the authors in embarking upon this chapter had been based on knowledge of the extent of the Oxford Nutrition Surveys and Sinclair's work, only to find that so little emanating from these surveys has ever been published.

## References

Barker, M.E. and Burridge, J.D. (2013) Nutrition claims in British women's magazines from 1940–1955, *Journal of Human Nutrition and Dietetics*, DOI: 10.1111/jhn.12075. Accessed on 24th February 2014.
Bruce, P.J. (ed.) (1942) *The Kitchen Front*, Nicholson and Watson, London.
Burger, G.C., Sandstead, H.R. and Drummond, J.C. (1948) *Malnutrition and Starvation in Western Netherlands, September 1944 to July 1945. Part I and II*, General State Printing Office, The Hague.
Charman, T. (2009) in association with the Imperial War Museum, *Outbreak 1939*, Virgin Books, London.
Charman, T. (2010) Imperial War Museum's Ministry of Food. Published at: www.culture24.or.uk/history_&_heritage/war-and-conflict/world-war-two/art76114. Accessed on 20th February 2014.
Darke, S.J. (1979) A nutrition policy for Britain, *Journal of Human Nutrition*, 33, 438–444.
Dennehy, I., Drummond, J.C. and Duckham, A.N. (1940) *A Survey of Wartime Nutrition with Special Reference to Home Production Foods and Import Policy*, MAFF 98/46 National Archives.
Department of Health (1991) *Dietary Reference Values for Food Energy and Nutrients for the United Kingdom*, The Stationery Office (TSO), London.
Drummond, J.C. and Wilbraham A. (1939) *The Englishman's Food: A history of five centuries of English diet*, Jonathan Cape, London.
Ewin, J.H. (2001) *Fine Wines and Fish Oil: the life of Hugh Macdonald Sinclair*, Oxford University Press, Oxford.
Fisher, P. (1977) The promotion of nutrition and food by the Ministry of Food in 1940–54, *Proceedings of the Nutrition Society*, 36: 349–353.
Hansard (1943) Railings Removal (Allotments, Ilkley), *House of Commons Debates*, 387(February): 155–156.

Harrison, J. (n.d.) *Allotment History – A Brief History of Allotments in the U.K.* Published at: http://www.allotment-garden.org/allotment/Allotment-History.php. Accessed on 22nd February 2014.

Hollingsworth, D.F. (1979) A national nutrition policy: can we devise one? *Journal of Human Nutrition*, 33: 211–220.

Hollingsworth, D.F. (1983) Rationing and economic constraints on food consumption in Britain since the Second World War, *World Review of Nutrition and Dietetics*, 42: 191–218.

Hollingsworth, D.F. and Wright, N.C. (1954) Sir Jack Cecil Drummond, D.Sc., F.R.I.C., F.R.S. (1891–1951), *British Journal of Nutrition*, 8(4): 319–324.

Huxley, R.R., Lloyd, B.B., Goldacre, M. and Neil, H.A.W. (2000) Nutritional research in World War 2: The Oxford Nutrition Survey and its research potential 50 years later, *British Journal of Nutrition*, 84: 247–251.

League of Nations (1946) *Food, Famine and Relief 1940–1946*, League of Nations, Geneva.

Magee, H.E. (1946) Application of nutrition to public health, *British Medical Journal*, 1: 475–482.

Martin, J. (2011) British game shooting in transition, 1900–1945, *Agricultural History*, 85(2): 204–224.

McCarrison, R. (1953) *Nutrition and Health: Being the Cantor lectures delivered before the Royal Society of Arts, 1936, together with two earlier essays*, Faber and Faber, London.

Ministry of Food (1946) *How Britain was Fed in War Time: Food Control 1939–1945*, HMSO, London.

Mitchell, B.R. and Deane, P. (1962) *Abstract of British Historical Statistics*, Cambridge University Press, Cambridge

Moss, R. (2010) Ministry of Food – Imperial War Museum shows how Britain fed itself in WWII. Published at: www.culture24.org.uk/history_&_heritage/war_&_conflict/world_war_two /art76042. Accessed on 7th June 2012.

Mouré, K. (2010) Food rationing and the black market in France (1940–1944) *French History*, 24(2): 262–282.

Neugebeuer, R., Hoek, W.W. and Susser, E. (1999) Prenatal exposure to wartime famine and development of antisocial personality disorder in early childhood, *Journal of the American Medical Association*, 4:282(5): 455–462.

Stephen, A.M. and Sieber, G.M. (1994) Trends in individual fat consumption in the UK 1900–1985, *British Journal of Nutrition*, 71: 775–788.

Theien, I. (2009) Food rationing during World War Two: a special case of sustainable consumption? *Anthropology of Food*. Published at: www://aof.reveues.org/index6383.html. Accessed on 16th April 2012.

Williams, C.A., Taylor, R. and Martin, J. (2012) *Wartime Farm*, Open University, Milton Keynes.

www.birmingham.gov.uk *'Lest we Forget' Online Exhibition*. Published at: http://www.birmingham.gov.uk/cs/Satellite?c=Page&childpagename=Lib-Central-Archives-and-Heritage%2FPageLayout&cid=1223092756358&pagename=BCC%2FCommon%2FWrapper%2FWrapper. Accessed on 20th February 2014.

www.livingmemory.org.uk/Homefront/homefront_rationing_1.htm#FoodShortage. Accessed on 20th February 2014.

# CHAPTER 9
## BEYOND THE RATION: ALTERNATIVES TO THE RATION FOR BRITISH SOLDIERS ON THE WESTERN FRONT, 1914–1918

*Rachel Duffett*

### Introduction

Private A.E. Perriman summed up the bitterness of many British soldiers when he complained after one particularly poor breakfast in the trenches 'the buggers don't intend us to die on a full stomach do they?' (Perriman IWM 80/43/1). Perriman's complaint, one echoed in many rank and file soldiers' accounts, undermines the official view that military provisioning was an unmitigated success for the British Army of the First World War. The men were often disappointed not merely by shortfalls, but also by rations that though high in calories, failed to tempt the palate and did not reflect the civilian meals that had shaped their eating preferences. Whether driven by hunger or boredom, supplementing the official diet was a preoccupation for the men, whether through parcels from home, visits to the canteens or less legitimate means. Scrounging opportunities included fruit stolen from French orchards, opportunistic raids on chicken coops and the theft of bread from local citizens. This chapter demonstrates the extent of the role played by this extra food in the men's diet and explores the significance of the way in which it was obtained and consumed. Whatever the source of the food, its even-handed division was a subject repeatedly referenced in the soldiers' diaries, letters and memoirs. The sharing of food between pals in a just and proper fashion recreated, to some small degree, a microcosm of an ordered, civilised world in the ranks.[1]

Despite its best efforts, the army did not always meet the challenge of feeding its troops on the Western Front; numbers had reached over 1.8 million by March 1918 and the generous frontline ration scale of almost 4,200 calories per man per day presented an unprecedented logistical challenge. As it had

**Table 9.1**  British Army rations 1917–1918.

|  | Frontline (4,193 calories) | Lines of Communication (3,472 calories) |
|---|---|---|
| Bread | 16 oz | 14 oz |
| Meat | 16 oz | 12 oz |
| Bacon | 4 oz | 3 oz |
| Vegetables | 9 6/7 oz | 8 oz |
| Sugar | 3 oz | 2 oz |
| Butter or Margarine | 6/7 oz | 1 oz |
| Jam | 3 oz | 3 oz |
| Tea | ½ oz | ½ oz |
| Cheese | 2 oz | 2 oz |
| Condensed Milk | 1 oz | 2 oz |
| Rice | – | 2 oz |

Source: War Office (1999: 586)

been since its formal introduction at the beginning of the nineteenth century, the ration was founded upon bread and fresh meat, a daily pound of each for the frontline soldiers. Initially the army had issued the same amounts of food to soldiers whatever their position, but as the war progressed and supplies became increasingly limited the rations for those in training or reserve were reduced in order to ensure that those in the line of fire received the best that was available. The details of the daily scales for the last two years of the war are shown in Table 9.1. This table indicates the importance of the key items of bread and meat in the British soldiers' diet, a significance that dates from the initial establishment of formal rations during the Peninsular Wars of the preceding century. The combined quantity of meat and bacon for men in the frontline – equalled only by the US Army – was almost double that provided for German soldiers.

Shortages were never as severe nor as prolonged for the British as those experienced in both the German and the French armies. At times of rapid movement the British supply lines did break down completely, for example during the Retreat from Mons in 1914, and the fallback before the German army's Spring Offensives of 1918, but this was unusual. However, in the more distant and exposed parts of the frontline, food, as Private Perriman noted, was often limited in both quantity and quality; it could be difficult to get sufficient tins of bully beef and hardtack biscuit forward, let alone the hot stews and the fresh bread that the men preferred.

The detailed ration scales and army recipe books appear impressive, but analysis indicates their reliance on the restricted nutritional science available at the time (see also Lightowler and Macbeth this volume). A limited understanding of the role of minerals, vitamins and variety in the diet resulted in a ration where the delivery of calorific values was usually the only objective. This lack of dietary knowledge combined with problems in transportation, conflicting priorities – for example, food for the horses and mules that pulled the ordnance wagons was a higher priority than that for the men – and unskilled cooks, frequently resulted in rations that left much to be desired.

The repeated references to food in the soldiers' letters, diaries and memoirs demonstrate its significance in their lives and indicate an importance that extended beyond purely physical hunger. For the rankers,[2] calorific concerns did not address the central complexity of eating, which is not about nutrition alone but comes freighted with a wealth of psychological, social and cultural associations that may have little to do with physiological need (see also Campbell this volume). While the official rations met calorific targets in theory and frequently in practice, many men remained unhappy: army food did not taste like home – it carried with it an unpalatable flavour of their new, institutionalised lives. The lack of enthusiasm for the monotonous iron ration of tinned beef and biscuit could be as significant as actual hunger in generating the longing for alternative supplies.

When opportunities to obtain extra food presented themselves, the rankers took whatever they could find: from the simple scrumping[3] of fruit to more complex chicken and pig-stealing strategies. Scrounging – stealing was far too loaded a word – was a key part of the men's experience and the supplies taken from farms, fields, orchards and abandoned homes all enhanced their diet and forced French and Belgian citizens into the role of unwilling, and frequently unwitting, benefactors. Additions to the diet were not always stolen; there was a range of establishments where the soldiers could purchase extra food: canteens, rest huts and *estaminets*,[4] selling everything from tea and buns to egg and chips, sprang up along the Western Front. In addition, most Regiments had their own Comforts Funds, organisations often run by the senior officers' wives dedicated to providing the men with food treats absent from the daily ration. It was, however, the steady flow of food parcels from Britain which was the greatest source of comfort to the soldiers. These gifts delivered a welcome taste of home and, in the correspondence with their relatives, food provided a vocabulary for the expression of familial love and concern founded upon past meals and sustained by the regular packages.

## Parcels

By 1915, four thousand mail bags crossed the channel daily, a number that rose to over fifty thousand a day in the period before Christmas 1917. The tide flowed in both directions and soldiers sent tokens back to their loved ones: keepsakes, lace, handkerchiefs, shells, grenades, and also butter from French markets all found their way home. The latter items were soon prohibited, as melting butter was deemed almost as much a hazard to the postal system as the explosives (Robinson 1953: 237). In the main the direction was eastward from home, and the parcels were proof to the men that they were not forgotten, that their sacrifices were acknowledged and appreciated (McCartney 2005: 96). The soldiers' accounts indicate the men's reliance on them, both in terms of nutrition and as tangible indications of love and support; for Private Percy Jones, hell was defined as 'the Front without any parcels' (Jones, IWM P246).

The majority of the rank and file soldiers came from the working and lower-middle classes and were aware that for many families the parcels represented a significant portion of household income. The men's longing for the extras could be tempered by a concern that they were consuming precious, limited resources, but conditions on the Western Front militated against unselfish behaviour. As the war progressed, the food shortages at home made sharing with the men abroad difficult for many families. Initially, soldiers such as Lance-Corporal Lawrence Attwell viewed the privations in Britain with some scorn. He wrote to his family in March 1917: 'the food shortage at home will soon seem a small item when the clash of the great offensive begins to fill the granaries of death' (Attwell 2005, 4.3.1917). Irritation caused by the complaints from home passed however, and those pressed into their country's service became increasingly resentful of the food deprivations endured by their families.

Family or friends were the issue point for the majority of parcels, but there were other donors, including employers. On Christmas Day 1916, the tobacco company J. Player of Nottingham gave each Sherwood Forrester (a local Regiment) a gift of twenty cigarettes, chocolate and a card (Bacon and Langley 1986: 51). Schools encouraged pupils to use their pocket money to send letters and gifts to soldiers as a token of appreciation of their sacrifice. There were the 'comforteers', women whose – often anonymously donated – packages, knitting and letters helped to sustain the men at the front (Watson 2004: 109). Some soldiers such as George Hewins could be very calculating in the cultivation of alternative sources of supply. In his training camp in England, Hewins formed a relationship with a woman who was unaware of his wife and numerous children, with the sole intention of ensuring extra parcels of sweets and chocolate. He laughed about her with his pals, calling her his 'Cadbury's Girl' – Cadbury's being the leading chocolate producer (Hewins 1981: 143).

All extra food was welcome, but it was the parcels from home for which the men longed; they were 'the most powerful emblem of sentiment and affection' and carried with them their families' love (Herbert 1970: 83). A tangible reminder of the world the men had left, but to which they longed to return. A regular supply of parcels embodied the care and affection that families, deprived of the physical presence of their loved ones, communicated through the postal service. Consequently, an interruption of the supply caused dismay and men would chide their relatives if they felt that they were not sending packages as often as they should. Private C.R. Jones, wrote home wistfully, 'I am rather in the cold because the other fellows are continually getting parcels . . .' wondering why he was not in receipt of similar care (Jones, IWM 05/9/1). It is touching to note that after his death in 1916, before his family gave his letters to the Imperial War Museum archive in London, they annotated this complaint with the explanation that they had sent out four to six parcels a month for fear that subsequent readers might doubt their love and concern.

## A Taste of Home

Parcels did not consist entirely of foodstuffs and soldiers requested a range of items from camp cookers to lice powder, but it was the edible items that brought the greatest happiness. For the men unwrapping their packages in the distant trenches, billets and camps, each represented a piece of home. The touch and taste of the items reconnected soldiers with their loved ones nutritionally, but also emotionally, stimulating their memory and imagination. In the manner of Proust's *madeleine*, the parcels from home carried with them a whole structure of recollection, and those fragments of food had the power to evoke an entire and comforting world of family love. Homemade food was especially important, as Lieutenant Kenneth Addy wrote in a letter home: nothing is 'as good as mother makes' (Addy 1916). Deborah Lupton has highlighted the special significance of the giving of homemade food: the food is prepared with its recipient's preferences in mind and is therefore imprinted with both the identity of the giver and that of the receiver (Lupton 1996: 48). David E. Sutton has explored the role of food gifts from home in the lives of Greek émigrés in the United States, describing how these 'pieces of homeland' allow a distant group to recall the comforting whole of their once familiar society. Sutton writes of the creation of an imagined community implied in the act of eating food from home while in exile 'in the embodied knowledge that others are eating the same food' (Sutton 2001: 78–84), experiences which echo those of the soldiers of the First World War. It was not the food alone that triggered comforting memories. Lance-Corporal W.H. Petty wrote in his diary how delighted he was with the cake his wife had baked and sent to him, but it was the container in which it was sent that seemed to give him even greater satisfaction. He ended his diary entry with the comment '[the cake tin] reminded me very much of home as I recognised the tins that are usually on the kitchen shelf' (Petty, London Scottish). An apparently inconsequential, domestic object, perhaps even to the wife who packed the parcel, had a disproportionate impact on the recipient; items from home allowed soldiers to imagine an escape from their military world and envision themselves inhabiting their past civilian lives.

## Food and Comradeship

Ironically, while so many of the parcels were the quintessence of a deeply
personal relationship, they were simultaneously public property. Their receipt
was a matter of celebration, not just for the addressee, but also for his particular pals. Sharing was both a manifestation of friendship and a practical
survival tool. In the ranks, giving and receiving food were not isolated acts, but
mechanisms for drawing the men into what Mauss called 'cycles of exchange'
(Mauss 1980). Cycles that sustained the soldiers during periods of hunger. For
example, Private A.P. Burke was able to reassure his family that even though
their parcel had not arrived and rations were stretched '[I] never go short of
anything, there are some good lads here' (Burke, IWM Con Shelf). Burke was
grateful for the regular gifts from home, but not all men were so privileged.
Cavalryman Ben Clouting remembered that the more fortunate in his unit
pooled their gifts with the two orphans who received nothing, saying that 'it
was only fair that those who received parcels from home shared out the contents, particularly food' (Emden 1996: 92). The rankers' writings repeatedly
stress the importance of the available food being divided equally between the
men. In practical terms, the sharing of food was a pragmatic act: a soldier's
chance of satisfying his physical hunger increased if he worked on the principle of regularly pooling resources with a group of pals. In addition to the
practical physiological advantages, there were psychological and emotional
benefits. Comradeship, which is described by many men in their personal
accounts as the only enriching aspect of their war service, was frequently
constructed within the framework of eating. Food was an object around which
acts of kindness, generosity and nurture were enacted. Equally, if individuals
failed to share or, even worse, stole food from fellow soldiers, their behaviour
was condemned.

The pooling of parcels extended beyond a soldier's life when packages sent to
men killed in action were shared amongst the survivors. It was regarded as only
sensible to open them and eat the contents which, after all, were likely to spoil
if returned to the sender. Private Jack Ashley recounted the experience of the
majority of the rankers when he wrote in his diary: 'There were a week's parcels
and, as two thirds of the men were killed or wounded, there was plenty for everybody' (Stone 1982). A few were more diffident but still pragmatic, F.E. Noakes
recalled 'it was not pleasant to think that we might be enjoying dainties which
had been prepared with loving care for someone we had known and who might
now be dead – but we did not refuse them on that account' (Noakes 1953: 177).

## Scrounging and Stealing

The generous flow of parcels did not fully compensate for the shortfalls in,
and boredom with, army rations and additional food scrounged from the

local population was another source for the soldiers. Shortages of supplies and a resigned tolerance meant that officers generally preferred to ignore the illegality of their men's efforts. Indeed, in certain circumstances they encouraged, even ordered, the soldiers to take whatever extra food they could. Often their only interventions were steps to avoid confrontation with the locals, such as ensuring that orchards were raided under cover of darkness (Dunn 2003: 138). At times of real crisis, scrounging was insufficient and a concerted raid on available provisions was required. During the fallback from the German Spring Offensives in 1918, Private J. Sanderson noted in his diary that 'some of the men had actually been detailed by the Major to go out looking for food, wines etc in the deserted houses . . .' (Sanderson, IWM 87/33/1). Sanderson's use of 'actually' implies that it was unusual for such a direct order to be issued, although his diary has numerous matter-of-fact references to his and others habitual scrounging. All such actions contravened the letter from Lord Kitchener, held in each soldier's pay book, which advised them to always look upon looting as a disgraceful act. Unsurprisingly, direct orders to undertake such raids were rare and rankers regarded discretion as the better part of valour when it came to stealing. Cavalryman Ben Clouting was typical when he noted that pilfered chickens were always skinned never plucked, ensuring that evidence of the crime could be more easily concealed (Emden 1996: 79).

At the start of the war, the civilians on whose land the battles were fought were generous to the soldiers and provisions were given freely. Sergeant E.C.H. Rowland noted that during the retreat from Mons in 1914, the French 'have been more than kind to us giving us of their best food, fruit, wine . . .' (Rowland, NAM 1986–01–31). Local enthusiasm, like the food supplies, had worn thin after four years of the hungry presence of the armies on the Western Front. When a ranker was especially hungry he could commit outright theft; Private T. Dalziel shamefacedly noted in his diary that he had taken the bread of the French workers who passed through his sentry post that morning (Dalziel, IWM 85/51/1). The principled certainties of respectable civilian life, where theft was both morally and legally defined, were blurred by military service, and the taking of food was mitigated by both hunger and the general frustrations and perceived exploitations of military existence. Life in the army partly redefined the men's civilian views of ownership, as the soldiers found themselves in a world where normal determinations of property were less applicable. Clearly, the British army's ranking of its needs above the concerns of local farmers when they commandeered agricultural land was a visible demonstration of the fragility of civilian ownership in wartime (Gibson 2003); the exigencies of warfare made the appropriation of food a less heinous crime.

The Western Front was not as well stocked with game as the grouse moors of Scotland, but its rabbits and game birds did provide opportunities for both sport and an enhanced dinner table. It was not only fur and feathered game that was under threat; Private F.A.J. 'Tanky' Taylor wrote that he had used purloined grenades to stun the fish in the local river (Taylor 1978: 158). Farm animals were taken too and the many rural households which kept a pig for their own meat faced disappointment if it crossed the paths of the hungry soldiers. Although it took time and immobility to butcher and cook the animal, in the rapid and hungry retreat of March 1918, Lieutenant William Carr's unit killed an abandoned sow and carried the carcass off with them but had no opportunity to deal with it before it rotted, a misfortune he described as a 'tragedy' for the hungry men (Carr 1985: 111).

Sometimes opportunities to supplement the diet were a direct consequence of shelling. Horses were frequent victims of the barrage, but the response to their meat was mixed – horsemeat, while popular amongst the French working classes as the poor man's steak, was alien to the British diet. In addition to the unfamiliarity of the meat, given the widespread use of horses in the war effort many men would have been eating their own charges. Close relationships with the horses may have influenced the ability of some of the soldiers to ingest what the day before had been a carefully nurtured dependant.

## Estaminets

Not all food extras were the result of opportunism or gifts from home – the local communities provided other dining possibilities for the men stationed in their midst. Low pay and lack of transport ensured that the rankers gravitated to the more convenient, smaller, local *estaminets* where prices were lower than in the town restaurants populated by the officers. Perhaps many of them were attracted to the homely environment of these establishments, which was less daunting than the formal establishments. The restricted menus in the smaller venues did not present a problem as the British soldier was not renowned for his sense of culinary adventure. Forays into unfamiliar food types were infrequent and usually doomed to failure; there were numerous jokes about the smell of French cheese, which was widely rejected as, to quote George Herbert Hill, it was 'white and soapy, looking and tasting like curdled milk' (Hill 2005: 163). In fact, the staple, often the only dish on the *estaminets'* menus was egg and chips, for which the men had an enormous passion. The number of eggs men were able to consume was impressive. A.P. Burke wrote home that he was delighted to have found a place where he could indulge: '[I] have had 3 everyday for my dinner . . . & 4 today – one extra as a souvenir – what a treat from stew' (Burke, IWM Con Shelf).

Around the Western Front, women who did not run an actual *estaminet* were often happy to provide *ad hoc* private dining arrangements for soldiers. They had both the cooking skills and the domestic space for men who had purchased foodstuffs and wanted them prepared and served in a more convivial environment. The provisions for such meals tended to be purchased locally, as parcels often contained ready-prepared foodstuffs. Buying food was not always easy; in busy centres such as Poperinghe the problem was the high prices and in smaller places supplies were limited and concerns regarding civilian requirements resulted in local orders limiting soldiers' access to food. One man noted in his diary that bakers were forbidden to sell bread to the troops and in another village soldiers were banned from entering food shops until after 4.00 pm, presumably to allow the locals first choice (Eachus, IWM 01/51/1). If the makings of a good meal could be obtained, a sympathetic local woman might transform it into a feast; the men's accounts indicate that such meals were always shared between a group of soldiers – there was little pleasure to be gained from solitary dining.

## Conclusion

It was the sharing of extra food that was so important to the soldiers. In practical terms this was due to the failures of military provisioning, where it compensated for shortages and relieved the monotony of the relentless bully and biscuit. However, it also proved to be an important source of emotional and social comfort for the men, offering as it did the opportunity to form groups of particular pals within which the food obtained could be pooled. Army practices facilitated this in that the distribution of rations often required the men to share a loaf of bread or a tin of jam passed to a group – the size of which depended upon the availability of supplies – to be divided up. Extras, whether scrounged, purchased or gifted, did not have to be shared between the soldiers, they could have opted to consume all the food themselves, but they chose to share. Pooling food became a talisman for the men; a vindication of working-class values in the face of an army hierarchy that all too often appeared as the embodiment of greed to its rankers. The sharing of their supplies in a just and proper fashion recreated, to some small degree, a microcosm of an ordered, civilised world in the ranks. This element of justice, so often denied the rankers in their position at the bottom of the military barrel, could be reinstated in one part of their lives: the equitable apportionment of food.

## Notes

1  For further reading on the topic, see Duffett (2012).
2  Rankers: short for those in 'other ranks', i.e., the ordinary soldiers of an army and not the officers.
3  Scrumping: stealing fruit from an orchard or garden.
4  *Estaminet*: from the French a small café.

# References

Addy, G.H. (1916) *A Memoir of his Son Kenneth James Balguy Addy, Second Lieutenant, Killed in Action October 3rd 1915*, Privately published, London.
Attwell, W.A. (ed.) (2005) *Lawrence Attwell's Letters from the Front*, Pen and Sword, Barnsley.
Bacon, M. and Langley D. (1986) *The Blast of War: A History of Nottingham's Bantams, 15th (S) Battalion Sherwood Forresters 1915–1919*, Sherwood Press, Nottingham.
Burke, A.P. *Letters*, Imperial War Museum (IWM), Con Shelf.
Carr, W. (1985) *Time to Leave the Ploughshares: A Gunner Remembers 1917–18*, Chivers Press, Bath.
Dalziel, T. *Diary*, Imperial War Museum (IWM) 85/51/1.
Duffett, R. (2012) *The Stomach for Fighting: Food and the Soldiers of the Great War*, Manchester University Press, Manchester.
Dunn, Captain J.C. (2003) *The War the Infantry Knew 1914–1919*, Abacus, London.
Eachus, S.T. *Diary*, Imperial War Museum (IWM) 01/51/1.
Emden, R. van (1996) *Tickled to Death to Go. Memoirs of a Cavalryman in the First World War*, Spellmount, Staplehurst.
Gibson, C. (2003) The British Army, French Farmers and the War on the Western Front 1914–1918, *Past and Present*, 180: 175–239.
Herbert, A.P. (1970) *The Secret Battle*, Chatto & Windus, London.
Hewins, A. (ed.) (1981) *The Dillen: Memories of a Man of Stratford-upon-Avon*, Elm Tree Books, London.
Hill, G.H. (2005) *Retreat from Death*, I.B. Tauris, London.
Jones, C.R. *Letters*, Imperial War Museum (IWM) 05/9/1.
Jones, P.H. *Letters, Diary and Memoir*, Imperial War Museum (IWM) P246.
Lupton, D. (1996) *Food, the Body and the Self*, Sage, London.
McCartney, H.B. (2005) *Citizen Soldiers*, Cambridge University Press, Cambridge.
Mauss, M. (1980) *The Gift: Forms and Functions of Exchange in Archaic Societies*, Routledge, London.
Noakes, F.E. (1953) *The Distant Drum*, Privately published, Tunbridge Wells.
Perriman, A.E. *Unpublished Memoir*, Imperial War Museum (IWM), 80/43/1.
Petty, W.H. *London Scottish Regimental Archive*.
Robinson, H. (1953) *Britain's Post Office*, Oxford University Press, London.
Rowland, E.C.H. *Diary*, National Army Museum 1986–01–31.
Sanderson, J. *Diary*, Imperial War Museum (IWM) 87/33/1.
Stone, P. (ed.) (1982) *War Diary of Private R.S. (Jack) Ashley 1914–1918*, Privately published, South Woodford.
Sutton, D.E. (2001) *Remembrance of Repasts. An Anthropology of Food and Memory*, Berg, Oxford.
Taylor, F.A.J. (1978) *The Bottom of the Barrel*, Chivers Press, Bath.
War Office (1999) *Statistics of the Military Effort of the British Empire during the Great War 1914–1920*, Naval and Military Press, Uckfield.
Watson, J.S.K. (2004) *Fighting Different Wars: Experience, Memory, and the First World War in Britain*, Cambridge University Press, Cambridge.

# CHAPTER 10
## SUSTAINING AND COMFORTING THE TROOPS IN THE PACIFIC WAR

*Katarzyna J. Cwiertka*

> *In tough circumstances, as a war prisoner or under siege or waiting for Godot, what was most on the soldier's mind was not women nor politics nor family nor, for that matter, God. It was food.*
>
> (Terkel 1997: 6)

## Introduction

War creates extraordinary circumstances of multicultural encounter for soldiers and civilians involved in military conflicts. Along with landscape, climate and language, food constitutes the most immediate articulation of the unfamiliar for soldiers fighting on a foreign soil. The potential meaning of food at the front sharpens – it can become a weapon, an embodiment of the enemy, but also a token of hope, a soothing relief. The commitment of massive armed forces to battle, brought about by twentieth-century modern warfare, along with intensified mobility of the troops, turned the feeding of soldiers into a complex logistical operation that could involve thousands of civilians stretched over continents. On the other hand, when these complex logistics failed, the tried and tested methods of barter, scavenging and looting that had been practised for centuries were the last resort for survival.

Supplying the troops with imperishable and easily portable rations not only enabled them to concentrate on fighting and reduced the risk of ingesting contaminated food, but also eliminated the anxiety of encounter with unfamiliar diets. Yet, the very same rations which represented the taste of home for invading or occupying troops could function as gateways to 'the cultural other' for the hungry populations who were forced to rely on them when indigenous sources of nutrition were no longer available. The same holds true for trespassing soldiers, who at times had to depend on unfamiliar local food – traded or bartered, offered as gifts, stolen, or acquired through the application of force. Wartime experiences of eating unfamiliar food often left a lasting impression, affecting not only individual tastes and preferences, but in some cases even consumption practices of entire populations. Among the most striking examples of war-induced culinary transformations are Spam and the *gyōza* dumplings (in English known as 'potstickers'). The former – branded American canned luncheon meat – turned into a fixture of the Okinawan, Philippine and South Korean diets under the impact of prolonged presence of the US military on the three territories after 1945 (Matejowsky 2007; Cwiertka 2012: 130–131). The latter – thinly rolled pieces of dough with a meat and/or vegetables filling – were brought to Japan from northern China by the returnees from Manchuria, including thousands of soldiers, who had acquired a taste for them. In contemporary Japan, *gyōza* are among the top five dishes most frequently served at dinner tables (Cwiertka 2006: 140).

The objective of this chapter is to illuminate the intricacies behind subsistence supply of the two major troop contingents involved in the Pacific War (1941–1945) – the Japanese and the American forces. I hope to be able to demonstrate how the circumstances of war elevate the multiple functions and meanings of food and drink into extreme dimensions, and to underline frictions between military logistics, the hard reality of military conflicts and the vulnerability of the human condition.

## Provisioning Japanese Forces in Theory and Practice

In the circumstances of the early 1940s, when the Pacific War unfolded, considerable discrepancies could be identified between the logistical planning and the actual support that the Japanese troops received. This was true for all forces involved in the conflict, but was particularly relevant in the case of the Imperial Japanese Army (IJA), which followed the principle of local procurement of food. The supply programme for forces stationed overseas aimed at complete self-sufficiency in terms of subsistence supply within each theatre. In Korea, Formosa and China, for example, rice requirements were met locally. In Manchuria, the army obtained its rice from Korea, securing wheat and barley from local sources. In the Philippines, the army received its rice from French Indochina and in Malaya from Java and other nearby areas (The United States Strategic Bombing Survey 1947: 25). In theory, if the tactical situation, the nature of the terrain or other conditions prevented a battalion from securing its food, the divisional headquarters, district area army or the general army headquarters was to provide as much of these deficiencies as possible from its own resources. Deficiencies which could not be met from any source in the theatre were placed on requisition from other areas or from Japan itself. However, in practice, this kind of operation rarely succeeded, partly due to shortages of food resources themselves, and partly due to priority in shipping being given to gasoline and ammunition. Shortage of shipping space was aggravated in particular from 1944 onward, as the domination of American forces in the region vastly increased. According to the estimates provided by the Japanese officials of the Ministries of War and Navy, who were questioned by the Americans after Japan's surrender, thirty to fifty percent of shipments from Japan had been destroyed or damaged by ship sinking, spoilage or other causes (The United States Strategic Bombing Survey 1947: 25–26).

Provisioning the IJA was a complex logistical operation for two reasons: its size and a vast territorial stretch of the troops. In December 1941, the army's strength totalled 1.7 million men and increased to 5.5 million by 1945; at the height of its power in 1942, the Japanese Empire ruled over a land area spanning 7,400,000 square kilometres (Figure 10.1).

In theory, the principle of local procurement entailed purchasing food from professional traders or directly from the producers. In practice, forced requisition and looting were the prevailing methods carried out by the soldiers of IJA. For example, Japanese forces are reported to have regularly plundered rice in the lower Yangtze River delta famous for its rich crop. There are accounts of Japanese troops shooting water buffaloes for food and other examples of using brutal force while acquiring food for the troops (Ienaga 1978: 95, 166). Oral historical records suggest that during the Burma campaign, however,

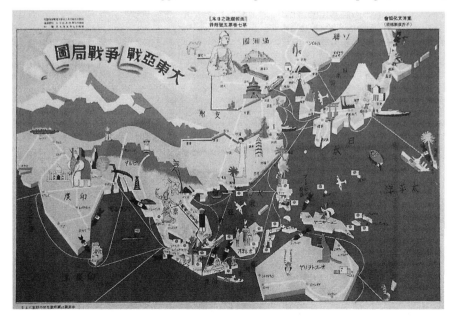

**Figure 10.1**   The extent of the Japanese Wartime Empire, 1942. Reprinted courtesy of Rotem Kowner.

this kind of behaviour was not officially sanctioned, and that the Japanese military authorities took precautions not to alienate the local population there (Tamayama and Nunneley 2000).

Whenever the tactical situation allowed, IJA soldiers were encouraged to supplement food supplies through self-sustaining activities, such as raising vegetable gardens, keeping livestock, fishing, hunting and even gathering (The United States Strategic Bombing Survey 1947: 24). This was particularly relevant on tropical islands of the southwest Pacific. Detailed advice on making use of local food resources in the tropics appeared regularly in internal publications of the Army Provision's Depot. For example, the magazine, *Ryōyū*, featured recipes for army cooks that utilised such exotic ingredients as papaya and pineapple in the preparation of *miso* soup and other Japanese dishes (Iso 1940: 66–67). Yet, the supplementary character of self-sustaining activities that were envisaged by the Japanese military authorities in practice developed into the sole method of provisioning for many Japanese battalions fighting in the southwest Pacific. Perhaps the most striking example of the logistical difficulties that the Japanese army troops encountered is given in the account of the New Guinea Campaign, provided by Keith Richmond (2005). From the summer of 1944 the supply of rice to the troops fighting in the southwest Pacific effectively ended. At this point the Japanese suspended much military activity over many months while they lived off the land. The troops were allocated large tracts of land, began self-sufficiency operations on them in order to regain strength, and then used the territory as a home base from which to engage the enemy when necessary.

A great proportion of the Japanese troops in New Guinea spent the bulk of their time searching for sago palm trees in the areas allocated to their units, and extracting starch from them, inspired by the practices of the local population. The starch was generally known under the name *sacsac*, and was acquired from sago palms through a labour intensive process of felling the palm, removing the pith, crushing and kneading it to release the starch, and then washing and straining it to extract the starch from the fibrous residue (Richmond 2005: 28–29).

The situation was very different in the Imperial Japanese Navy (IJN), where a system of central food control had been in operation since 1890 (Cwiertka 2006: 71). All provisions were distributed centrally by the Munitions Bureau of the Naval Ministry. Moreover, the guidelines concerning the content of meals to be served on board each vessel were specified by the central authorities, determining in detail the kinds and amounts of food that each sailor was to consume regardless of the location, even suggesting how the food was to be cooked.

The sophisticated nature of the navy system of provisioning is perhaps best illustrated by the state-of-the-art catering ships. For example, *Mamiya* carried a 350-man staff engaged in full time food processing for the entire fleet; it could produce daily 1,000 kg of noodles, 14,000 bottles of lemonade, 2,000

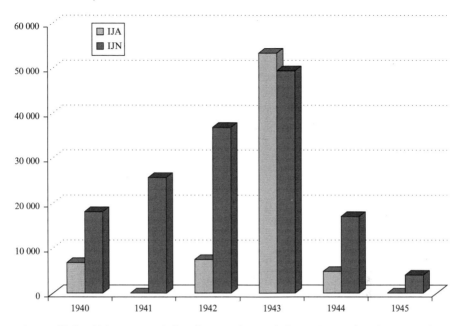

**Figure 10.2**   Shipments of rice (in metric tons) from Japan for the Imperial Japanese Army (IJA) and the Imperial Japanese Navy (IJN).

portions of ice cream and fresh-baked bread for 7,500 sailors. The largest catering ship of the Japanese navy, *Irako*, had a capacity of feeding 25,000 men for fourteen days (Cwiertka 2006: 73).

The differences in the strategies of IJA and IJN during the Pacific War are clearly demonstrated by the data on shipment of rice from Japan between 1940 and 1945 (Figure 10.2). Additional evidence that these data provide concerns the rapidly shrinking shipments during the last two years of the conflict. Logistical support from Japan became increasingly uncertain, and most likely a gap between theory and practice in subsistence supply of the IJN began to resemble that of the IJA.

## The Best-Fed Soldier in the World

Contrary to the infamous unreliability of food logistics of the Japanese armed forces, the Americans enjoyed the reputation of being the 'best-fed army in the world'. The attribute had surfaced in the media already at the time of the First World War (*The Free Lance* 1918: 5), but by the 1940s achieved an impossible-to-argue-against 'matter of fact' status. The American armed forces followed the principle of consolidated procurement – food for the troops was purchased by centralised agencies and distributed to each area via a complex web of depots, bases and dumps. In the case of the Pacific theatre, the San Francisco Port of Embarcation functioned as the central agency charged with the task of filling Pacific requisitions. The needed items were ordered from the Utah General Depot and some other installations along the west coast. If stocks were limited, an item might have been handled directly through a procuring agency, possibly even the Office of Quartermaster General in Washington (Stauffer 1990: 140). The system was far from perfect; long lines of communication, shipping and stock shortages, and storage deficiencies delayed the delivery of supplies, which could take as long as 116 days.

In no other theatre of operations of the US forces during the Second World War did local procurement become quite as extensive as in the South Pacific areas. However, the meaning of the term 'local' was quite different from the practice of the Imperial Japanese Army. It implied that rations were not purchased individually by each unit, but contracted from commercial producers and processors in Australia and New Zealand. For example, during 1943 and 1944 these two countries together furnished the major part of the meat consumed by the US armed services below the equator (Stauffer 1990: 98, 128).

Industrially processed food, such as canned vegetables, dehydrated potatoes and onions, dried eggs and candy formed the bulk of supplies for the US troops in the Pacific. All the rations served in the US military during the Second World War were classified into five categories: A, B, C, D and K. The 'A ration' corresponded roughly with the regular peacetime ration of soldiers in the United States, but storage and transportation conditions seldom permitted the use of perishable food items such as fresh fruit, vegetables and meats. The so-called 'B ration' was basically the same as the 'A ration', except that no perishable items were used, only canned and dehydrated products. The Field 'C ration' was intended for front-line troops to be consumed in battle conditions either cold or heated. It consisted of a combination of ready-to-eat meat units, such as pork and beans, meat and vegetable hash, meat and vegetable stew, supplemented by jam and crackers, hard candy, soluble coffee, cocoa powder, and since the mid-1940s also chewing gum, water purification tablets, toilet paper and cigarettes. The 'D ration' functioned as both a reserve and emergency ration. It consisted of a four-ounce chocolate bar that contained six hundred calories, could withstand high temperatures, and tasted 'just a little better than a boiled potato' (Fisher and Fisher 2011: 148). The developers of the 'D ration' were concerned that if the bar tasted too good soldiers would eat it like candy rather than retaining it for emergency. 'K rations' were compact, light-weight rations developed especially for paratroopers, containing canned meat products, biscuits, cereal bars, granulated sugar, salt tablets, soluble coffee, bouillon powder, confections and chewing gum (Fisher and Fisher 2011: 150).

In comparison with the Japanese forces, food shortage was rarely a problem for the US troops fighting in the Pacific Theatre. However, scarcity of manpower and equipment, coupled with difficulty of the terrain of combat zones, made the supply of hot meals to front-line troops extremely difficult. The emphasis on portability and lasting qualities of C, D and K rations was primarily achieved at the expense of taste appeal. Moreover, despite continuous efforts, the lack of variety haunted the US Quartermasters until the very end of the Second World War (Stauffer 1990: 302–313).

## PX and *Shuho*

Along with the daily food ration provided to the troops fighting in the Pacific War, the military authorities of both sides provided their men with additional comfort in the form of goods that they remembered from home, but were not part of the regular food ration, such as soft drinks, candy, cigarettes and alcohol, which could be purchased at a small expense. The same branches of military organisation were also in charge of operating clubs and recreational canteens for the officers and the servicemen. Post Exchange stores, better known under the abbreviated form of 'PX' followed the American GIs anywhere in the world, with the articles for the frontline troops provided free of charge. The NAAFI (Navy, Army and Air Force Institutes) were the British Commonwealth equivalent of the PX, and the Japanese forces had their so-called *shuho* (Cole 1982; Cooke 2009, Fujita 2009).

While the former two were highly centralised, the regulations left decisions concerning the Japanese *shuho* entirely to the discretion of the commander of each regiment (Rikugunshō 1943: 149). It was up to him to decide about the location, opening hours and items in stock. For example, the *shuho* managed by Otoshi Butai in the bay of Manila resembled a splendid restaurant (including hostesses) rather than a military canteen (Mishima 2005: 81). With notable exceptions such as this, most establishments were simple and sold freshly cooked snacks, Japanese and Western-style confectionery, soft drinks, cigarettes and alcoholic beverages (Yoshida 2005: 68; Fujita 2009: 161). These last two articles constituted the main source of profit for a *shuho*, as they did for the PX and NAAFI. Officially, the US army was 'dry', insofar as there was no free issue of alcohol. Enlisted men were allowed to buy beer when off duty, and officers were entitled to purchase half a bottle of liquor per month (Ellis 1990: 289). In reality, however, a fair amount of drinking went on wherever the US armed forces were stationed. GIs desperate for a drink resorted to substitutes, such as 'torpedo juice' – high-proof alcohol utilised for driving torpedoes – and other forms of doctored industrial alcohol sold by local entrepreneurs (Michener 1947: 181). James Jones, who experienced the Guadalcanal campaign first hand in the 25th Infantry Division, recalls that the Aqua Velva aftershave, available at a poorly stocked PX in Guadalcanal, went like hotcakes.

> Mixed with canned grapefruit juice ... the shaving lotion did not taste at all. Grapefruit juice seemed to cut all the perfume out of it. It made a drink rather like a Tom Collins. Everyone loved it. (Ellis 1990: 291)

## The Taste of the Enemy

An important source of food supply for the soldiers of the Imperial Japanese Army, which, as mentioned above, operated on the basis of local procurement of food, were enemy rations. Diaries of Japanese soldiers and sailors are replete with descriptions of 'gifts from Churchill', 'Roosevelt's supplies' and 'American supplies' anticipated with excitement; the promise of feasting on captured supplies not infrequently functioned as a motivation for battle (Kamei 1994: 403–404, 431, 481, 595, 662; Tamayama and Nunneley 2000).

Taking over the enemy's premises and consuming captured food and drink was an established practice in the battlefields of the Pacific War. The US authorities also encouraged the consumption of captured Japanese rations. As the end of the war in the Pacific drew closer and instances of Japanese troops retreating leaving their supplies behind became more frequent, encounters with the enemy's rations increased. For example, the October 1944 edition of *Intelligence Bulletin*, a monthly journal issued by the Military Intelligence Service with the aim of informing 'officers and enlisted men of the latest enemy tactics and weapons', included a multi-page article with detailed information on Japanese rations and how to consume them. The rationale behind propagating the consumption of the enemy's rations was explained as follows:

> Some enemy foods, such as canned crabmeat, salmon, tuna, mandarin orange sections, canned pineapple and other fruits, rice, tea, and sugar, are familiar to American tastes. These items can easily be used provided that they are in good condition. Certain other Japanese foods, including dried fish, edible seaweed, pickled radishes, and pre-cooked rice flour, are strange to most American tastes. But, if rations are short, these items may be eaten and will supply nourishment. (*Intelligence Bulletin* 1944)

The article described in detail the packaging of different kinds of Japanese rations. Illustrations of a number of emergency rations, with English translation of inscriptions on the packaging, were also featured. A translation of the method of preparation included a note indicating that the amount of water called for was roughly one third of a US canteen cup. Such details clearly indicate that the information was indeed intended to be followed if necessary by the American soldiers in the Pacific.

No mention was made in the article about the consumption of captured alcoholic beverages, but evidence suggests that the practice was indeed widespread. Second World War memoirs of American servicemen are full of accounts of captured Japanese alcohol. For example, the inventory of the abandoned Japanese headquarters described by Richard Tregaskis (2000: 51–52) in *Guadalcanal Diary*, at the very beginning of the land offensive against the Japanese, included 'big bottles of saki, small bottles of wine', 'cases of a soda pop labelled "Mitsubichampagne Cider" and two varieties of Japanese beer'.

With the arrival of American troops on Japanese soil soon after Japan's capitulation, incidental consumption of alcohol manufactured in Japan became officially sanctioned and its volume skyrocketed (Figure 10.3). Within only a few months between their arrival in Japan in September 1945 and the end of the year, the occupying forces drank 76,000 *koku*[1] of Japanese beer through official channels alone, distributed either directly to the regiments or supplied through a network of brothels managed by Recreation and Amusement Association (RAA). During 1946 and 1947, roughly twenty percent of beer manufactured in Japan was consumed by the American occupying forces (Kirin biiru kabushikigaisha kohoshitsu 1969: 36). Japanese whisky was widely consumed by the officer cadre. Along with social occasions at which it was served, General Headquarters distributed whisky allotments to officers and civilian personnel for private use (Gayn 1948: 81). The Japanese beer and whisky producers proved quite successful at changing horses from the patronage of the Imperial Japanese Army and Navy – dissolved in 1945 – to the US military.

There is some evidence that the 'taste of the enemy' applied, on occasions, not only to their foods. On 25th December 1942, the Allied Translator

**Figure 10.3**  US Parachute Glider Regiment soldiers enjoying Japanese beer and a meal on Japanese soil (September 1945). Source: US National Archives and Records Administration, photo no. 342-J-54G-63284ac.

and Interpreter Section (ATIS) – a joint Australian-American intelligence agency set up in 1942 for the purpose of translating intercepted Japanese communications, interrogations and negotiations in the Pacific Theatre of Operations – received the diary of a Japanese commander who was captured south of Gorari, New Guinea. In one of his October entries, the commander documented the gradual starvation of his platoon and their frantic efforts to get food. He then noted that meat had been carved from a dead American prisoner. He concluded, 'This is the first time I have ever tasted human flesh – and it was very tasty' (Bradsher 2006: 152). Due to the incredible implications of the statement, this fragment of the diary was translated by three independent translators. This was the first documentary evidence of cannibalism committed by Japanese soldiers in the southwest Pacific. Many more followed. Four decades later, the issue received public attention worldwide through a highly acclaimed 1987 documentary, *Yuki Yukite Shingun* (known in English as *The Emperor's Naked Army Marches On*), which attempted to confront Japanese veterans, who had allegedly survived the New Guinea campaign owing to cannibalism.

## Conclusion

Despite the fact that over half a century divides us from the Second World War its full story remains hidden behind accounts of military logistics, political espionage, and international peace negotiations. While memoirs written by soldiers and civilians provide first-hand accounts of individual experiences of heroism, horror and deprivation, we know relatively little about the impact wartime encounters had on the lives of populations at war, especially in the Far East. The focus on food has a potential to fill in these gaps, and provide us with insights into the role war has played in the construction of post-war societies.

The aim of this chapter was to demonstrate how the circumstances of war elevated the multiple functions and meanings of food and drink into extreme dimensions, and to underline frictions between military logistics, hard reality of military conflicts and the vulnerability of the human condition. The instances of cannibalism in the southwest Pacific represent an extreme accumulation of all these features. Equally shocking are the estimates of the Japanese historian, Akira Fujiwara, who argues that more than half of the troops that the Japanese armed forces lost between 1937 and 1945 did not die on the battlefield, but perished due to malnutrition-related diseases and starvation (Fujiwara 2001: 3). These data confirm from yet another angle the profound significance of food in zones of conflict.

# Note

1  *Koku* is a Japanese unit of volume, equal to approximately 180 litres.

# References

Bradsher, G. (2006) The Exploitation of Captured and Seized Japanese Records Relating to War Crimes, 1942–1945. In Drea, E., Bradsher, G., Hamyok, R., Lide, J., Petersen, M. and Yang, D. (eds) *Researching Japanese War Crimes Records: Introductory Essays*, National Archives and Records Administration for the Nazi War Crimes and Japanese Imperial Government Records Interagency Working Group, Washington, DC: 151–168.
Cole, H.N. (1982) *Naafi in Uniform*, The Forces Press (Naafi), Aldershot.
Cooke, J. J. (2009) *Chewing Gum, Candy Bars and Beer: The Army PX in World War II*, University of Missouri Press, Columbia, MS.
Cwiertka, K.J. (2006) *Modern Japanese Cuisine: Food, Power and National Identity*, Reaktion Books, London.
Cwiertka, K.J. (2012) *Cuisine, Colonialism and Cold War: Food in Twentieth-Century Korea*, Reaktion Books, London.
Ellis, J. (1990) *The Sharp End: The Fighting Man in World War II*, Pimlico, London.
Fisher, J.C. and Fisher, C. (2011) *Food in the American Military: A History*, McFarland & Company, Jefferson, NC.
*Free Lance, The* (1918) 'Best fed and best clothed army in world: Better cared for than any soldier at front' *The Free Lance*, vol. 33 no.12, 23rd February 1918: 5. Published at: http://news.google.com/newspapers?nid=1296&dat=19180223&id=slwzAAAAIBAJ&sjid=h48DAAAAIBAJ&pg=1744,325832. Accessed on 14th February 2013.
Fujita M. (2009) *Shashin de miru Nihon rikugun heiei no shokuji*, Kōjinsha, Tokyo.
Fujiwara, A. (2001) *Uejini shita eireitachi*, Aoki Shoten, Tokyo.
Gayn, M. (1948) *Japan Diary*, William Sloane Associates, New York.
Ienaga, S. (1978) *The Pacific War: World War II and the Japanese, 1931–1945*, Pantheon Books, New York.
*Intelligence Bulletin* (1944) 'Captured Japanese Rations May Be Eaten', *Intelligence Bulletin*, 3(2). Published at: http://www.lonesentry.com/articles/japanese-rations/index.html. Accessed on 14th February 2013.
Iso, K. (1940) Netchi muke tokushu chōrihō, *Ryōyū*, 15(4): 65–69.
Kamei, H. (1994) *Gadarukanaru senki*, vol. 2, Kōjinsha, Tokyo.
Kirin biiru kabushikigaisha kohoshitsu (1969) *Kirin biiru no rekishi, sengohen*, vol. I, Kirin biiru kabushikigaisha, Tokyo.
Matejowsky, T. (2007) Spam and Fast-food 'Glocalization' in the Philippines, *Food, Culture and Society*, 10(1): 23–41.
Michener, J. (1947) *The Tales of the South Pacific*, Macmillan, New York.
Mishima, S. (2005) *Biruma gun'i senki*, Kōjinsha, Tokyo.
Richmond, K. (2005) Some logistical challenges for the Japanese in the New Guinea campaign, 1942–1945, *Sabretache: The Journal of the Military Historical Society of Australia*, 4: 21–32.

Rikugunshō (1943) *Guntai naimurei*, Senryudo, Tokyo.

Stauffer, A. P. (1990) *The Quartermaster Corps: Operations in the War against Japan*, Center of Military History, United States Army, Washington D.C.

Tamayama, K. and Nunneley, J. (2000) *Tales by Japanese Soldiers of the Burma Campaign 1942–1945*, Cassell & Co, London.

Terkel, S. (1997) *The Good War: An Oral History of World War II*, The New Press, New York.

Tregaskis, R. ([1943] 2000) *Guadalcanal Diary*, The Modern Library, New York.

United States Strategic Bombing Survey, The (1947) *The Japanese Wartime Standard of Living and Utilization of Manpower*, US Government Printing Office, Washington.

Yoshida, S. (2005) *Kotō senki: Wakaki gun'i chūi no Guamu-tō no tatakai*, Kōjinsha, Tokyo.

# CHAPTER 11
## ENEMY CUISINE: CLAIMING AGENCY, SEEKING HUMANITY AND RENEGOTIATING IDENTITY THROUGH CONSUMPTION

*K. Felicia Campbell*

### Iraq 2003

I remember MREs (Meals Ready to Eat). Scrounging through the boxes when no one was looking in order to try to find a coveted hamburger patty package. I remember the MKTs (Mobile Kitchen Trailers), which were just large-scale versions of MREs served buffet style.

I remember the Iraqi chicken and warm flatbread that we devoured like animals. I remember the ketchup packets decorated with the picture of a little boy's head, grinning manically between two giant tomatoes. I remember the Iraqi Coca-Cola, still identifiable with its red and white packaging, despite the flowing Arabic script that covered it. I remember the atrocious 'pizza' on soggy flatbread, covered in ground meat with crunchy pebbles of blackened cartilage, bitter raw onions and a flavourless crumbled cheese. I remember the strange desserts of flaky pastry surrounding a green mush of chopped nuts, so unexpected in appearance that I was immediately repulsed. I remember being afraid of the food because I didn't understand the people preparing it. I spent my time looking for the familiar. But then too, even after they built us a chow hall filled with 'safe' food, I remember returning ironically to the Iraqi 'clubs' to satisfy my lingering craving for that simple chicken and flatbread.

In this chapter, themes of subversive personal agency, humanisation and the renegotiation of identity are explored through the narratives of American veterans and their consumption of rations and Iraqi cuisine during and post-Operation Iraqi Freedom. Food is often overlooked in the examination of wartime interactions, but the use of food as a psychological tool of classification in conflict has a long history, from the perceived threat of dehumanisation or barbarisation of the Greeks through exposure to Roman consumption habits in the third century (Purcell 2003) to the feminisation of the Indian vegetarian body in the subcontinent during the colonial era (Arnold 1994). I argue that disgust for the other and his food is a mechanism that mentally aids in the execution of the unnatural acts of war, thus, the adoption of enemy cuisine signifies much more than a change in palate, it signifies a defiant act of agency and the first step in the difficult process of shifting from soldiers fighting faceless enemies to men and women engaging with other men and women on a battlefield whose psychological reach extends far beyond the borders of Iraq.

## Agency and Consumption

One could say, with a reasonable amount of confidence, that personal agency is not one of the cornerstones of American military rhetoric, or probably any military's rhetoric for that matter. Soldiers are trained to do as they are told and to follow orders. They react instinctually, not with natural intuition, but with the synthetic instinct that comes from having reactions drilled into them. This is necessary, I think, for the rigours and horrors of war. In a fire fight, it would be disastrous if the platoon's gunner needed to debate and psycho-analyse the skirmish before laying down protective cover. I was told on many occasions, 'Campbell, you aren't paid to think, so why don't you take a load off and just do what you're told'; that being said, there is a rebellious side to every soldier, a human side that screams for attention even in the dehuman-ised, robotic mental space that must be occupied when fighting abroad. That primal scream often comes out as little more than a whisper, least subtle of which can be seen in consumption practices.

Using the definitions of 'agent' and 'actor' provided by anthropologist Laura Ahearn (2001), I observed that soldiers in combat generally exhibit the behaviour of actors following rules and commands as a means of survival, the deviation away from this highly governed behaviour in the pursuit of food choices and subsequent adoption of Iraqi local cuisine is a clear move from actor to agent. Ahearn (2001) states that agency is an expression of empow-erment, and nods to the possibility of change. When we engaged with Iraqi nationals and ingested their food not only into our bodies, but also into our identities, we were unconsciously exercising agency as the following vignettes demonstrate.

## Actor, Agent and MRE

I remember that we were hungry; hungry in a way the utilitarian plastic pack-ages of dehydrated sustenance could not satisfy. We sat in the shade of our LMTV (Light Mechanised Transport Vehicle), a behemoth truck with hard wooden benches and a tarpaulin roof, able to carry twenty of us packed like gun-bearing cattle in the back as we rolled north through the Bedouin southern deserts of Iraq. It was sweltering, causing our rationed litres of water nearly to boil, preventing them from providing any sort of refreshment.

The only living thing aside from us soldiers, who looked for all the world like storm troopers or aliens in our head to toe chemical suits, tanned by the dust which covered our faces rather than by the blazing sun, were the flies. These were no ordinary flies. They were bold and mean, crawling on our lips and biting our arms, despite the dangerous swats of our hands threatening them with death. They were our alarms, waking us from restless sleep at the first light, buzzing and tormenting us. We often wondered what kept the demon flies alive, what they feasted on in our absence. As for our own sustenance, an overzealous commander, seeking his third star, had decided to earn that shining accolade by sending us into Iraq as the first wave of soldiers during the invasion. It seemed to be of little consequence that our supply chain was not as well developed as his ambitions.

This left our rag-tag group with two litres of water a day and one MRE. This was certainly enough to survive on, as the MRE contained within its compact form about 2,500 calories. We were not infantry after all. We did not need three meals a day to sustain the energy needed to run through jungles, scale walls or clear buildings. We were simply pushing our way through the country in trucks, like a battle fitted centipede. Sure we dug a foxhole here or there, but mostly we just drove; eyes peering through the scopes of our weapons at the vast desert horizon.

After only a few weeks in-country, sitting under those trucks at the first stop on our journey – FARP (Forward Arming and Refuelling Point) Shell, a random patch of sand which became a base only by virtue of being the place we decided to stop – the fantasies about meals and showers and beds began. We would sometimes draw pictures of our 'wish lists' in the dust covering the large metal sides of the trailers we were hauling; outlining the curves of a steak, the stream of free-flowing shower water and soft pillows. One of the favourite conversation starters was, 'When I get home, I'm gonna ...' But that was just the beginning; shortly thereafter the fights over the hamburger patty MRE began.

All the MREs were similar, containing a squeeze packet of cheese (in jalapeño or regular flavour) or peanut butter, a dessert or candy, crackers or flatbread and an 'entrée'. To try and describe the aforementioned, I suppose I could say that all the products bore a resemblance to cheap American snack foods; the cheeses were something like squeeze-bottled Cheese Wiz, the peanut butter fairly normal, the desserts tasted similar to the dusty 'diet chocolate desserts' à la Snackwell or Jenny Craig (containing twice the calories instead of half), the candy was Skittles, a product we grew to loathe, or the occasional M&Ms. The crackers were a drier, harder, starchier version of a Matzo cracker and the flatbread was a nightmarish hunk of dry, tasteless, chemical 'bread'. The entrées ranged from the deeply dreaded Country Captain Chicken and Turkey Tetrazzini, gray masses with fear-inducing bits of meat-like product, to the ever-coveted hamburger patty.

Though none of the meals tasted like real food, the hamburger patty was the most evocative of deliciousness. It contained two pieces of the tasteless flatbread, laced with the faintest chemical preservative flavour, a thin packet of the cheese spread product, a packet of BBQ sauce, a bag of Skittles and the beefesque patty. We attempted to make the other meals palatable, adding crushed cracker to the 'entrée' to give texture, spreading peanut butter on the dry, malicious 'pound cakes' or stealing the miniature bottles of Tabasco from a fellow soldier's MRE in order to mask the flavours of the paste underneath the heat sufficiently, but the hamburger patty was palatable as it was. With only one meal a day, the importance of your selection was intense. People began digging through the crates of MREs at night in search of the hamburger patty, some getting in physical altercations over the 'golden ticket' of meals. Were our bodies starving to death? Certainly not, but some part of us was.

The MKTs (Mobile Kitchen Trailers) appeared at our next stop, Camp Freedom. It was another tent village in the middle of the desert, but it was slightly more civilised due to the arrival of the kitchens. We eagerly waited in line, the smells of cooking wafting over us. Prior to their arrival, our 'smells-cape' (to use Zardini's 2005 term) had been limited to the ever-present odour of burning that seemed to hang over the entire country of Iraq, the by-product of large garbage dumps which burned night and day, and the intense chemical smell of the water activated heating element which accompanied each MRE meal.

The plastic package of MRE entrée food was placed into a pale green bag, the tiny square nitro-pac lying dormant inside until a small amount of our precious water was poured atop. The bag had to be quickly closed as the chemical steam tried to escape. The boiling water shook the bag for a few minutes before fizzling out, an indication that dinner was ready. Upon opening the bag, you were hit with the nauseating scent of chemical vapours. The MKTs offered us the smell of edibility, though it was a deep emotional let-down when, with the first bite, it became apparent that they were no more than oversized MREs, served buffet-style. Despite this fact, many of us still went to stand in that line, if only to savour the fantasy of the smells, the idea that what we might encounter one day would taste something like the promises of its scent. Our cravings grew, though our stomachs did not grumble.

## Rebellious Consumption

It was at our final destination that our hungers were realised. I can still feel the knot of desire, anxiety and ferocious need that encompassed the rumours of 'real food' on base. It was known only as 'The Club', an Iraqi shop selling roast chicken and flatbread. Our leaders had not yet authorised us to go in search of this place, and as one of the few women in the platoon, I knew my turn would come later, if ever. Across the airfield, another soldier, who would become my best friend, had heard about another food vendor. A soldier had come back to the avionics platoon from guard duty, wielding a plate of *kofta* and fresh vegetables. He was swarmed with questions as to where he got the meal. In typical defensive military fashion, he refused to give up his secret so easily, but eventually explained that there was a man who came intermittently to the gate selling the barbecued meats.

We waited; she for a chance at the *kofta* and I for the roast chicken. These hungers seemed to preclude all others, including the need for survival, approval and safety. We were not encouraged to express or indulge our desires, so it is nothing short of extraordinary that we collectively roared in acknowledgement of our banal longings for this 'dirty', 'enemy' cuisine. We were in survival mode: trained and indoctrinated to feel nothing and need nothing. But the machines we were taught to be, the robotic ways in which we were socialised to eat, walk, dress and live, the inscriptions and embodiments of our lack of humanity, could not suppress the humanity that lay just underneath our fatigues.

Soldiers risked their lives to take trucks outside the gated walls of our base to meet the *kofta* man in back alleys of the adjacent town. Entire companies of soldiers fell ill with dysentery from improperly washed produce, yet continued to dine voraciously at the 'unauthorised food stands'. We ingested the foods of a people we were taught to be disgusted by. Those 'dirty, primitive, dangerous Iraqis' touched and cooked foods that we ingested into our bodies. Our basic needs had been met by our government and by our leaders, but that was not enough. The cultural needs, the needs of the humanity dwelling within our disciplined, civilised bodies, drove us across enemy lines in order to be satisfied.

We drank hot tea from their worn, cracked mugs; the very mugs that their Iraqi lips had touched earlier in the day. We ate foods of unknown origins, crunching ominous, dark ground meats covering flatbreads, a bit frightening, but so much more satisfying than the safe, precisely labelled bags of rations waiting for us at camp. The hamburger patties were no longer fought over, they began to collect dust. Survival had lost its supremacy in the face of visceral, human pleasure.

As soldiers we did not feel very much, feelings were dangerous in a place like Iraq, but we hungered. America (or the embodiment of it in our military structure) provided sustenance for our bodies, so why did we feel as though we were starving? How was it that we found ourselves at 'enemy' tables; the drive to satiate ourselves eclipsing our drive to survive?

Don Slater (1997) describes the concept of basic need, need devoid of meaning and sensuality, stripped down to its most utilitarian and mechanical form. 'For people to be entirely reduced to pre-cultural basic needs, for example to a point of starvation, where any food will do because the cultural person has been reduced to a "natural" body' (Slater 1997: 134–135). He asserts that this condition is not indicative of the underlying human condition, but rather the failure of the human social structure. It is therefore a concept that has no place in the examination of our human nature (whether naturalised or socialised). As he eloquently states:

> It is only at the most horrific extremes of inhumanity, economic catastrophe, war, when social and cultural life has broken down, when – as we say in these circumstances – 'people have been reduced to animals', that 'basic needs' might emerge. Even then, however, it is brutally but often heroically obvious how catastrophic things must be before 'trivial' and 'superfluous' culture gives way to 'basic need' . . . carrying out the rituals and cultural activities by which [people] socially define themselves as fully human . . . this is what we call human dignity. And even if a breaking point comes at some degree zero of human existence at which 'basic need' emerges, this is surely no basis on which to define human need, for what we observe in these catastrophic conditions is not the 'truth' of need, but the extremes of social failure. It is evident that people do not take such a degree zero of existence as the baseline for assessing their own needs, nor do they prioritize staying alive over living a meaningful life . . . we invariably assert a right to more than a basic body. (Slater 1997: 134–135)

I have seen such extremes and I can attest to the fact that basic need, as defined by scientists assessing the physical requirements to keep the human body alive, are so grossly inconsequential, that to use them as the benchmark for quality of life, as is the case within the wartime American military, is dehumanising in and of itself. Perhaps there is a 'basic need', but it is not of the physical kind.

Through consumption of 'enemy cuisine' the consumer was humanised, opening the possibility of humanising the producer. Our initial fear of the other was overcome by our desire for humanity, but the humanisation of the other was not immediate. Emerging cravings for Iraqi cuisine, which came only after returning to the United States, highlighted an internal struggle to renegotiate our ideology in a way in which our 'enemies' could be humanised. This was an impossibility within our military ideology of super-nationalism, under which we were the 'good guys', leaving only the position of the 'bad guys' available to 'the other'. Craving enemy cuisine was the first step in the long process of humanising our 'foes'.

Perhaps it is the culture that feeds our sense of living with which we most closely identify. Perhaps this is why food is so distinctive of our homelands, or of our mothers. I remember that upon returning to America, rather than going out and enjoying our new found freedom and choice, we cloistered ourselves in barracks rooms, drinking away the nights. I cannot remember what we ate upon our return to America, and whatever it was I am sure it did not taste like much of anything at all. The culture that had sustained our humanity and fed us was not the American culture from whence we came. The military culture that fed our bodies and kept us alive had done nothing to feed our souls, instead it tried to manage our humanity. The culture that had met our needs, our truer, deeper needs, was the one that we had been sent to destroy. American culture had become no more than a memory, a dream, and coming 'home' had become an oxymoron. We no longer found comfort in our dreams of America. The life we had fought for suddenly felt empty and flavourless, as much a tease and disappointment as the misleading aromas of the MKTs. We began to seek the flavours of 'enemy cuisine'.

## Renegotiating Identity: Craving Enemy Cuisine

Holt (1995) puts consumption into four categories, ranging from the meaning-less level 'play' to the highest level of adoption 'classification', in which the consumer comes to see the consumed as a part of their identity. The consumption and continuing search for Iraqi food by members of the veteran popula-tion falls into the classification category, as it became a tangible element of their identity, in contrast to those who rejected the cuisine upon return to the United States. My research has shown an interesting correlation between this repulsion and an inability to rectify the contradiction between the humanity of the Iraqi people and our nationalist indoctrination due to their inability to process especially traumatic wartime encounters.

### Repulsion

Soldiers, such as my interview subject Matt,[1] who engaged in especially hor-rific acts of war, seem to feel repulsion towards Middle Eastern food. The 28-year-old white male from New York, who served with interviewee Richard in Iraq in 2005, returned home with a deep hatred of the Iraqi people. Matt calls all Middle Eastern people 'Iraqis' and his resentment of them emerges in occasional raging outbursts. After leaving the military he began working in a restaurant where he subsequently lost his job after exploding in a racist tirade against a Middle Eastern family who did not tip him appropriately. Richard attempted to explain the disparity between his cravings and his platoon mate Matt's disgust by describing the one experience they had not shared during their time in Iraq.

He began, 'You remember how Iraqi's drive like idiots, right?' I nodded and he continued, 'Well they were stupid. We had all these huge red signs posted telling people they had to stop at the checkpoint or we would shoot. Well, they were stupid. Matt was at the checkpoint and saw this car barrelling towards them. They yelled for the car to stop, but it kept coming, so they all opened up on the car. Blew the shit out of it, I mean, really opened up on it until it rolled to a stop. They went to inspect the car and it was just a family inside. There were no weapons or anything in that car, just this family, all blown to shit. Matt had to pick up the pieces of that family and clean up the scene. I think that messed him up pretty bad.'

Some, like Matt, seem still to cling to ethnocentric nationalist rhetoric specifically because of the inherent principals of dehumanisation and superiority it extols. He is haunted by a past he cannot confront without the armour of super-nationalism. To humanise the other would require an acknowledgement of the horrific acts committed against a fellow human, a burden too great for many, like Matt, to bear.

## Adoption and Ideology

For those veterans who during re-acculturation into civilian life do experience cravings for foods evocative of deployment, there seems to be a common underlying shift in ideology and move away from nationalist rhetoric. Our sense of extreme nationalism, or even ethnocentrism, which pitted us against an inhuman enemy, began to crumble when we came face to face with human adversaries rather than faceless, soulless enemies. The consumption of Iraqi food, or its substitutes in America, speaks to the fact that though the past cannot be mended, there is a desire to make peace with it through a new forged sense of self.

Renegotiating the ideologies of nationalism post-Operation Iraqi Freedom and processing the reality of encounters with the Iraqi population are challenges faced by many returning veterans; consuming foods evocative of those consumed in Iraq is one way in which this process is externalised.

The shift in perspective I observed while investigating the adoption of Iraqi cuisine as comfort food for the Operation Iraqi Freedom veteran population, is a shift away from nationalism which is reminiscent of a similar shift I have observed in ethnic diasporas around the world. I have found cuisine to be a tangible way in which people renegotiate their identities in relation to the world around them, especially in places where they are not members of the majority (Tam 2001). I have found, in both the veteran population and among ethnic diasporas, that the supremacy of nationalism in their definition of self is undermined. It appears that flavours evocative of a communal history and memory (Halbwachs 1992) bring together unlikely bedfellows, like the veteran and the Iraqi, or the Lebanese and the Israeli abroad. Perhaps the commonality is the desire for the most basic and banal of human needs; the need to be fed, both body and soul.

The adoption of 'enemy cuisine' is a tangible way in which veterans try to come to terms with who they were before the war and who they are now, by framing the otherness of former foes as familiar by integrating it into their own identities; a tangible reminder of humanity in the face of the dehumanising acts of war.

## Conclusion

As humans, we operate on a basis of more than survivalism, requiring more than rations to feed our needs for choice and comfort. In demanding to be fed as humans and not as chattels, in demanding choice, we exercised personal agency. The significance of this lies in the fact that soldiers are conditioned so effectively to operate as actors rather than agents. The fact that the subversion of this ideology played out in the form of culinary consumption points to the basely human nature of this need, a social rather than purely physiological need. It logically follows that in overcoming preconditioned feelings of disgust and engaging with the Iraqi other through the deeply human act of commensality (when engaged in voluntarily by both parties) would have deep and lasting psychological impacts on returning veterans struggling to make meaning of their wartime experience. The degree to which this affected the Iraqi population is a subject that demands further investigation. What is clear is that such culinary consumption during wartime is more than a utilitarian or a political act (Roy 2010), it is a tool of personal agency and subversion, a core element of humanity, a form of intercultural communication and a deeply engrained aspect of identity (Bourdieu 1984) and thus a device through which one may re-examine identity.

War is filled with paradoxes. Returning to commensality, the most basic of human acts, is a way in which to make sense of the juxtapositions and perhaps a way in which to reclaim humanity, so often the first casualty of a foreign war.

## Note

1  All names have been changed to protect the identity of interviewees.

## References

Ahearn, L.M. (2001) Language and agency, *Annual Review of Anthropology*, 30: 109–137.

Arnold, D. (1994) The 'discovery' of malnutrition and diet in colonial India, *Indian Economic Social History Review*, 31: 1–26.

Bourdieu, P. (1984) *Distinction. A Social Critique of the Judgment of Taste*, Harvard University Press, Cambridge, Mass.

Halbwachs, M. (1992) The Reconstruction of the Past. In Coser, L.A. (ed.) *On Collective Memory*, University of Chicago Press, Chicago: 46–51.

Holt, D.B. (1995) How consumers consume: a typology of consumption practices, *Journal of Consumer Research*, 22(1): 1–16.

Purcell, N. (2003) The way we used to eat: diet, community, and history at Rome, *The American Journal of Philology*, 124(3): 329–358.

Roy, P. (2010) *Alimentary Tracts. Appetites, Aversions, and the Postcolonial*, Duke University Press: Durham.

Slater, D. (1997) *Consumer Culture and Modernity*, Polity Press, Oxford: 134–135.

Tam, S.M. (2001) Lost and found? Reconstructing Hong Kong identity in the idiosyncrasy and syncretism of yumcha. In Tan, C.B. (ed.), *Changing Chinese foodways in Asia, Hong Kong*, The Chinese University Press, Hong Kong: 49–69.

Zardini, M. (2005) *Sense of the City: an alternative approach to urbanism*, Lars Müller Publishers, Centre Canadien, Zurich.

# CHAPTER 12
## THE MEMORY OF FOOD PROBLEMS AT THE END OF THE FIRST WORLD WAR IN SUBSEQUENT PROPAGANDA POSTERS IN GERMANY

*Tania Rusca*

### Introduction

Using the memory of the famine which occurred in Germany during and after the First World War, the political parties of the Weimar Republic utilised food as one of the main tools of conviction in their propaganda posters: political opponents were castigated as the cause and source of the misery, while each poster presented its party as the one and only possible solution. The 'evil' attributed to the political enemy was often connected with the 'famine menace', and bread became the symbol of personal and common wealth, of the country's bright future and of honest work. This widespread use of food in political propaganda was due to the significance of the memory and the fear of famine in the post-First World War era, and was something that remained unchanged up to the advent of the National Socialist dictatorship, where food acquired the value of a material weapon once again.

### Famine in Germany during and after the First World War

The First World War was fought with new weapons and military strategies. The domestic front was important in ensuring the support of the population for the government. In this context, the British came to view blockade as a tool of war to prevent Germany from receiving supplies of necessary food and raw materials. From November 1914 the British stopped all sea traffic between northern England and southern Norway, and the British Consuls in the ports of Rotterdam, Oslo, Goteborg and Copenhagen were able to control all ships carrying goods destined for Germany. Not only was food supply obstructed, but also the supply of nitrate from Chile, necessary for gunpowder and fertiliser production. The consequences of these actions were especially severe for the populations in German cities. Between 1914 and 1918, 750,000 persons starved to death in Germany (Hosfeld and Pölking, 2007: 443); starvation in 1918 alone killed some two million people in the whole of central Europe (Hamann 2008: 322). The winter of 1916–1917 was the worst of the century and was dubbed the *Steckrüberwinter*, the 'winter of the turnips', because this was the only kind of food available. Food was rationed and state inspectors controlled the dietary behaviour of the population. Even baking cakes was forbidden. Contemporary diarist, Arthur Schnitzler, recorded: 'The market inspector [Marktkommissar] keeps watch on our fat supply and apologises; he is ashamed of his own job' (quoted in Hamann 2008: 231). In Germany, several posters incited people (especially children) to collect plants and the stones from fruit. During the war, the British blockade caused widespread feelings of hatred against the British, spread by propaganda in the German press.

After the war, the sea blockade continued until the summer of 1919, extending the privations of the population, together with famine and hyperinflation. The memory of starvation remained deep in the German psyche after the war and constituted one of the most important symbols in the popular imagery in the Weimar Republic. In fact, an experiment conducted in 1944 by researchers of the University of Minnesota, demonstrated how food privation influences the whole life of a person who experiences it. The analysed subjects 'became highly distressed, agitated and bewildered . . . not just during the experiment but, in some cases, for the rest of their lives' (Penny 2010: 27). One of the participants remarked that 'food became the one central and only thing real in one's life'.

This provides an explanation of the central role played by food in the propaganda of the political parties in the Weimar Republic. One can sense that each image of food (especially of bread) used on the posters immediately reminded the observer of the recent famine and played on their very deep emotions and fears. A significant aspect of the political posters of that time dealt with food; this can be understood as an instrumental appeal to the memory in the postwar decades of the famine experienced during the war.

## The Use of Food in the Propaganda of the Early Weimar Government (1918–1919)

### Order, Work and Bread

After the fall of the monarchy and the foundation of several 'Workers' Councils' in November 1918, the National Assembly of the Councils (Berlin, December 1918) voted for a democratic solution and decreed the creation of a parliamentary Republic (instead of a socialist one, as the extremist left forces wanted). The new Republic needed to gain the confidence of the population and to stem internal divisions. Democratic forces confronted two opponents. On one side were the reactionary parties, which were against the Republic itself and sought the reintroduction of the monarchy, and on the other side were the leftist extremists (the Spartachists, after 1919 the Communist Party, and the Independent Social Democratic Party), who wanted to keep on fighting for a socialist revolution. The German Propaganda Office[1] was founded in 1918 to spread democratic ideas. The months between November 1918 and April 1919 were particularly active for this office, which produced many posters in this short period of time. Food was a dominant theme, as food was still a very real problem for many people.

The biggest problem for the new provisional government (from November 1918 until January 1919, when the first election took place) and for the National Assembly (whose members were elected on 19th January 1919) was the demobilisation of soldiers returning from the front. They had no work at home. Located mostly in the cities, they could easily become an extremist and dangerous revolutionary mass poised to move against the government. To avoid that, the illustrators of the German Propaganda Office produced posters which used food – and in particular the lack of food – as a potential menace, in order to convince the veterans to keep in order. With the memory of the lack of food still alive, the government counted on this kind of propaganda specifically directed at the veterans in order to convince them not to join the revolution, which might cause another war.

For a similar reason, food was also used in many other posters directed at the workers. The main weapon of the revolutionary fighters was the collective withholding of their labour. By striking, the workers wanted to show their opposition to the government and to prevent it from getting the means to create a democratic Germany. Thus, the posters of the German Propaganda Office often voiced appeals to the workers to continue working. An explicit link was drawn between work and bread, suggesting that only by their continuing to work would there be food, a better future and an end to misery.

These appeals are evident in the posters of Alexander Cay and retained by the Friedrich Ebert Foundation, Bonn (FEF). For example the picture of the sailor waving red flags, warning the observer with the words: *Comrades, warning! Perturbations of the traffic cause starvation!* (FEF KA001400). In another poster by the same author, showing no pictures but written in large, bold text, is the epithet: *Work or starvation! If you want to go hungry – strike on. If you want to live – work! Without imports – starvation is certain. No imports without financial means. Therefore work! Produce coal, steel, potash. Produce exports! Work means food assurance* (FEF KA001607). Two other posters are preserved in the German Historical Museum (GHM) in Berlin. Their origin is not clear, but they were also commissioned by the government in 1919. They make a distinct connection between corn and coal. The first one shows a large skeleton (Death) rising up beside a factory. In his hand he holds some corn, withholding it from a group of striking workers close by. The words on the poster explain all: *Coal is bread* (GHM PLI16768). The second one shows a big piece of coal with an ear of wheat next to it. The writing is similar to the first one: *Coal brings corn – Without coal misery!* (GHM PLI16773).

Women became an important target for the German Propaganda Office. For the first time in German history, women could vote. They represented an important pool of voters who had to be convinced to take an active role in the political life of the country. During the war, children were a common target of the posters, which incited them to collect all kinds of objects which could be reutilised in the kitchen, like the stones from the centre of fruit to make oil and nettles for cooking. Women were often very busy, working for their family in the fields or in the factories, and they probably suffered from feelings of humiliation and helplessness due to their inability to provide adequately for their hungry children. Thus, the posters exploited the feminine sense of duty towards the family, especially children, sending a message to women that they could now be capable of meeting their family's food needs if they embraced the republican system, which wanted to help them. A famous poster by Max Pechstein retained by the Friedrich Ebert Foundation, Bonn (FEF) shows a little child hugging a red flag. This could be understood as an appeal both to the men: *Don't strangle the young freedom through disorder and fratricide* ... and to the women, through the picture of a baby and the conditional sentence ending the caption: *Or else our children will starve to death* (FEF KA00072). Another poster held by the Folkwang Museum, Essen (FME) of the 'Association of the German Women's Organization',[2] on the occasion of the election for the National Assembly, shows a woman cutting a large slice bread for her two children, who gaze expectantly at her. The words offer clear warning: *Your children need peace and bread. Therefore women: Vote!* (FME 4707) (Figure 12.1).

In this way, the posters displayed various associations promoted by the government. On the one hand, they displayed a positive image – showing that a better future could be reached. On the other hand, they were widely used as a threat and an appeal to keep people doing their duty. In this sense, they furnished an effective method of communication with the country folk. In addition to the urban workers, the farmers were asked to do their duty and to supply food to feed the population in the cities, who still had almost nothing to eat. Previously, during the war, farmers were often blamed for retaining the output of their production for themselves, and causing starvation among the urban population. For example, the poster in Figure 12.2, designed by Heinrich Hönich for the Central Committee for Popular Education and Instruction (Bavaria),[3] retained by the Friedrich Ebert Foundation, Bonn (FEF), shows the miserable situation of a family in the city: around a little empty table, an old woman is covering her face with her hand, a little child is crying and four others are standing in the scene. The youngest is a baby in a

**Figure 12.1** *'Your children need peace and bread. Therefore, women vote!'*, a poster of the Association of the German Women's Organization. Reprinted with permission of Folkwang Museum, Essen.

cradle, the eldest is a young girl looking hopelessly into an empty cooking pot. The dark colours and the sad atmosphere give a strong impression of poverty and misery. The caption warns: *Farmers! Do your duty! The cities are starving!* (FEF KA000754).

## The Fight against Bolshevism (1918–1919)

### Bolshevism Means Starvation and Death

Another organisation working in the first few months of the Weimar Republic was the 'Association to Fight against Bolshevism'.[4] At that time there were many movements aimed at preventing the spread of Bolshevism, an ideology particularly strong in Germany following the First World War. Among them, the Association to Fight against Bolshevism was the one which produced most

**Figure 12.2** *'Farmers! Do your duty! The cities are starving!'* a poster
designed by Heinrich Hönich for the Central Committee for Popular
Education. Reprinted with permission of Friedrich Ebert Foundation, Bonn.

posters of a good quality. Although information is very limited about this
association, it is known that it dedicated much attention to visual propaganda
and used the posters as its main propaganda tool. Many skilled illustrators
worked for it, producing a kind of horror picture to induce fear about the
spread of Bolshevism. This was very similar to the propaganda of the Allies
in the First World War, which already used the image of food as an internal
propaganda tool.

The images used by this Association could be very realistic, offering a grim
view of the Soviet Union, where Bolshevism ruled, and again employing food
or the threat of hunger. This is the case in a poster, now held by the Friedrich
Ebert Foundation, Bonn (FEF), showing the misery of a farming family having
their farm forcibly appropriated by the Bolshevists. While the woman is hiding
her face with her hand and hugging a little child with the other, the elder son
is wordlessly observing the scene and the father burns with powerless anger.

The writing explains: *Bolshevism brings misery, poverty, hunger, destruction. Therefore keep away from all Bolshevist supporters* (FEF KA000734). Another realistic poster, also with the Friedrich Ebert Foundation, Bonn (FEF), shows the picture of a thin and poor woman, sitting down, looking at the observer with wide open, scared and helpless eyes. On her legs lies a child, with closed eyes and no expression on the face: probably dead. The warning tells the observer: *Bolshevism brings starvation and death, but never peace* (FEF KA001530). In fact, a connection of Bolshevism with hunger emerged in almost all the posters of this Association. The claim was that Bolshevism did not only bring hunger, but it was hunger itself. Bolshevism was often represented through violent pictures, which seemed to describe real war scenes. By invoking the recent memories of the war, such posters were designed to associate Bolshevism with famine in observers' minds.

Whilst these posters employed horror to convey their message, a small anti-Bolshevist poster, retained by the German Historical Museum, Berlin (GHM), used the weapon of humour to describe Bolshevism to the population. In this image a standing man, dressed in middle-class urban clothing, is talking to a farmer, evidently a Russian, who is sitting doing nothing: *Hey, you, Ruski! Bolshevism: what is it? – Bolshevism is the greatest equality: nobody has anything to eat* (GHM PL009636).

## Revanchism

### What We Are Losing

An important issue throughout the time of the Weimar Republic was revanchism. Revanchist sentiments were manifest across the political spectrum, and found common acceptance amongst those who rejected the prescriptions of the Treaty of Versailles. Independent and military organisations used posters as a tool to engender the hatred of the population against the Treaty. Lack of food provided a visceral and concrete image of the losses and privations imposed upon Germany by the Allies. This matter was especially connected with the memory of the war, because the Treaty was a direct consequence of it, and because the Treaty itself was viewed by the German press to be the most glaring evidence of the exploitative aims of the Allies towards the German people. Thus, the privations of the war, already ascribed to the starvation strategy of the Allies, was portrayed as being intimately connected to the Treaty, aimed to deprive the Germans of their own resources. For example, a poster of the military authority produced in 1919, now in the German Historical Museum, Berlin (GHM), shows an angry thin woman, surrounded by four hungry children. The word *famine* stands in the centre of the poster, written in bold red letters. The lower part of the poster declares: *The loss of the Eastern provinces means famine! Half your bread ration comes from the*

*Eastern provinces. Half your potato ration comes from the Eastern provinces.
Do you want to let them be stolen by the Polish? Upper Silesia provides half
our coal. Without coal no warmth, no light, no work, no life! Germans! Save the
East! Volunteers forward!! Come forward to your district commands!* (GHM
XP995827). This wording clearly links loss of food with the terms of the
Versailles Treaty, and the famine that followed it.

This kind of propaganda took advantage of the lessons learned from the
German posters of the First World War, which utilised charts and graphics
to convey a sense of objectivity and credibility to the viewers. German territorial losses were represented as loss of food, comparing the contemporary
German production with production levels before the war. A case in point is
a poster of 1919 (Figure 12.3), retained by the Friedrich Ebert Foundation,
Bonn (FEF), which adopted a typical pre-war design. The pictures show all
kinds of German losses: *What we have to lose! 20 percent of our production
areas; 10 percent of our population; one third of our production of coal; one
quarter of our total production of bread-cereals and potatoes; four fifths of our
coal deposits; all our colonies and our merchant navy* (FEF KA002368).

It is interesting to note that women were a popular subject in these posters.
Typically, it was the women who worked in the kitchen and prepared the
family meals. Consequently, women were acutely aware of, and sensitive to,
the problems of food supply already experienced during the war. Exploiting

**Figure 12.3** *'What we have to lose!'*, a poster of 1919, which adopted
a typical pre-war design. Reprinted with permission of Friedrich Ebert
Foundation, Bonn.

the frustrations and anxieties of the housewives, a poster of the 'German Women's Committee to Fight against the Guilt-Lie (Berlin)',[5] retained by the Friedrich Ebert Foundation, Bonn (FEF), shows a large spider spinning its web all over Germany. Underneath are pictures of the products which were 'stolen' by the victors of war. Then the description clearly stimulates the memory of the hard times at the end of the war: *German women! Have you already forgotten the real origin of our increasing misery, of our dreadful impoverishment? It is the Versailles Treaty! . . . Versailles plunders you: Bread cereals, potatoes, sugar, butter, milk, coal. How can we escape this fatal net? Not by quarrelling and striking. France enjoys the German fratricide . . . German sisters! The way is hard! Don't droop! We want to remove the Versailles net by working together without rest. . .!* (FEF KA003234).

## The Political Fight 1919–1932: Propaganda of the Parties

The propaganda strategy followed two strands: a positive message to enlist support, and a negative message to engender fear. Common themes in them were chimneys, the family, grain and, once again, explicit links between work, grain and bread.

An example is seen in a poster of the 'Bavarian Order Group',[6] an association of right-wing parties in Bavaria. Now retained by the City Archive, Munich (CAM), it shows a flour mill (the place for producing flour, and thus a symbol of both work and food), with four large, whirling blades. On each blade is written the word, 'Bread'. An appeal incites the individual to: *Fight Bolshevism. Join the Bavarian Order Block* (CAM 4102). In this case, bread (which also represents work) is pictured as a weapon capable of defeating the enemy.

An example of positive propaganda is a poster of the Communist Party created in 1924, held by the Friedrich Ebert Foundation, Bonn (FEF). In this picture, a small crowd, composed of poor women and children, is looking at a poster on the wall (a kind of 'meta-poster'). This poster illustrates Communist promises and ideals. It was intended that the observer should identify with the crowd. Written on the wall in red letters is the message: *What do the communists demand? Better salaries! 8-Hour Working days! Work for the Jobless! Milk and bread for hungry children! Vote Communist* (FEF KA003217). Another poster produced by the Communists in the same year shows a marching crowd, similar to the famous painting, *La Fiumana*, by Pellizza da Volpedo (1891). Also at the Friedrich Ebert Foundation, Bonn (FEF), the poster is in black and white and on a red banner the following words stand out: *Fight against hunger and freezing.* Here the Communists show themselves as the saviour of the poor population, enthusiastically distributing food to the hungry. An explanation is given on the left side of the poster: *3 million tons rye – exuberance. 25 Million ctw. potatoes – exuberance. 12 million tons coal – exuberance. Come on with bread, potatoes, coal* (FEF KA003218). The name of the party is not shown on the poster. Evidently, the style, message and content of the poster were sufficient to make the identity of the party evident to the observers of the time.

Another method of using food as a propaganda tool was caricature. It was already adopted in the war by the Allies in order to mock German food supply problems, but it was not commonly used in post-war posters; it was nevertheless a popular rhetorical device in postcards and newspapers. Dualistic representations of 'fat and thin' were a common theme. This device was utilised initially by both the Communists and the National Socialists. The Communists portrayed the Capitalists as fat men eating heartily, in contrast to the privations of the starving population. In the propaganda of the National Socialists, a similarly obese Jew was illustrated, whereas the Marxists were usually depicted as thin and malnourished. An early poster by the National Socialist caricaturist, Fips (Philipp Rupprecht), now held by the Folkwang Museum, Essen (FME), serves as an example. An obese Jew, with his whole body painted red and dressed only in a pair of shorts in the colours of the national flag (black, red and gold) smokes a cigar and is laughing. The writing provokes the observer: *Shall he grow fatter and fatter? No!* (FME 4814) The posters of the solidarity associations employed a more realistic style. Käthe Kollwitz produced beautiful pictures of great aesthetic merit. An artist, whose work began towards the end of the nineteenth Century, Kollwitz described through her drawings the miserable conditions of the workers and the proletariat. Famine was a common theme of her works. Held by the German Historical Museum, Berlin (GHM), the drawing, *'German children go hungry!'*, shows a few children asking for something to eat; stretching out their arms with empty plates. It was utilised as a poster in 1923 by the 'International Worker Solidarity Association of Berlin'[7] (GHM P 56/37). Another work of the artist, produced in 1924, became a poster for the 'Karlsruhe Solidarity Association'[8] in 1931. Entitled *'Bread!'* it portrays a woman bent double, from whose dress hang two crying children (Exhibition Brotmuseum Ulm, 1997).

Thus, the memory of the famine was exploited most of all in the period when the economic situation caused a genuine fear of a possible return to the worst months of the war. Pictures of food were especially common on the posters in the first years of the Republic, when the famine was ongoing, until the so called 'golden Twenties', when the economic situation became better for the first time since the war. In fact, in reviewing some eight hundred posters, an average of fourteen percent dealt with the matter of food. In the first two years of the Weimar Republic, and in the last two, this rate was considerably higher (Figure 12.4). The rate of posters dealing with food grew again in the last years of the Republic, probably because of the New York Stock Market crash in 1929, whose consequences were especially hard in Germany, thus raising the fear of famine again.

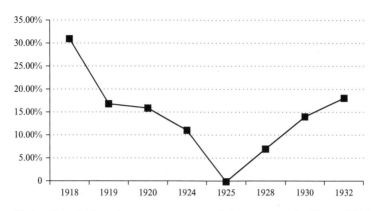

**Figure 12.4**   Graph showing average rate of the posters dealing with food according to the years when elections occurred, i.e., 1919, 1920, 1924, 1925, 1928, 1930 and 1932.

By observing the connection between the economic situation and the rate of the posters including images of food, one can understand the meaning and the impact which food had in the concepts of the population in the years after the famine. Without such a shocking experience, it might never have acquired such importance among the people, exploitable by the political parties as a 'constantly alive' frightening menace.

## The Last Battle: Political Posters in 1932

### Back Again?

According to the graph (Figure 12.4), it is interesting to observe the re-emergence of topics which were prevalent at the beginning of the Weimar Republic in the propaganda of its final year of 1932. Fears of a new famine following the financial crisis of 1929 were soon exploited by political propaganda. The old themes of the immediate post-war years became popular once again. For example, the matter of Bolshevism, of the 'resurgence' of the country, of reconstruction, and especially of hunger once again became common themes.

The Communist and National Socialist Parties, which used propaganda to greater effect than other political parties throughout the Republic, continued this pattern during its final years. In particular, the visual propaganda of the National Socialists, already well-developed by 1930, really matured in 1932. Although increasingly militaristic, it should not be forgotten that the Nazis held power legally and democratically, and that they enjoyed the support of the greatest part of the population for a time. It is not possible to establish a firm correlation between propaganda and electoral success, but it is notable that as Nazi propaganda became more sophisticated and effective, they enjoyed growing success and popularity. It is not unreasonable to suppose that they understood and exploited the fears of the population in a very deliberate and targeted way, devoting particular attention to the matter of food in the propaganda of the final years of the Weimar Republic. Substantial differences can be observed in the propaganda of the Nazis and the Communists during these final years. The Communists favoured negative pictures of misery and oppression, whilst the Nazis preferred positive images of hope for a better future and a flourishing of German pride. Two posters for the Communist Party by John Heartfield in 1932 illustrate the point. One, held in the City Archive, Munich (CAM), shows the photograph of a very young, poor and thin child. He bites into a large piece of bread with a wistful and sad expression. The warning reads: *Capitalism steals from you the last piece of bread. Fight for yourself and your children! Vote Communist! Vote Thälmann!* (CAM 2263). The other photograph, at the German Historical Museum, Berlin (GHM), shows the close-up face of a tired woman. She looks at the observer, seemingly awaiting an answer. The poster is related to the politics of the government: *Margarine duty, Herring duty, Civil duty, Butcher duty, Salt duty. The people are fed up with being hungry! We fight with the communists. Vote list 3*[9] (GHM PLI14624). Although the Communists did use positive propaganda, their pictures generally conveyed a sense of oppression and sadness without a positive answer or solution.

In contrast, the National Socialists, whilst not providing solutions, did provide answers: dreams and hopes, which the population, tired of several years of political disorder and financial difficulties and humbled by the conditions of the Versailles Treaty, needed. An example is the Nazi propaganda particularly directed at farmers that was produced for the 1932 election. The picture of the farmer working the land and pushing the plough or sowing the field was a common theme of posters of the Weimar Republic. But the Nazis invested a new significance into this image. The farmer is shown as a proud man – not seeking intervention and aid, but courageously working towards his own future. This can be seen in the poster by Felix Albrecht (1932), retained by the Central State Archive, Munich (STAM), captioned: *Work, freedom and bread!* (STAM 10975). Here a farmer is sowing whilst looking bravely and proudly ahead, presumably to a brighter future. In 1930 the National Socialist Party produced an impressive poster, also at the Central State Archive, Munich (STAM), showing a wide cornfield, above which shines a large bright sun. In the centre of the sun is a large white swastika. In bold red font, the following words complete the scene: *Freedom and Bread. Vote National Socialist* (STAM 10975). This poster is a good example of the representation of a better future, hoped for and anticipated by the people. It is a simple illustration, which used an image of the corn as the promise of a forthcoming abundance of bread. There is no logical relationship between the scene and reality, nor with the political programme of the Nazis. It simply appealed to the imagination of the population, whose wartime experience had generated a painful awareness of the importance of the food supply.

Also the workers were an important political target for the propaganda of the later Weimar Republic. The message was positive: their expectations could be met and their dignity maintained. An example of a poster at the City Archive, Munich (CAM), which enjoyed great success at the time, shows the arms of an SS soldier raised above the outstretched hands of several workers, giving them tools. The objects are in black and white, whilst the background is red. The writing is very simple: *Work and bread through list 1* (CAM 2901). The message of the poster is clear. The Nazis presented themselves as the solution, providing the structures by which the workers could sustain themselves rather than relying on an uncertain culture of dependency through food hand-outs.

These examples demonstrate how the National Socialists came quickly to understand the importance of food in the political sphere. For the duration of the dictatorship, a sustained programme of propaganda relating to food was maintained. For example, the posters of '*Winterhilfe*' (a solidarity association to help the poor in the winter months) were used throughout the National Socialist dictatorship to show the provision of food and clothes for the poor. These posters were well-designed, and are commonly recognised to this day. Furthermore, biological and racial constructs related to the State were continually connected to food.

## The Second World War

Further evidence for the memory of the effects of food shortage in war is the central place the famine strategy acquired in the German war tactics in the Second World War. This was evident not only in the *General Plan Ost* for the subjugation of the Soviet Union, calculated to cause the starvation of about thirty million people (Paggi 2009: 45), but also in the renewed war against Britain (see also Lightowler and Macbeth this volume). These actions soon acquired the meaning of a 'food war', based on the memory of the similar kind of conflict in the First World War. A German publication of about 1941 is significantly called '*Englands Ernährungskrise*' (England's Food Supply Crisis). This short booklet is clearly a propaganda product, but it harks back to the food supply war of the First World War. The huge political value of food to the Weimar Republic was therefore recognised and re-adopted by Nazi propaganda. Fear of a return to the most extreme privations of the war years were exploited by all political parties, in a desire to present themselves as the solution to this problem.

## Conclusion

In summary, it is clear that the issue of food remained politically significant from the time of the First World War, throughout the Weimar Republic and in the propaganda of the National Socialists up to and during the Second World War. In particular, the memory of the starvation of the latter months of the First World War furnished one of the most common motives of the political propaganda of the parties. The same pictures helped to keep the memory of that experience alive. Furthermore, thanks to this wide diffusion and thumping representation of images of food during the political campaigns, the food itself acquired a political value, which was recognised by the Nazis and exploited in their propaganda (see Trostel 1997: 89–123). Finally, during the Second World War, food once again became a valuable weapon of war. A later National Socialist poster in the Folkwang Museum, Essen (FME) clearly demonstrates this. In the picture, a hand holding a sword is seen in front of a wide corn field and cloudy sky. The slogan delivers an uncompromising message: *Food is a weapon* (FME 5060; 1943).

## Notes

1  Deutscher Werbedienst.
2  Ausschuss der Frauenverbände.
3  Zentrale für Aufklärung und Volksbildung, Bayern.
4  Vereinigung zur Bekämpfung des Bolschewismus.
5  Deutscher Frauenausschuss zur Bekämpfung der Schuldlüge, Berlin.
6  Bayrischer Ordnungsblock.
7  Internationale Arbeiterhilfe, Berlin.
8  Karlsruhe Notgemeinschaft.
9  The word 'list' means the electoral roll, including all candidates of a party, who could be chosen by the voters. Each 'list' was called with a number.

## Archive sources

The archive number and abbreviation of the institution where the poster is retained can be found in the text alongside the description of each poster.

- Friedrich Ebert Foundation (*Friedrich Ebert Stiftung*), Bonn (FEF)
- German Historical Museum (*Deutsches Historisches Museum*), Berlin (GHM)
- City Archive (*Stadtarchiv*), Munich (CAM)
- Central State Archive (*Hauptstaatsarchiv*), Munich (STAM)
- Folkwang Museum (*Museum Folkwang*), Essen (FME)

# References

Hamann, B. (2008) *Der Erste Weltkrieg. Wahrheit und Lügen in Bilder und Texten*, Piper, Munich, Zurich.

Hosfeld, R. and Pölking, H. (2007) *Die Deutschen. 1815 bis 1918. Fürstenherrlichkeit und Bürgerwelten*, Piper, Munich, Zurich.

Paggi, L. (2009) *'Il popolo dei morti'. La Repubblica Italiana nata dalla guerra 1940–1946*, Il Mulino, Bologna.

Penny. L. (2010) *Meat Market. Female Flesh under Capitalism*, Zero Books, Winchester, Washington.

Trostel, W. (1997) *Schlagwort Brot. Politische Plakate des 20. Jahrhunderts*, Deutsches Brotmuseum, Ulm.

# CHAPTER 13
## ECHOES OF CATASTROPHE: FAMINE, CONFLICT AND RECONCILIATION IN THE IRISH BORDERLANDS

*Paul Collinson*

## Introduction

The focus of this essay is on the northwest of the Republic of Ireland, where I have been conducting anthropological fieldwork periodically since the late 1990s. This is an area of Ireland that has been shaped by a history of conflict, something which stems from events during the early 1920s and the traumatic partition of the country. The origins of the division of the island of Ireland can, of course, be traced back much further, to the Celtic (or Gaelic) Revival of the previous century, the various uprisings against colonial rule and, particularly relevant to this volume, the Famine of the 1840s. Furthermore, the 'Ulster Plantation'[1] of the early seventeenth century created a broad pattern of demographic divisions on the island of Ireland, which has persisted to the present day (Robinson 1984).

One of the most important themes in Ireland's history is access to land, and for much of the country's history, this meant access to food – something that was by no means always guaranteed. The failure of the potato crop in the 1840s led to one of the worst famines ever experienced in Europe, resulting in the deaths of over one million people and the emigration of a million more. According to the economist Amartya Sen (2006: 105), the mortality rate during the Irish Famine was higher than in any other recorded famine before or since. The horrors of the Great Hunger (*an Gorta Mór* in Irish), as it became known, threw into sharp relief the precarious condition of the subsistence economy of western Ireland, and its dangerous dependence on only one crop. The Famine also highlighted the unequal relationship between Ireland and its colonial master and, for many people in subsequent generations, it became a symbol of the oppressive nature of British colonialism. The event continues to resonate for Ireland's population today, commemorated in memorial gardens, sculptures, shrines, murals and museums throughout the island of Ireland.

The Famine and its legacy today form the primary themes of this chapter, which examines the relationship between access to food, identity and social and political change. It argues that the Famine's immediately devastating impact on the population and its effects on Irish society were of critical importance in the social and political upheavals which beset Ireland over the course of the nineteenth century, and which cumulated in the War of Independence and the partition of the country in the second decade of the twentieth century. This chapter also addresses the 'silence' which has characterised the Irish population's relationship with the Famine for much of the country's existence as a modern nation, something which has only recently been reversed following the 150th Anniversary of the Famine in the 1990s. Some commentators expressed the view that the commemoration should be used instrumentally as a means of reconciling previously divided communities on the isle of Ireland, and the Irish population with its past. Drawing on ethnographic research conducted in County Donegal in the late 1990s, the chapter considers how a Famine commemorative event could be viewed as a form of catharsis for the local population, and a way of understanding their identity and symbolising reconciliation between different religious communities in western Ulster (Figure 13.1).

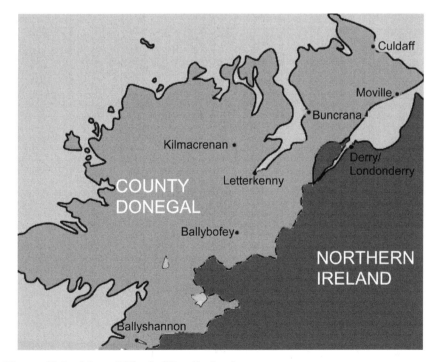

**Figure 13.1**  Map of North-West Ireland.

In summary, the chapter addresses the relationship between famine, memories of famine, and conflict. Furthermore, it considers how food can also be an instrument for reconciliation.

## Geographical Context: County Donegal

County Donegal is probably the most anachronistic of the twenty-six counties of the Irish Republic, sharing only a six-mile border with the rest of the country and being part of the nine counties of the Province of Ulster,[2] six of which form Northern Ireland, part of the UK. With the largest Protestant population of any county in the Republic and its proximity to Northern Ireland's second city, Derry (known to Protestants as Londonderry), the county's natural hinterland is just across the border[3] (Clifford 1992: 93). However, Donegal was cut off from the rest of the Province of Ulster when Ireland was partitioned in 1922, an event which left a deep and long-lasting legacy on the county's population.

The creation of the Irish border represents the most potent historical symbol of Ireland's troubled past. The peace process of the past twenty years has cemented the permanency of the border by removing the clause in the constitution of the Irish Republic proclaiming sovereignty over Northern Ireland and bringing most nationalists into the political fold, despite the small minority who maintain a focus on its dissolution. But the border continues to shape the lives of those who live in its environs, 'borderlanders' as anthropologists like to call them.

County Donegal is not a conflict zone. However, the conflict between the Catholic and Protestant (or, more accurately, Nationalist and Loyalist) communities of Ulster during the past century has never been far away. Nearby Derry/Londonderry has been one of the centres for this conflict, and was the location of the 'Bloody Sunday' shootings of 1973. These occurred in the Catholic area of the city and were one of the most controversial and long-lasting events of the entire history of the 'troubles'. From the early 1970s to the mid-1990s, the most fortified border in western Europe was between Northern Ireland and the Republic; the difficulties associated with crossing it meant that people living in Donegal who wished to travel to Dublin often preferred to travel via the six-mile isthmus in the south of Donegal, rather than using a more direct route by driving across Northern Ireland.

Donegal contains two distinct geographical zones. In the east, towards the border with Northern Ireland and around the Swilly Estuary, the land is low-lying and undulating, and represents the primary area of agricultural land in the county. This zone is known as the Laggan. In the south and west, in contrast, the land is mountainous, and the soils thin and acidic; sheep and dairy farming dominate here. There are also social and religious divisions between these areas, with the highest concentration of Protestants living in the eastern districts, most descended from the Scottish and English settlers who were 'planted' in Ulster in the early seventeenth century (c.f. Bell 1995: 471; Lecky 2007: 107). Whilst the relationship between Catholics and Protestant communities in Donegal is harmonious and the county has never experienced the same kind of 'troubles' associated with the sectarian conflict over the border, it is, to borrow a term from Nic Craith, a 'bicultural society' (2003: 1), with the two communities retaining distinctive identities. Many people living in the Laggan are discernibly different from those in the rest of Donegal: as well as worshipping in different churches, their children go to different schools and they have their own accent, a kind of hybrid of Scottish and northern Irish known as Ulster Scots.

Whether the contrasts between the two areas of the county are reflected in dietary variations of the population of each or not is a question beyond the scope of this chapter – but would be an interesting avenue for further research. It is likely, however, that today age, income and social class will be far more significant determinants of food choice than religious affiliation (c.f. Walsh and Nelson n.d.).

## The Famine and its Aftermath

The population of the Republic of Ireland today is around 4.7 million, just over half what it was prior to the Famine. From the early seventeenth century to the 1840s, the country's population had increased from two to over eight million. Donegal's population grew twenty percent between 1821 and 1841 (O'Donnell 1995), peaking at around 300,000; by the 1880s it was 100,000 less (MacLaughlin 2007: 363). Such significant growth, which was concentrated largely in the west of Ireland, had been made possible largely by the introduction of potato-cropping in the seventeenth century. The failure of the crop due to blight over three years starting in 1845 was felt most acutely in the marginal and congested lands of the south and west of the country, where the population was almost entirely dependent for their nutritional needs upon potatoes and buttermilk, supplemented to a limited extent by fish and seafood (Bolger 1995: 650). Whilst the Irish diet had become progressively more restricted during the eighteenth and early nineteenth centuries as produce such as grains, eggs and livestock came to be exported rather than consumed at home, the staple diet was nutritionally adequate – and, although by no means balanced, would also have been sustainable had the potato crop not failed (Crawford 1995: 60; Keating 1996: 62; Clarkson and Crawford 2001: 73–74; Nally 2011: 42).

Those living in the central and eastern areas of Ireland, although still affected by the Famine, did not suffer to the same extent. To claim that geography was responsible for the Famine's differential impact would be incorrect, however. The laissez-faire economic policies of the British Whig government meant that the export of agricultural produce from Ireland (mostly from the eastern areas of the country) continued unabated during the Famine (Kinealy 1997; Nally 2011: 12–13), something which gave rise to the claim that the Famine was actually 'man-made'. In support of this argument, critics at the time and subsequently pointed to, among other policies, the failure to impose embargos on food exports from Ireland, as had happened in previous subsistence crises in the 1740s, 1760s and in 1816–17 (Clarkson and Crawford 2001: 274; Nally 2011: 10). In the view of Kinealy, for example:

> The Irish poor did not starve because there was an inadequate supply of food within the country, they starved because political, commercial and individual greed was given priority over the saving of lives in one part of the United Kingdom. (Kinealy 2002: 90–91)

It is not the intention of this chapter to rehearse the arguments for and against the 'man-made' thesis. It is worth noting, however, that others have disagreed with this position, since it fails to take into account the fact that had the exported food remained in Ireland, it is very doubtful that this would have alleviated the Famine as most people would have been unable to afford to buy it (e.g., Clarkson and Crawford 2001: 276–277). From this perspective, variable access to food was the critical factor, itself a product of social class differentials which privileged certain groups over others (Cohen 2002: 117).

The pattern nationally was reflected in Donegal, with the most acute hardships experienced by the populations in the upland and coastal regions, while those living on the low-lying plains of the east were relatively less affected, having a more varied diet and being more closely tied into the economy of the rest of the British Isles (Begley and Lally 1997). These internal disparities were manifested, above all, in the fact that farmers in eastern areas of the county were still sending large volumes of agricultural produce, such as wheat, oats and butter, to markets in western Ulster during the height of the Famine in 1847 (Lecky 2007).

Another highly significant determinant of the impact of the Famine was the attitudes of landowners, which varied considerably across Donegal (Sheane 2008). Some landowners became notorious in the ways in which they treated their tenants, with their names living on through subsequent decades as bywords for cruelty, in contrast to many others who displayed more compassion, often at considerable personal cost to themselves. One such figure was Lord George Hill who owned an estate around the town of Gweedore and, as head of a relief committee, arranged for Indian meal to be sold (illegally) to the population at below the regulated cost during the height of the Famine (Begley and Lally 1997: 80). In contrast was the behaviour of John George Adair, the owner of another large estate in central Donegal called Derryveagh, from which he evicted 47 families from their homes in 1861 during a period of renewed agricultural hardship in the area (Vaughan 1983). The grandiose castle that Adair built for himself on the shores of Lough Garten is now an interpretative centre, much of which is given over to explaining the story of its former owner and those he cast out.

The work of relief societies that provided food to the poor – in which Protestants and Quakers played a prominent role – was also instrumental in ameliorating the worst ravages of starvation (Grant 1997). Much of this sustenance was provided in the form of a soup or broth, the nutritional value of which was questionable (Haines 2004: 308; Nally 2011: 145–146), but undoubtedly saved many lives during the Famine years. The broth was often served in large iron pots, which have become potent memorial symbols and may be seen at numerous locations throughout Ireland. The Irish word for broth, *brachan*, is also a common place- and road name in the country today, marking the locations where the starving were fed (Begley and Lally 1997: 97; Sheane 2008: 67).

The Famine was perhaps the defining event in Irish history and had profound and far-reaching effects on all aspects of Irish society, which, through emigration, was no longer confined to the country itself. One immediate impact in Ireland was to increase the variation in the diet, with other staples being introduced, such as maize, bacon and herring (Vaughan 1983: 160). The fat content in an average Irish diet rose six-fold between the 1840s and 1900 (Clarkson and Crawford 2001: 183), as livestock-raising came to replace cultivation in many areas (Burnet 1997: 8). The most potent political legacy of the Famine was to increase the pressure for land reform in Ireland. This gathered pace during the 1850s and 1860s and culminated in the Irish Land War of 1879–81, when many tenant farmers throughout the country refused to pay their rents, and in the founding of the Irish Land League, which pressed for a fairer distribution of land and an end to the absentee landowner system, whereby much of the land was held by (largely Protestant) landowners, at least one-third of whom did not live on their estates (Miller 1985: 44, cited in Nally 2011: 43). These events were prompted in part by another near-famine in the west caused by poor harvests, a depression in Britain and a cholera outbreak among the chicken population (Vaughan 1983: 220); a famine was averted only because of the willingness of shopkeepers to extend credit to the local population, often at the expense of their own livelihoods. The importance of subsistence featured prominently in the ideology of the Irish Land League; indeed, its second resolution stated:

That as the land of Ireland, like that of every other country, was intended by a just and all-providing God for the use and sustenance of those of His people whom he gave inclination and energies to cultivate and improve it, any system which sanctions its monopoly by a privileged class, or assigns its ownership and control to a landlord caste, to be used as an instrument of usurious or political self-seeking, demands from every aggrieved Irishman an underlying hostility, being flagrantly opposed to the first principles of humanity – self preservation. (Irish Land League, Second Resolution 1879, quoted in Vaughan 1983: 221)

In this way, the Famine and the importance of land and subsistence became central elements in the formation of Irish sociopolitical identity during the nineteenth century and the first part of the twentieth. The Irish Land League (together with its successor the National League) represented the nascent stirrings of a popular and militant Irish nationalism, and together with the Celtic revival, laid the foundations for the uprising of 1916, the War of Independence and the partitioning of the country, the effects of which are still being felt today.

## Remembering the Famine

## Popular Conceptions

> The changes wrought [by the Famine] on our language, our culture, our psyche, continue to impact on us as contemporary realities. The issues of the Great Famine are monumental and devastating, there are areas of immense sadness, anger, humiliation, confusion, dignity and healing. (O'Kelly 1995: 29)

Many have argued that the Irish population has had an ambiguous relationship with the Famine over the years, that the trauma and 'shame' associated with it means that there has been a tacit, largely unconscious undertaking to deliberately 'forget' the events of the 1840s (e.g., Lloyd 2011: 51–52). This attitude of silence, it is held, has had a detrimental impact on the development of Irish identity, since it has prevented a full understanding of how contemporary Ireland has been shaped by its past. In the view of Waters (1997: 28), for example, 'because we refuse to remember, we are doomed to repeat'. Arguably the fullest expression of this argument is found in the contributions to the volume *Irish Hunger, Personal Reflections of the Legacy of the Famine*, edited by Hayden (1997).

Whilst there is undoubtedly some truth in this type of perspective, the number of memorials to the Famine throughout the country – supplemented by museums, interpretative centres and historical societies – would suggest an alternative view (c.f. McLean 2004: 151–154), although many have only been established in the past fifteen years or so. There is also a very large corpus of art, music, poetry and literature devoted to remembrance of the Famine. Probably the most famous of all Irish popular songs, *The Fields of Athenry*, for example, posits an explicit relationship between the Famine, colonialism, rebellion and (forced) exile.

Although it is likely that for most of the Irish population today, the Famine is something buried deep in the country's past and is not something that particularly stirs the conscious on a day-to-day level, it may be that it has left its imprint on the character of the Irish population in less tangible ways. Some have made the point that one of the Famine's most measurable legacies is to be found in the volume of charitable giving in Ireland in comparison to other countries in Europe, particularly for causes associated with the alleviation of poverty and starvation. According to the polling company Gallup, Ireland was the most charitable nation in Europe in 2011 and the second most charitable in the world, measured in terms of the proportion of the population who regularly donate to charitable causes (reported in the *Irish Times* online, 20th December 2011). And this at a time when the country was experiencing one of the worst economic downturns in its history. Another possible 'survival' from the Famine lies in the hospitality of the Irish population – with the sharing of food very much a part of this tradition. Hospitableness is associated with rurality and a powerful community ethos, and remains strongest in the rural west of the country. Ireland's tourist image, in which the promise of a 'Hundred Thousand Welcomes' (*Cead Mile Failte*) often features prominently, is not simply something dreamed up by the ad men.

It may also be the case that, along with the other aspects of social change that Ireland has experienced in recent years, the relationship which the population has with the Famine has altered and Irish people have now come to accept what the events of the 1840s means to them. The Famine's 150th anniversary in the mid- to late-1990s heralded a collective outpouring of emotion as people in numerous towns and villages across the country held commemorative events, with many commentators calling for the occasion to be used instrumentally to promote reconciliation and forgiveness. It was in this spirit that the single most important political breakthrough of the Irish peace process, the Good Friday Agreement, was signed between the British and Irish Governments and the main Nationalist and Unionist political parties in Northern Ireland in 1998.

## The Famine Memorial Garden

One such commemorative event occurred in a village in eastern Donegal of some two hundred people, located in a mountainous area overlooking the Swilly Estuary and the Laggan. The village is an innocuous place, containing a small church, a village hall, a primary school, a playing field and a pub. It lies close to a main road, and one could pass by the village easily without quite realising it is there.

In 1996, a community group was established by the parish priest and others in order to promote social and economic development in the area. One of the first projects the participants became involved in was an attempt to secure funds to build a famine memorial garden, an endeavour that soon came to occupy the group fulltime. The centrepiece of the garden was to be a large

Famine soup pot, which had been found in the mudflats of the estuary a few years before and brought up to the village. The group applied for funding from the EU's Peace and Reconciliation Programme, which had been established by the EU after the first Irish Republican Army (IRA) ceasefire in 1994 in order to promote development in the border region and foster cross-border and community cooperation.

In their written application to the programme, the group highlighted the village's location on the boundary of what had been the Ulster Plantation, something that, the application argued, had been responsible for holding its population back over the centuries. It also drew attention to the marginal and isolated aspect of the settlement above the Swilly Estuary, the impact of the Famine in the area, and the fact that many of the forebears of its inhabitants had worked as day labourers (*spailpin fanachs*, in the vernacular) on the farms of the Laggan and had never owned their own land. Finally, it alluded to the conflict across the border, arguing that this had had a profound effect on suppressing economic development in the area. In this way, the geography of the Irish border, the historical events which created it, the area's underdevelopment and the conflict in Ulster were brought together in a powerful explanatory nexus.

Funding was secured from the EU and, over the course of the next few months, the garden was built using local labourers employed by the group. An organising committee met weekly to plan the garden's layout and organise the inauguration ceremony, which was to be a grand occasion attended by local dignitaries from the county. The latter included senior figures from the Protestant (Presbyterian and Church of Ireland) dioceses, whose presence was regarded as essential in order to acknowledge the role that the Protestant community had played in Donegal in alleviating suffering during the Famine years and symbolise the reconciliation between the two communities in Ulster.[4] Members of the Society of Friends (Quakers) were also invited for the same reason. The garden was officially opened in the summer of 1997 by the US Ambassador to Ireland, Jean Kennedy Smith, with local TDs (members of the Irish parliament), councillors, clergy and most of the population of the area in attendance. Local TV and radio were also present to record the event. The ceremony was followed by a reception in the village hall, and music and dancing in the local pub until late into the evening.

Whilst the garden yielded few tangible economic benefits for the population and did not create significant amounts of employment beyond the labourers tasked to build it, its creation was seen as a significant achievement in the village. It symbolised the struggle of its population over the adversity they felt they had suffered through the years; it brought its inhabitants together in a collective endeavour in which all could share; it helped cement relationships between the religious communities in Donegal; and it commemorated an event which, all recognised, was of critical importance in the history of modern Ireland and which continues to have a significant resonance.

## Famine Murals

Across the border from Donegal, in Northern Ireland, the Famine has, conversely, been seen by some as a reason for continued division, and has been adopted as a rallying cry for militant Republicanism. In reflecting this, nationalist murals in Northern Ireland have often drawn on images from the Famine to reinforce what their creators hold are the parallels between the colonialism of the past and the ongoing partition of the island. Most murals of this genre reproduce – usually in meticulous detail – well-known paintings and drawings from the 1840s which depict the destitute and starving, and are often supplemented by lines from poetry or by more politically explicit phrases (such as 'Britain's genocide by starvation', which appeared on a Famine mural painted in Belfast in 2007).

The political message that these murals convey has always reflected a minority view, however, and the peace process of the past two decades has taken much of the sting away from the argument. The statement made by British Prime Minister, Tony Blair, in 1997 concerning the Famine was also of considerable historical significance in this context, and did much to heal wounds on both sides of the community:

> [The Famine] has left deep scars. Those who governed London at the time failed their people through standing by while a crop failure turned into a massive human tragedy. We must not forget such a dreadful event. It is also right that we should pay tribute to the ways in which the Irish people have triumphed in the face of this catastrophe.[5]

## Conclusion

As with several chapters in this volume, this one is about a lack of food rather than food per se. Unlike most of the chapters, though, the geographical area on which it focuses is not a conflict zone today; but it is one which has been shaped by conflict, and cannot be understood without reference to it. The intersection between (lack of) food, conflict and social and political change is a theme that recurs throughout this book – how people respond to change and how change impacts on their lives.

The Irish Famine affected Ireland in profound and long-lasting ways. It certainly deepened the divisions between the Catholic and Protestant communities and sowed the seeds for the subsequent rebellions against British rule, cumulating in the War of Independence of the following century (Kinealy 2002). It also created borders – social, political and geographical – the effects of which are still discernable today.

However, ironically, perhaps, on the present day island of Ireland, food is undermining the significance of these borders, helping to ameliorate conflict and bring communities closer together. Cross-border food shopping is one notable trend in this regard, with the shopping habits of the populations on each side responding according to the relative strength of the two currencies, the Euro and Sterling. In 2008 and 2009, for example, with the Euro stronger in value than Sterling, customers from the Republic flocked to supermarkets in Northern Ireland; the Asda superstore in Enniskillen, a town of around 14,000 people, was the sixth busiest store in the whole of the worldwide Walmart group in the pre-Christmas period of 2008 (*Belfast Newsletter* 9th January 2009). At other times, conversely, shops in the Republic have prospered as Sterling has risen against the Euro. A dual currency area exists on both sides of the border, with all shops accepting both currencies as a matter of course; in practical, everyday terms the concept of being in Ireland and being in the UK for border-landers in Ireland is becoming increasingly blurred. Food is also being used to promote cross-border development. One such scheme is the Killybegs-Tyrone Good Food Initiative, which is funded by the EU Peace and Reconciliation Programme and was set up in the early 2000s to promote networking between those involved in the food and tourism industries in Donegal and Northern Ireland. In establishing tourist trails and recipe books, it has promoted the area as a single region – a trend that is increasingly evident in other areas along the border. With the border's permanency has come its permeability.

This chapter has looked at the relationship between the Famine and political change in Ireland. It has demonstrated how the origins of the division of the country in the 1920s and the continuing sectarian conflicts on the isle of Ireland lie partly in the Famine years. Whilst emphasising the impact of the terrible events of the 1840s in sowing divisions in Ireland, it has also noted the way in which the remembrance of the Famine in recent years has been used as a symbol for healing and reconciliation, and has enabled Irish people to come to terms with their past. Perhaps no-one has expressed this better than Mary Robinson, former President of Ireland:

> I think it marks our maturity as a people that our remembrance is becoming an act of self-awareness. It marks our maturity as a people and as a nation that we are able to break the silence on the disaster that overcame us in ways which are both rigorous and challenging ... We need to help [our young people] to face the future with the understanding that famine is not something which can be understood only through history. It must be understood with every fibre of our moral being.[6]

## Notes

1  The Ulster Plantation was the most extensive of the various 'plantation' schemes initiated by the British government during the seventeenth century, when English and Scottish settlers ('planters') were granted plots of land in Ireland.

2  The Province of Ulster is one of four Provinces on the island of Ireland, the others being Connaught, Leinster and Munster.
3  Wherever the word, 'border', is used, it refers to the border between the Republic of Ireland and Northern Ireland.
4  It is notable that the Anglican Archdeacon of the Raphoe Diocese in which the village falls had provided £400 for the local relief committee in 1847 (Grant 1997: 190).
5  Text contained in a statement from Tony Blair read by Irish actor Gabriel Byrne on 31st May 1997 in Cork, Ireland (quoted in McCaffrey 2006: 175).
6  International Conference on Hunger Keynote Address by President Mary Robinson, President of Ireland 1990–1997, United Nations High Commissioner for Human Rights 1997–2002. New York University, Glucksman Ireland House, 19–20 May 1995. Text published at: http://gos.sbc.edu/r/robinson.html. Accessed on 1st May 2012.

# References

Begley, A. and Lally, S. (1997) The Famine in County Donegal. In Kinealy, C. and Parkhill, T. (eds) *The Famine in Ulster*, Ulster Historical Foundation, Belfast: 77–98.

*Belfast Newsletter* (2009) Enniskillen Asda Second Best in UK, 9th January 2009. Published at: http://www.newsletter.co.uk/news/business/local-businesses/enniskil len-asda-second-best-in-uk-1-1880211. Accessed on 4th May 2010.

Bell, J. (1995) Changing Farming Methods in Donegal. In Nolan, W., Ronayne, L. and Dunleavy, M. (eds) *Donegal – History and Society. Interdisciplinary Essays on the History of an Irish County*, Geography Publications, Dublin: 471–490.

Bolger, P. (1995) The Congested Districts Board and the Coops in Donegal. In Nolan, W., Ronayne, L. and Dunleavy, M. (eds) *Donegal – History and Society. Interdisciplinary Essays on the History of an Irish County*, Geography Publications, Dublin: 649–674.

Burnet, J. (1997) The Irish Famine: Ethnic Groups as Victims, *Lectures and Papers in Ethnicity*, 23(March), University of Toronto, Toronto.

Clarkson, L.A. and Crawford, E.M. (2001) *Feast and Famine. Food and Nutrition in Ireland 1500–1920*, Oxford University Press, Oxford.

Clifford, B. (1992) *The Economics of Partition*, Athol Books, Dublin.

Cohen, M. (2002) Towards an Historical Ethnography of the Great Irish Famine. The Parish of Tullylish, County Down 1841–51. In Nugent, D. (ed.) *Locating Capitalism in Time and Space*, Stanford University Press, Stanford: 113–136.

Crawford, M. (1995) Food and Famine. In Póirtéir, C. (ed.) *Famine Echoes*, Mercier Press, Dublin: 60–73.

Grant, J. (1997) Local Relief Committees in Ulster. In Crawford, M.E. (ed.) *The Hungry Stream. Essays on Emigration and Famine*, Institute of Irish Studies, Belfast: 185–198.

Haines, R. (2004) *Charles Trevelyan and the Great Irish Famine*, Four Corners Press, Dublin.

Hayden, T. (ed.) (1997) *Irish Hunger. Personal Reflections on the Legacy of the Famine*, Wolfhound Press. Boulder, Co.

*Irish Times* online (20th December 2011) Ireland second most charitable nation. Published at: http://www.irishtimes.com/newspaper/breaking/2011/1220/breaking37. html. Accessed 10th June 2012.

Kinealy, C. (1997) Food Exports from Ireland 1846–7, *History Ireland*, 5(1): 32–36.

Kinealy, C. (2002) *The Great Irish Famine. Impact, Ideology and Rebellion*, Palgrave, New York.

Keating, J. (1996) *Irish Famine Facts*, Teagasc, Dublin.

Lecky, A.G. (2007) Outer and Inner Donegal [1909]. In Maclaughlin, J. (ed.) *Donegal: the Making of a Northern County*, Four Courts Press, Dublin: 107–108.

Lloyd, D. (2011) *Irish Culture and Colonial Modernity 1800–2000: The Transformation of Oral Space*, Cambridge University Press, Cambridge.

MacLaughlin, J. (2007) Conclusion. In MacLaughlin, J. (ed.) *Donegal: The Making of a Northern County*, Four Courts Press, Dublin: 358–364.

McCaffrey, C. (2006) *In Search of Ireland's Heroes*, Ivan Dee, Chicago.

McLean, S. (2004) *The Event and its Terrors. Ireland, Famine, Modernity*, Stanford University Press, Stanford, Calif.

Miller, K. (1985) *Emigrants and Exiles: Ireland and the Irish Exodus to North America*, Oxford University Press, Oxford.

Nally, D. (2011) *Human Encumbrances: Political Violence and the Great Irish Famine*, University of Notre Dame Press, Notre Dame.

Nic Craith, M. (2003) *Culture and Identity Politics in Northern Ireland*, Palgrave Macmillan, Gordonsville, Va, USA.

O'Donnell, M. (1995) Settlement and Society in the Barony of East Inishowen c1850. In Nolan, W., Ronayne, L. and Dunleavy, M. (eds) *Donegal – History and Society. Interdisciplinary Essays on the History of an Irish County*, Geography Publications, Dublin: 509–546.

O'Kelly, A. (1995) Introduction to her Exhibit 'No Colouring Can Deepen the Darkest of Truth', opened at the Irish Museum of Modern Art in September 1992. In Mullan, D. (ed.) *A Glimmer of Light. An Overview of Great Hunger Commemorative Events Throughout the World*, Concern Worldwide, Dublin: 61.

Robinson, P. (1984) *The Plantation of Ulster. British Settlement in an Irish Landscape 1600–1670*, Ulster Historical Foundation, Belfast.

Sen, A. (2006) *Identity and Violence. Illusion and Destiny*, W.W. Norton, New York.

Sheane, M. (2008) *Famine in the Land of Ulster*, Arthur H Stockwell, Ilfracombe.

Vaughan, W.E. (1983) *Sin, Sheep and Scotsmen. John George Adair and the Deeryveagh Evictions, 1861*, Appletree Press, Belfast.

Walsh, A. and Nelson, R. (n.d.) *Northern Ireland Food Culture: Moving Beyond Spuds*. Published at: http://arrow.dit.ie/cgi/viewcontent.cgi?article=1001&context. Accessed on 4th July 2012.

Waters, J. (1997) Confronting the Ghosts of Our Past. In Hayden, T. (ed.) *Irish Hunger. Personal Reflections on the Legacy of the Famine*, Wolfhound Press, Boulder, Co.: 27–31.

# CHAPTER 14
## 'LAND TO THE TILLER': HUNGER AND THE END OF MONARCHY IN ETHIOPIA

*Benjamin Talton*

**A** decade before the historic Ethiopian famine of 1984–1985, university student activists in Addis Ababa rallied around the crisis of peasant hunger. The plight of the peasantry was, for the students and their colleagues attending universities in North America and Europe, evidence of Emperor Haile Selassie's callous disregard for the welfare of his subjects and exposed him as unfit to rule. Hunger in and of itself was not the student activists' primary concern in 1972 and 1973. Yet, among their many differences the leaders of the various organisations and factions that comprised the Ethiopian student movement agreed that widespread hunger had no place in modern Ethiopian society. They embraced hunger as a stand-in for political issues on which they had neither consensus nor control: political corruption, economic stagnation, the Amhara's political and economic dominance, an antiquated land tenure system and the national language policy (Zewde 2010). The government's treatment of the peasantry, close to ninety percent of Ethiopians at the time, exemplified the Emperor's detachment from the realities of life in Ethiopia and provided the students with common ground and, for many, justified revolution. In this way, the student movement showed the efficacy of hunger as a political tool for those who sought to cultivate a sense of common cause toward social and political change.

In 1973, at the height of the food crisis, students, primarily from Haile Selassie I University in Addis Ababa, with help from their colleagues abroad, launched food relief programmes, while they held street demonstrations to compel the Emperor either to enact agricultural and educational reforms or to abdicate. Their activism created the political breach into which military officers launched the coup that ended Ethiopia's almost two thousand years of monarchy (Zewde 2001). Gradually, methodically throughout 1974, junior military officers took over the students' movement and either co-opted or

marginalised its leaders. The soldiers' activities began as non-political defi-
ance by rank-and-file soldiers and junior officers discontented with their living
conditions and pay, rather than with the country's social and political condition. Yet, many of the mutiny's leaders sympathised with and gained inspira-
tion from student activists. What is significant, particularly for the purposes
of this essay, is that the more radicalised members among the junior officers
broadened the mutiny's rather narrow focus to include national, populist
concerns, peasant hunger in particular, as a platform for a coup against the
Emperor and his government. By adopting the student movements' stand
against hunger, the Derg ('the committee' in Amarinya), as the military
leaders called themselves, initially gained popular support.

From this foundation, during the middle months of 1974, the leaders of the
broadened revolution – students, military officers, labour leaders, and leftist
activists – engaged hunger as a social, political and moral problem. Activists
within this movement sought to delegitimise politically those it cast as com-
plicit in creating or allowing widespread hunger or famine. In the context of
Ethiopia's revolution, holding aloft the banner of hunger cloaked political
actors with authenticity and a connection with masses of people that the monarchy considered at the time to be beyond the realm of political relevance. The
activists moved beyond the Emperor's political authority by responding to
the critical needs of the Ethiopian people, while he ignored them. Therefore,
from 1972 to September 1974, for the first time in Ethiopia's modern history,
commoners subverted state power with political rhetoric and protests that featured a food crisis among rural peasants as a principal grievance. University
student activists, as would military leaders, ascribed a political significance to
both hunger and the peasantry that departed from previous generations and
provided a viable justification for revolution.

The students' humanitarian and political responses to hunger are all the
more noteworthy in light of the predominant discourse on famine in Ethiopia
and elsewhere in Africa over the past thirty years, which has largely rendered
Africans agentless observers in their own tragedy. If one places students'
activities at the centre of this history, the diverse and dynamic response to
hunger among Ethiopians becomes evident. Moreover, one sees the ways in
which the students' politically charged engagement with hunger was critical in
reshaping Ethiopia's political history.

## Grassroots Humanitarianism and the Ethiopian Student Movement

1972 and 1973 were the most severe years of the prolonged crisis in the Horn
of Africa and across much of the Sahel. Nature combined with public policy to
hobble a large swath of the peasant population. An extended drought struck
key agricultural areas of the north and around Hararghe in the east which

accelerated rising food prices. The government compounded the peasant's problems maintaining access to food by tightly controlling its distribution throughout the country. It directed the preponderance of produce to urban centres, which inflated food prices in rural areas. Moreover, Emperor Selassie did not approach agricultural and land tenure reforms as a priority. For 1972–1973, the monarchy allocated US$191,797,669 for defence, internal law and order, and information, compared to US$14,983,789 available to support agricultural production (Ethiopian Student Union of North America 1974). The hardest hit communities were the Afar camel herders in the lowlands and Oromo tenant farmers on the escarpment, although farmers of the highlands suffered the highest death rates. In Wello and Tigray provinces alone 40,000 and 80,000 people respectively died.

Until the rise of the student movement, Ethiopians did not valorise the peasantry. Whether urban or rural, a majority of Ethiopians defined themselves, first and foremost, through an Ethiopian hierarchy wholly based on class and ethnicity (Donham 1992). The country's unique power dynamic, in which the monarchy, nobility and the church owned much of the land, entrenched deep social and political inequality. Exorbitant tax practices which targeted the peasantry ensured that they rarely had a surplus from agricultural production, remained in debt and were denied the luxury of political participation. The resulting tensions periodically bubbled to the surface in peasant protests and uprisings (Rahmato 2008).

Despite palpable links between government policies and peasant hunger, many Ethiopians accepted episodes of extreme hunger as part of a natural order (Pankhurst 1985). Just as many Ethiopians spoke of social stratification – another target of the Ethiopian student movement – as God's will; they also seldom questioned the origins of drought, famine and poverty (Molver 2008). After the revolution, journalist Ryszard Kapuściński conducted extensive interviews with members of the Emperor's staff. In one, a palace official described famine to Kapuściński as an expected occurrence. It was natural, he suggested, that droughts arrived, the earth dried up, the cattle dropped dead and the peasants starved. Then, as he described it, the rains would finally arrive and the cycle would begin anew (Kapuściński 1978). Another palace official blamed Westerners for blowing hunger in the north out of proportion and interfering in Ethiopia's domestic affairs. Hunger and suffering were 'in accordance with the laws of nature and the eternal order of things', the official contended. 'Since this was eternal and normal, none of the dignitaries would dare to bother His Most Exalted Highness with the news that in such and such a province a given person had died of hunger' (Kapuściński 1978: 111).

Students in the early 1970s had only recently taken a social and political interest in hunger and the peasantry. Indeed, they remained relatively quiet politically until the mid-1960s. Some of the early activists were inspired by the failed 1960 coup against the Emperor led by Germame Neway and his brother, Brigadier General Mengistu Neway. But most students remained politically ambivalent. A critical force for change came from abroad. Emperor Selassie welcomed students from newly independent African nations to Haile Selassie I University, beginning in 1960 and established a scholarship programme to attract them. Many of the foreign African students who arrived at Haile Selassie I University over the course of the decade imported a strident nationalism, pan-Africanism and anti-imperialism that had a profound effect on their Ethiopian counterparts. Similarly, the sizeable population of Ethiopians who went to study in the United States took in the American civil rights and anti-Vietnam War protests that swept across American universities and cities during the period. These movements – African and American – shaped what many Ethiopian activists believed was politically acceptable for a government and possible for citizens (Zewde 2010). Yet the students' politics remained complex and fluid. Within and outside of the country, their activism reflected Ethiopia's complex ethnic and class dynamics. Student organisations at Haile Selassie I University pushed their own agendas, some of which placed these organisations in opposition to each other. Shared frustration with the Emperor alone was not an effective enough glue to bind these factions into one movement.

Emperor Selassie, furthermore, seems to have regarded widespread hunger as beneath Ethiopia's dignity. His responses to the problem suggest that he feared that highlighting the peasants' plight would threaten Ethiopia's international standing and internal stability. Ethiopia was the only African nation to stand as a political equal to the powers of Europe in the signing of the Geneva Conventions in 1949 and as a founding member of the United Nations. In the period of decolonisation, when the promise and hope of African independence was threatened by a proliferation of coups d'état, ethnic and regional violence, political corruption and neo-colonialism, hunger was poised to expose the Ethiopian government's soft underbelly of class exploitation, cronyism and imperialism. The students and the government recognised hunger's potential to subvert Ethiopia's place in the world, but in fundamentally conflicting ways.

Students in North America and leftist intellectuals were aware of Ethiopia's economic and political deficiencies relative to many of their African neighbours. For them, Ethiopia's economic and political stagnation undermined its prestige from never having experienced formal European colonial rule. Student activists and intellectuals argued that famine did not emerge from the absence of food, but, rather, from the peasants' lack of access to it. The Emperor had clearly defined duties and responsibilities to his subjects, but evidently did not foresee the political costs of his negligence. News of the famine, spread to students through their colleagues who either hailed from or had worked in the northern provinces and Hararghe. It became the Ethiopian government's ultimate shame and failing. A shift emerged in the perceptions of the urban-common elite with regard to the relationship between government policy and famine, government action and the persistence of hunger.

The peasants' hardships in the midst of drought were compounded by exploitative taxes and rents that increased continuously. These factors rendered living conditions for peasants in northern and eastern Ethiopia unsustainable. Activists described northerners in 1972 and 1973 as living, 'in the grinding teeth of starvation' (Ethiopian Student Union of North America 1974: 38). They railed against exorbitant tax practices that targeted the peasantry and ensured that they rarely had surplus agricultural production, remained in debt and were denied the luxury of political participation and organised protest. 'The fundamental causes of the present famine in Ethiopia,' The Ethiopian Student Union of North American (ESUNA) leaders argued in December 1973, 'are feudal stagnation and imperialist exploitation ... We thus strongly and angrily denounce the criminal government of Haile Selassie and his cohorts for playing jokes until death of the Ethiopian people whom we regard more precious than anything in the world' (Ethiopian Student Union of North America 1973: 39).

In Addis Ababa during the first years of the 1970s, students often staged their demonstrations beyond the university's gates, along King George Street. On occasion, they took their protests a mile down the road to hold protests near Emperor Selassie's Menelik II Palace. They chanted popular slogans that reflected their politics and linked the persistence of hunger with the broader issue of ethnic and class-based social and economic inequality. 'Land to the tiller,' they shouted, and 'self-rule for all nations,' and 'democratic and human rights.' In *Combat*, mouthpiece of the World Federation of Ethiopian Students, activists stated that it had, 'since 1965 made the land question the heart of the national problem by agitating for "land to the tiller". The implementation of this crucial watchword,' the activists editorialised, 'will once and for all remain the spectre of famine from Ethiopia. The antagonistic existence of abject poverty on one side and luxury on the other, grain exports by some and famine for the multitude and potentially rich country and an actually poor one will be made to vanish never to return again' (Ethiopian Student Union of North America 1974: 44). The students' demands that the land be turned over to 'those who till it' reflected Marxism's influence within the students' evolving ideologies. This rallying cry, as Kifle Selassie describes, 'became steadily louder, year after year, up to the fall of Haile Selassie and the adoption of a radical agrarian reform in 1975 by the Derg' (Selassie 1987: 19).

With the increased anti-government agitation in Addis Ababa, the government tried to block news of the famine from urban residents and the international community. Still, Western journalists and humanitarian organisations took note of the famine, and compelled Selassie to acknowledge the crisis, which he did, but refused to admit that it had grown beyond his control. In June, he met privately with humanitarian relief organisations, but did not follow these up with a comprehensive relief programme. Jack Shepherd, a US State Department official who served in Ethiopia during this period, described the Emperor as seeking, 'to create the impression that they weren't just another Sahel country coming apart at the seams' (Shepherd 1975: ix). Selassie did not invite officials from humanitarian organisations to assess the food crisis. In addition, government officials blamed foreign journalists and aid workers for inciting students to protest and denounce the Emperor (Kapuściński 1978).

In the absence of an effective government response to the food crisis, a group of university students and their allies on the faculty at Haile Selassie I University organised a food relief regimen. They started with an ad hoc research group comprised of three professors to examine the food situation in the north and issue a report. 'The situation is extremely grave and urgent' they related (Ethiopian Student Union of North America 1974: 33). More than simply filling the humanitarian void, students acted out of a sense of national purpose. From abroad, leaders of the World Wide Federation of Ethiopian Students demanded that the government use a portion of the food set aside for university students' meals for food relief for the peasants in the north and that the Emperor organise the relief operation. Ethiopian students in Addis and those abroad were not always coordinated in message and action. Foreign-based activists were essential in voicing the grievances and advertising the efforts of their Ethiopia-based colleagues (Zewde 2010). Indeed, the Emperor's aggressive response to students' humanitarian initiatives illustrates the tremendous risk that the students took. It was dangerous to protest and organise hunger relief. These remained the preserve of students within Ethiopia, while those abroad risked their scholarships through their vocal opposition to the monarchy and their fundraising on behalf of Addis Ababa-based activists.

During the first week of March 1973, students from Haile Selassie I University organised trips to Wello to distribute to peasants food they had collected. On 17th March, police arrested students for no apparent reason except that their initiative embarrassed the Emperor. The following week, students held political marches in Wello to draw attention to the famine and protest about their fellow students' arrests. The police fired on the crowd of peaceful demonstrators and killed seventeen students. Despite the government's willingness to use deadly force to put down the student movement, the propaganda campaign against the Emperor and the students' relief programme continued throughout 1973. Police action stifled student humanitarianism but strengthened their resolve to push the government to enact education reforms, end police brutality and address famine. The more radical students sought the end of the monarchy itself. Government violence against the students speaks to Haile Selassie's concern for the message that protests sent to the rest of the population. Evidently, however, he did not perceive the student movement as an existential threat, nor that the junior military officers would use the student movement to bring down the monarchy and implement elements of reform that the university students and leftist intellectuals had demanded. This evolved rapidly over eight months, beginning in 1974.

## The Double Usurp: Military Takeover of the Student Movement and the State

In Addis Ababa, students coined a popular aphorism that proved to be prescient: 'the students prepared the meal, the taxi drivers are cooking it, but the army will eat it' (Darch 1976: 12). While activists unwittingly prepared for the fall of the Emperor's government, their movement reached a tipping point. In January 1974, students at Haile Selassie I University boycotted classes and held large street demonstrations to protest government repression and violence directed at students and journalists. In the midst of this civil unrest, the government enacted policies that infused the movement with energy and broadened support, including raising petrol costs. Taxi drivers in Addis Ababa might have settled for higher fuel costs had the Emperor allowed them to raise taxi fares. He refused, and, in so doing, precipitated the taxi drivers joining the national protests. On 18th February 1974, the drivers and school teachers launched a city-wide strike, beginning four days of extensive protests, which encouraged the students. At the same time, however, student leaders within the broad administrative structure of the World Federation of Ethiopian Students struggled to keep their coalition of student organisations together. With the added pressure of coordinating with non-unionised striking workers and civil servants, and with the regime turning more liberal in its use of violence toward activists, the student movement floundered. The progression of the army's mutiny is not as clear as the student movement, but from January 1974 the revolution evolved with striking speed (Zewde 2001). Soldiers of the Fourth Division, in the southern frontier post of Nagelle Borana, were the first to mutiny.

In the early stages of what became a revolution, the government operated with a diminished capacity to discern the nature of the unfolding events and no palpable inclination to erect even a veneer of consideration for the concerns of protestors and mutineers. Both the military and civilian movements capitalised on the government's weakness and an unravelling of Ethiopia's social fabric, which had, for so many generations, successfully checked challenges to its social and political hierarchy. Apart from this context, the soldiers and the students aspired to distinct goals. The mutineers sent radio messages throughout the country in which they made their demands clear: increased pay and better living conditions. They did not make any political demands. As their message echoed throughout the country, other divisions joined the rebellion. When the army's Second Division, stationed in Asmara, joined its leaders and demanded not just reform but regime change, this was the beginning of the coup (Tareke 2009).

Rather than assess the forces that drove the movements for change, the Emperor and his government responded to the events taking place around them on the basis of centuries of tradition. As a result, junior officers freely formed an ad hoc branch of the central government that became the Coordinating Committee of the Armed Forces, Police and Territorial Army.

With the Emperor's tacit approval, the Committee, or Derg, investigated the soldiers' grievances. At its inception, therefore, the Derg was neither revolutionary nor populist. The issues that spawned it were specific to the military, and unlikely to be the basis for broad civilian support, but its agenda changed rapidly. Many activists welcomed the Derg, for its capacity to use force with the monarchy in ways that the coalition of activists and labourers could not. Derg leaders welcomed many leftist leaders and intellectuals into its fold. With its leadership and composition heavily in flux throughout the course of the revolution and its aftermath, they adopted much of the left's social and political positions, particularly with regard to the monarch.

The Derg, initially under the leadership of Aman Andom, and then Mengistu Haile Mariam, had, by November 1974, embraced the peasant-centred themes that brought the student movement popular support. It set up a commission to examine the causes of famine in Hararghe and the northern provinces, which announced its findings in a fifteen-page report on 27th August 1974. The commission condemned the entire imperial government for neglecting 'the problem of drought' in the north and accused Prime Minister Habte Wold and his cabinet of suppressing news of the drought. The Derg ordered the Prime Minister and the thirty-four people who served under him to stand trial. By contrast, Derg leaders remained respectful toward the Emperor, while they culled members of his government and family. But as they solidified the Derg's political position, its leaders turned to undermine Haile Selassie's credibility directly. Just as university student activists had done, Derg officials used the existence of pervasive hunger in the north to indict him for wilful neglect. The commission's report quoted an August 1970 memo from Mamo Seyoum, Governor and Special Imperial Envoy in famine-stricken Wello, to Selassie that warned him of the likely effects of prolonged drought in the region. Seyoum explicitly requested that Emperor Selassie take immediate action to 'save the lives of thousands of starving peasants' (Shepherd 1975: ix–x).

On the evening of 11th September 1974, a radio announcer read the names of the sixty-five government officials and members of the royal family who had been executed, and instructed listeners to turn on their televisions and await a special programme to be aired that evening. Derg officials also directed the Emperor to watch the scheduled television programme, British journalist, Jonathan Dimbleby's documentary, *Ethiopia: The Unknown Famine*. He reportedly did so, alone in his palace, except for a single aide (Kapuściński 1978; Shepherd 1985; Tareke 2009).

When Dimbleby arrived in Ethiopia in 1972, he was an admirer of the Emperor and of Ethiopia. Haile Selassie permitted him to travel freely throughout the country. But while Dimbleby travelled through Wello and Tigray, he realised the famine's extent. Dimbleby edited images from the Tigrayan crisis with footage of the Emperor hosting a lavish feast and feeding mounds of food to his caged, pet lions in one of his gardens. When he returned to Britain, Dimbleby reported that Selassie was slow to respond to the emergency in the north and had actively worked to conceal its seriousness from the outside world. *The Unknown Famine* is historic for its place in the dramatic end to Ethiopia's monarchy and the Haile Selassie regime. However, journalist Peter Gill describes the film as unwatchable: 'There is film of the bodies of children who have died overnight which would almost certainly be banned by modern broadcasters on the grounds that it was too upsetting. The twenty-five minutes comprise relentless images of suffering, a sparse script, and a veiled appeal for assistance' (Gill 2010: 29). The morning after the film was shown on Ethiopian television, the Derg forced the Emperor to abdicate. Chief among the indictments that the military officers used to justify seizing power was that Selassie fomented and ignored famine among the peasants. Hunger, therefore, served as the cornerstone of Ethiopia's revolution, waged in the midst of and justified by famine.

In October, the Derg cemented its political hold on the country and hunger, again, was central to this process. Yet the continuously revolving door of leaders and the growing list of condemned political and social elites made it difficult to gauge the direction of the revolution. It took on a vague meaning. At the very moment that the military dethroned Selassie, the Derg issued the more ominous *Ithiopya tikdem* (Ethiopia First) as the new slogan for revolutionary Ethiopia. This was a deliberate move away from the students' populist slogans and a clear nod toward the nationalist approach that the new regime would take toward separatist movements in Eritrea and the large Somali-speaking Ogaden. Still, hunger remained a core political issue for the Derg. In addition to establishing the Commission of Inquiry to investigate the famine, it enacted extensive and dramatic land reforms geared toward empowering the peasantry (Rahmato 1991).

## Conclusion

Ethiopia's relationship with hunger in the mid-1970s was not simply as victim. Hunger was deeply politicised as an issue, as I have argued, and students' responses to it were historic and transformative. It is essential to recognise student engagement with hunger during this period, considering the broader significance of the 1973–1974 famine in international affairs. As historian, Hussein Ahmed, wrote, 'the prevailing economic and social malaise, aggravated by the famine and the global energy crisis, and by the mutinies of army divisions stationed in sensitive regions in the south and in Eritrea in the north combined to provide the complex backdrop to the revolutionary upsurge that finally swept away the monarchy and its institutions' (Ahmed 2006: 298). In distinct and significant ways, chronic hunger and famine were not only the experiences of millions of Ethiopian peasants during the early 1970s. Student activists reshaped them as symbols of political corruption, underdevelopment and, for many, political illegitimacy. For the Derg's leadership as well, effectively responding to chronic hunger legitimised it in the eyes of many activists, and Ethiopians in general, and enabled it to cast its military coup as a populist revolution.

Ethiopian student activists of the 1960s and 1970s have been called 'the grave diggers of the old regime and the generators of the Ethiopian revolution' (Zewde 2001: 220), for precipitating events that ultimately ended the monarchy. It is likely that this revolution would not have happened if they had remained the sole political agitators. Indeed, one former student described the movement as ultimately powerless without the army. 'As radical as we students were voicing the misery of the peasantry,' he recalled, 'we would have been protesting for many more years without any result had the military kept its pledge to protect the throne. It did not, and that made the whole difference'.[1] In response to the crisis of chronic hunger and in stark contrast to the role of the international humanitarian regime in the decades to come, student and leftist activists spearheaded their own, independent, humanitarian relief initiatives among peasants. The 1972–1974 famine, therefore, marks a moment in Ethiopian history in which perceptions of the peasantry among urban elites was transformed along with their conceptions of the government's responsibility to its people. It marks the end of a period, moreover, after which the obligation to respond to hunger in Ethiopia and elsewhere in Africa was embraced by Western humanitarian relief organisations. Their well-funded and well-publicised humanitarian interventions did not exclude local voices and relief initiatives, yet their predominance in famine relief in Africa after 1975, palpably defined during the 1984–1985 famine in northern Ethiopia, politicised hunger in a profoundly new and enduring manner (de Waal 1997; Gill 2010; Polman 2010). As with the junior officers of the Ethiopian military, who in 1974 embraced the rallying cry of hunger relief to accomplish their political goals, hunger during the 1980s and 1990s, as Alex de Waal, among others, has demonstrated, would legitimise international interventions in African affairs elsewhere (de Waal 1997).

## Note

1 Personal correspondence with Professor Teshale Tibebu, 18th December 2012.

## References

Ahmed, H. (2006) Addis Ababa University, Fifty-Three Years on an Insider's View, *Cahier d'Etudes Africaines*, 6(182): 291–312.
Darch, C. (1976) The Ethiopian Student Movement in the Struggle Against Imperialism, 1960–1974. Paper Presented at the Annual Social Science Conference of the East African Universities, Dar es Salaam: 1–15.

de Waal, A. (1997) *Famine Crimes: Politics and the Disaster Relief Industry in Africa*, Indiana University Press, Bloomington, Indiana.

Donham, D. L. (1992) Revolution and modernity in Maale: Ethiopia, 1974 to 1987. *Comparative, Studies in Society and History* 34(1): 28–57.

Ethiopian Student Union of North America (ESUNA) (1973) Report of the 21st Congress of ESUNA, *Combat*, 2(1): 36–40.

Ethiopian Student Union of North America (ESUNA) (1974) The Dilemma of Famine in Ethiopia, *Combat*, 2(2): 1–46.

Gill, P. (2010) *Famine and Foreigners: Ethiopia since Live Aid*, Oxford University Press, Oxford.

Kapuściński, R. (1978) *The Emperor: Downfall of an Autocrat*, Vintage Books, New York.

Molver, R.K. (2008) *Tradition and Change in Ethiopia: Social and Cultural Life as Reflected in Amharic Fictional Literature*, Tsehair, Addis Ababa.

Pankhurst, R. (1985) *The History of Famine and Epidemics in Ethiopia Prior to the Twentieth Century*, Relief and Rehabilitation Commission, Addis Ababa.

Polman, L. (2010) *The Crisis Caravan: What's Wrong with Humanitarian Aid*, Metropolitan, New York.

Rahmato, D. (1991) *Famine and Survival Strategies: A Case Study from Northeast Ethiopia*, Nordiska Afrikainstitute, Uppsala.

Rahmato, D. (2008) *The Peasant and the State: Studies in Agrarian Change in Ethiopia, 1950s–2000s*, Custom Books Publishing, Addis Ababa.

Selassie, K. (1987) The Class Struggle or the Struggle for Positions? A Review of Ethiopian Student Movements between 1900 and 1975. UNESCO Symposium on 'The Role of African Student Movements in the Political and Social Evolution of Africa from 1900 to 1975', Dakar, Senegal, 5–9 April 1988.

Shepherd, J. (1975) *The Politics of Starvation*, The Carnegie Endowment for International Peace, Washington, DC.

Shepherd, J. (1985) Ethiopia: The Use of Food as an Instrument of U.S. Foreign Policy, *Issue: A Journal of Opinion*, 14: 4–9.

Tareke, G. (2009) *The Ethiopian Revolution: War in the Horn of Africa*, Yale University Press, New Haven.

Zewde, B. (2001) *A History of Modern Ethiopia, 1855–1991*, 2nd Edition, Ohio University Press, Athens, Ohio.

Zewde, B. (2010) *Documenting the Ethiopian Student Movement: An Exercise in Oral History*, Forum for Social Studies, Addis Ababa.

# CHAPTER 15
## PROSPECTS FOR CONFLICT TO SPREAD THROUGH BILATERAL LAND ARRANGEMENTS FOR FOOD SECURITY

*Michael J. Strauss*

The growth of international trade and the expansion of global commodity markets in the twentieth century dramatically increased the ability of nations to achieve food security, and consequently to enhance their security more generally. The fact that countries could be viable without necessarily having the territory to be self-sufficient in food alleviated a source of conflict by diminishing the importance of direct control over agricultural land. Today, many nations routinely import food in large quantities, a practice supported by growing populations, urbanisation and farming costs that differ with location.

This reliance on food imports has made foreign agriculture[1] a structural component of the stability and strength of many states, requiring them to adapt to constantly evolving market prices. Many food-importing nations began to question this market dependence in 2007–2008, when global prices of cereals and other food commodities surged higher with a severity and breadth not previously experienced. This prompted them to seek alternative ways to access foreign agriculture that offered greater supply stability with less price risk, and what emerged was a movement to secure long-term rights on farmland abroad (Strauss 2010).

This quickly developed into a large-scale international scramble to buy or lease substantial amounts of foreign land that would be used specifically to satisfy the food requirements of importing countries. The trend has often been derided as a neo-colonial 'land grab', but many host nations where the farmland is located became eager participants as the movement represented a new source of foreign investment and held out the promise of further developing their agricultural sectors (Lampietti *et al.* 2009).

Previously, the food security of a state had three pillars, described by Christopher Stevens as 'its production entitlements, which reflect the food that can be produced domestically; its trade entitlements, which reflect its ability to earn sufficient foreign exchange with exports to purchase imported food; and its transfer entitlements, which cover food that can be obtained either directly through food aid or indirectly by (semi-) commercial imports financed through financial aid' (Stevens 2000: 2–3).[2] The important new network of bilateral food-supply arrangements being locked in by the transactions for foreign farmland has now created a fourth pillar – a nation's foreign land entitlements.

By restoring the importance of direct control over farmland, however, this fourth pillar generates new opportunities for conflict. The difference today is that the new arrangements do not transfer sovereignty over the land, but rather transfer rights on it while leaving sovereignty intact. The experiences of nations that have leased territory in the past suggest that this difference, seemingly just a legal technicality, may heighten the risk that conflict can spread by introducing a new factor: the interests of third countries.

This chapter describes the land transactions involved, and how they can channel conflict toward the country where the land is located. It assesses the political and military threats from abroad that can arise for the host country. It then presents the case of Madagascar, where a government was overthrown after agreeing to set aside much of the country's farmland for the benefit of South Korea; the cancellation of the arrangement was a strategic gain for North Korea – but was it involved? The chapter concludes by discussing how the geopolitical risks created by these farmland transactions might be countered.

## Nature of the Transactions

Today's bilateral farmland transactions now cover substantial amounts of territory in a number of nations. Global data is imprecise because many specific agreements lack transparency, but the known details allow us to realise the magnitude of the phenomenon and to identify its main characteristics.

By 2009, the UN special rapporteur on the right to food, Olivier de Schutter, estimated that more than thirty million hectares had become subject to such agreements (Rice-Oxley 2009), mostly in developing countries and particularly in Africa (de Schutter 2009). Researchers at the World Bank subsequently reported that foreign demand for African land alone, which had grown by an average of 1.8 million hectares annually between 1961 and 2007, increased by a remarkable 39.7 million hectares in 2009, an amount 'greater than the total agriculturally cultivated area of Belgium, Denmark, France, Germany, the Netherlands and Switzerland combined' (Arezki *et al.* 2011: 9–10). Many individual transactions involve more than 100,000 hectares and some exceed one million hectares; one report citing 177 arrangements in 27 African nations showed an average size of more than 290,000 hectares (Friis and Reenberg 2010). In one very large case, China obtained agricultural rights on 2.8 million hectares in the Democratic Republic of Congo – more than one percent of the country's sovereign territory (*Economist* 2009).

The land subject to these arrangements is typically purchased or leased in accordance with the laws of the host nation, and when leases are involved they are generally for extended periods such as 30, 50 or 99 years (Cotula *et al.* 2009). Despite the potential of the transactions to broadly impact the host state – they can affect local farmers' livelihoods, land use patterns, water demand and even the food security of the host nation itself – many of the agreements are brief in form, indicating that only limited attention is given to addressing problems that might arise; de Schutter notes that some accords are only three or four pages long (quoted in Laishley 2009).

In seeking long-term access to foreign agriculture, the governments of food-importing nations have become major drivers of these bilateral trans-actions, but agribusiness companies and financial investors are also among the actors (Deininger and Byerlee 2011). The governments of some import-ing nations have encouraged private-sector entities to invest on their behalf through financial and other incentives (Laishley 2009; *Oryza Rice News* 2009). Likewise, governments in the countries where the farmland is located are also heavily involved. 'In many host countries, land is legally claimed, owned, or otherwise controlled by the state', according to experts at the Food and Agriculture Organization (FAO) (2011: 17). Thus, a transaction may be done between two governments, between the government of one of the states and a private-sector entity in the other, or between private-sector entities in both states. It may involve partnerships of two or more entities on one or both sides, or entities that are not based in either state but that act on behalf of one or both of them (Strauss 2011).

## How Conflicts May Spread

Regardless of the parties involved 'on paper', these arrangements have the effect of redistributing territorial rights among nations without formal ces-sions or changes in national boundaries. They erode a traditional function of borders by permitting a state that benefits from farming rights abroad to rein-force its sovereign situation on its own territory through activities it performs outside of that territory. The circumstances thus created essentially parallel those generated by traditional bilateral leases of state territory by treaty, and consequently the lessons from treaty-based leases are relevant.

One lesson is that a leased area may be perceived as a *de facto* territorial extension of the nation that has rights there, rather than as part of the nation where it is physically located; the Canal Zone, for example, was leased by the United States from Panama from 1903 to 2000 and 'was popularly perceived as

American territory' (Smith 2005: 142). This can affect other states' behaviour toward the countries involved. A century ago, the international law scholar George Grafton Wilson remarked that nations making lease agreements for military bases do so with a view 'specifically to a condition of war' (U.S. Naval War College 1912: 97). In other words, the host country accepts the risk that the zone on its territory where the foreign base is located becomes vulnerable to attack by a third country – an enemy of the nation that operates the base.

A transaction for foreign agricultural land can generate the same risk for a host nation. When a country at war derives some of its strength and national security from its farming rights abroad, its adversary may act to neutralise the advantage, and the state where the land is located may find itself in a conflict in which it had no prior involvement or interest.

In fact, a country that allows another state to use its agricultural land may actually face greater risks than if it had allowed the other nation to have a military base on its soil. There are several reasons for this. First, a military base normally occupies a very limited portion of the host state's territory, but a farmland agreement must entail a large enough area to justify another country's interest in using it for food security. Second, a military base normally has armed forces and military equipment stationed on-site and is prepared to deter or counter attack. This is not the case with farmland used by foreign states. In view of the amount of land they cover, agricultural arrangements can expose far greater areas, and much larger proportions of a host state's total territory, to actions by an adversary of the state with farming rights there. Third, an attack on a military base is an obvious event, but an attack against agriculture may be far less obvious because of the ways it can be carried out (Strauss 2011).

In addition, a host nation may be drawn into a conflict involving the state with farming rights by becoming dependent on the bilateral arrangement and wanting to protect it. War scholars recognise the potential for conflict to spread through economic ties that generate shared interests between states (Vasquez 2009).

The drive by food-importing countries to use agricultural land abroad has created a new web of bilateral relationships through which armed conflict can expand geographically. Unlike classic paths that involve proximity to the initial belligerents or political alliances (Midlarsky 1993), these routes follow no spatial or political logic other than the pairing of countries that want more farmland with those that make it available, and the viability of transporting crops between the two. Such routes can be erratic, allowing conflicts to leap across the earth's surface in the same way that a theatre of war may be enlarged when the belligerents have far-flung military bases (Vasquez 2009).

Meanwhile, the long durations of the bilateral land deals entail their own conflict risks. Relations between any two countries can vary considerably over time, even dramatically in some cases, making it reasonable to assume that some nations with long-term rights on farmland abroad may become engaged in armed conflicts that could expose the host country to risks at some point while the arrangements are in effect.

## Risks for the Host State

When a food-importing country is at war, its enemy can be expected to try to neutralise any advantage the importer gains from physical assets, including foreign agricultural land. There are numerous ways it can do this on the host country's territory in addition to actions it takes on the food importer's own sovereign territory. The enemy can attempt to bring about the termination of the importer's farming rights through political or economic pressure on the host country's government; this can be done directly, but it may also involve indirect means such as providing financial or material aid to local groups that are disadvantaged by the farming arrangement or oppose it for other reasons. The food importer's adversary can also take more extreme measures, including open or covert efforts aimed at ousting a host-country government that does not cooperate with it. The US invasion of Iraq in 2003 illustrated that intervening militarily to overthrow another nation's leadership in order to achieve a policy change cannot be dismissed as unrealistic when the issue involved is sufficiently important to an affected nation.

The enemy of a food importing state may also seek to prevent the farmland in the host nation from providing the desired benefits. Besides attacking the host country's export infrastructure to disrupt shipments, this can involve attacks against the farmland itself. Throughout history, the destruction of crops has been a frequent tactic to weaken an enemy in wartime. It can result in famine, disrupting the population's survival and eroding its will to fight, and it can eliminate the agricultural trade that contributes to financing the conflict (Wise 1975). In the past, crop destruction was routinely achieved by burning crops, but today a nation with adequate resources has many other choices – notably chemical, biological and radioactive weapons that can affect crops over much greater expanses of land.

Chemical weapons can destroy agricultural output in several ways: herbicides kill or injure plants, defoliants cause leaves to fall off prematurely and desiccants cause plants to dry out. All of these can eliminate existing crops, while other chemical weapons known as soil sterilisers can contaminate the land and make it unsuitable for crops over periods that may span multiple crop seasons.

Biological weapons have been developed from naturally occurring plant diseases such as fungi (the most common), bacteria and viruses. They absorb or disrupt the flow of nutrients, disturb the plants' metabolism or consume their cells. Fungi in particular can affect vast areas of cereals and are responsible for common crop diseases such as rusts, blasts and smuts (Whitby 2002).

In the years since the Second World War, 'a number of nations have devoted considerable resources to the development of (biological weapons) in order to bring about the destruction, for hostile purposes, of the plant resources of an adversary', according to Whitby (2006: 223). The potential for this to occur is actually heightened by current farming practices: 'Modern agricultural methods dictate that large areas be planted with genetically identical crops. This genetic homogeneity leaves entire regions susceptible to attack with an antiplant agent to which the crop is not resistant' (Caudle 1997: 460).

Nuclear technology, too, may be used against crops. Plants can be killed or rendered poisonous by accumulating radioactive particles from contaminated soil, a fact that US nuclear scientists have recognised as being able 'to impair if not destroy the use of agricultural areas for the purpose of producing food crops' (Hamilton 1946: 1).

Today's anti-crop weapons can be dispersed from aircraft, balloons, missiles or land vehicles, or with bombs. Biological weapons may be the most difficult to guard against, as they can be spread by wind, water, insects or human or animal contact. Moreover, these weapons may be difficult to recognise or trace, according to Pearson (1998: 22), who notes that 'a biological agent can be disseminated without immediate and obvious signs that an attack is underway'.

This can create particular problems for a host nation. If the enemy of a country that uses its farmland has no quarrel with the host state itself, it can attack the farmland without necessarily being detected, to avoid reprisal or a deterioration in what might otherwise be positive relations with the host nation. In addition, biological weapons are self-propagating and the diseases they cause can easily spread to crops outside the area where the food-importing state has farming rights, even if the crops in that zone are the only intended target. Diseases associated with such an attack can also spread to crops in other states if the land that is targeted or otherwise affected is near a national boundary, creating further possibilities for the conflict to spread.

## Limits of International Law

Various international conventions and treaties exist to prohibit the production and use of the weapons noted above and to ensure that civilian populations are protected from the actions of an adversary. The Hague Regulations of 1899 and 1907 outlawed poison weapons, and the more expansive Geneva Protocol of 1925 prohibited the use of poisonous gases as well as weapons comprised of bacteria. Yet while these agreements ban such weapons from being used against human beings, governments have never resolved a critical issue: whether they apply equally to anti-plant agents.

The use of anti-crop weapons by the United States during the Vietnam War helped to spur a clearer ban on destroying crops intended for civilian populations, elaborated in 1977 in the Additional Protocol I to the Geneva Conventions of 1949. This protocol made it illegal during an armed conflict to starve civilians as a method of warfare, or to 'attack, destroy, remove, or render useless objects indispensable to the survival of the civilian population, such as foodstuffs, agricultural areas for the production of foodstuffs, crops, livestock, drinking water installations and supplies and irrigation works, for the specific purpose of denying them for their sustenance value to the civilian population or to the adverse Party, whatever the motive, whether in order to starve out civilians, to cause them to move away, or for any other motive' (Protocol Additional to the Geneva Conventions of 12 August 1949 1977, art. 54, para. 1–2).

Newer international treaties against the use of specific weapons have also appeared, such as the Biological and Toxin Weapons Convention of 1972 and the Chemical Weapons Convention of 1992. Like the earlier ones, these have been subject to inconsistent interpretations, and nations have sometimes defined chemical weapons in a way that excludes chemicals used for destroying crops (Verwey 1977).

Despite these potential safeguards for agricultural areas in times of war, research by the FAO shows that 'the use of hunger as a weapon is widespread in present-day conflicts' and that crop destruction is one of various means still used to achieve this (Teodosijević 2003: 17–18).

## Coup in Madagascar

It is too early for the rush of bilateral land transactions for food security to produce any history of interference in host countries by outside states whose interests are threatened by the arrangements, but the potential for this can be illustrated by one case in which there was reason for this to occur – and where it could have happened.

A 2008 agreement between a South Korean enterprise, Daewoo Logistics Corp., and the government of Madagascar gave Daewoo the right to lease 1.3 million hectares of agricultural land in Madagascar for 99 years, where it would cultivate food crops to export back to South Korea. In exchange, Daewoo would provide Madagascar with up to US$6 billion in payments and infrastructure investments (Park 2008).

The agreement occurred as the South Korean government was encouraging its companies to enhance the nation's food security by offering them loans and technology to develop farming projects abroad (*Oryza Rice News* 2009). As a mountainous country with a large population, South Korea has little arable land and was dependent on world markets for most of its food. The Madagascar arrangement was to alleviate its market dependence by increasing the amount of farmland available to South Korea by more than fifty percent (Strauss 2011).

The agreement, still in preliminary form, aroused substantial public opposition in Madagascar, as it would have involved roughly half of the nation's potential agricultural area and caused some disruptions for local communities. Before a final agreement was reached, a coup d'état occurred, and Madagascar's new president, Andry Rajoelina, immediately aborted the transaction (Lough 2009).

Its cancellation was advantageous to the military interests of North Korea, which has been at war with its southern neighbour for decades. Familiar with chronic food shortages, North Korean officials would have had a profound appreciation of the role that food security plays as a factor in the strength of a state.

Whether North Korea had any direct or indirect involvement in the coup in Madagascar is impossible to determine in the absence of available information that can allow the question to be explored. There are no known reports of a North Korean role, although it would have been logical for the country's strategists to view Madagascar's farmland as a source of material support for its enemy, as if it were South Korea's own territory. Regardless of whether any intervention actually occurred, North Korea benefited from the coup's outcome, which could induce it to proactively oppose other arrangements that South Korea makes for farmland abroad.

## Risks of Bilateral Conflict

At the time an agreement for farmland rights is concluded between a food importing country and a host nation, it holds the promise for enhanced bilateral relations. Each state helps the other achieve an objective – food security against investment – and the arrangement launches a stable, long-term bilateral trade relationship. But issues arising from the land arrangement may become sources of conflict within the countries involved, and also between them.

The agreement between Daewoo and Madagascar was far from the only one to generate substantial public opposition; such accords can provoke unrest by destabilizing local inhabitants' lives, and the threat of this was certainly a factor in Madagascar's coup.

As for bilateral tensions, a land agreement cannot take into account, much less foresee, all of the potential circumstances that can arise in the context of the political, economic and social changes that occur in either or both countries during its long duration. Contentious situations can develop from events, such as pollution or other factors in the host country that damage the importing nation's crop, or vice versa; competition between the two states for limited resources, such as water during a drought; or a disruption in port activity that can prevent the crop grown by the food-importing nation from leaving the host state.

Tensions can also develop if a nation that obtains farming rights abroad begins to use the land in the host state for purposes not covered in the agreement, with or without the knowledge of the host state; certain uses, such as the gathering of military intelligence, may even be prejudicial to the host state or its relations with other nations (Strauss 2010). Cases of unauthorised use of territories leased by treaty are not unknown; for example, the activities of the United States at Guantanamo Bay, a zone leased from Cuba, went far beyond the restricted set of uses that the lease stipulated for the territory (Strauss 2009).

A bilateral farmland arrangement also has the potential to erode the host country's own food security as circumstances change over time, because it blocks part of its land from being used for the benefit of its inhabitants. Among factors that can give rise to this scenario are demographic and climate changes; a period of rapid population growth in the host country, for example, would boost its internal demand for food. Meanwhile, the food security of the nation using the land cannot be assured either, according to the World Bank, which notes that 'capital locked up in land purchases and long-term leases cannot easily be freed up to buy food from other suppliers when there is bad weather or political disruptions in the host country' (Lampietti *et al.* 2009: 49).

It is relevant to ask if a food-importing nation would be willing to abandon an arrangement that satisfies its food-security needs if the host country no longer desires its presence on the land. The history of treaty-based territorial leases suggests that in some cases the answer would be no – and this is another potential trigger of conflict. If the country with rights on the farmland is stronger than the host state, it may refuse to leave, and the host country may consider this tantamount to an occupation of its land. Cuba's inability to evict the United States from Guantanamo Bay since the 1959 Cuban revolution is one such case. Another was temporarily averted in Ukraine when a new government took office in 2010 and renewed Russia's lease of a naval port at Sevastopol that the previous Ukrainian government wanted to end (Levy 2010), but Russia's continued military presence through the lease played a critical role when it won control of Crimea in 2014.

## Addressing the Risks

The likelihood that a specific bilateral farmland arrangement will cause a conflict or become a factor in one is probably quite small, but with hundreds of such arrangements being established for periods of many decades it is equally probable that at least some will be at the heart of conflicts during their duration.

Because of the abstract nature of the risks, which include the fact that an attack on agricultural land may not be obvious, it can be difficult to justify the costs and efforts necessary to prepare militarily to defend large expanses of farmland prior to the emergence of situations that introduce a more concrete potential for conflict. Countering the risks may therefore favour preventive measures such as negotiating clauses in the agreements that create frameworks for handling contingencies, systematic monitoring by each party of the other's evolving geopolitical circumstances, so that potential problems can be detected early, as well as greater transparency in the arrangements – including the identification of all direct and indirect actors and locations of the farmland – so that the conflict risks can be more comprehensively assessed.

## Notes

1  Farming done outside a nation's territory that serves its interests, e.g., food security or commercial activity.
2  These refer to ensuring sufficient food for a state's population. Viewing food security more conceptually, the Food and Agriculture Organization considers its three pillars to be availability, access and use.

## References

Arezki, R., Deininger, K. and Selod, H. (2011) *What Drives the Global "Land Rush"?*, Policy Research Working Paper 5864, World Bank, Washington.

Caudle, L.C. III (1997) The Biological Warfare Threat. In Sidell, F.R., Takafuji, E.T. and Franz, D.R. (eds) *Medical Aspects of Chemical and Biological Warfare*, Office of the Surgeon General, Washington: 451–466.

Cotula, L., Vermeulen, S., Leonard, R. and Keeley, J. (2009) *Land Grab or Development Opportunity? Agricultural Investment and International Land Deals in Africa*, International Institute for Environment and Development, Food and Agriculture Organization and International Fund for Agricultural Development, IIED/FAO/IFAD, London/Rome.

Deininger, K. and Byerlee, D. (2011) *Rising Global Interest in Farmland: Can it Yield Sustainable and Equitable Benefits?*, World Bank, Washington.

de Schutter, O. (2009) *Large-scale land acquisitions and leases: A set of core principles and measures to address the human rights challenge*, Briefing Note, UN Office of the High Commissioner for Human Rights.

*Economist* (2009) Buying farmland abroad: Outsourcing's Third Wave. 21 May.

Food and Agriculture Organization (2011) *Land tenure and international investments in agriculture*, Food and Agriculture Organization High Level Panel of Experts on Food Security and Nutrition of the Committee on World Food Security, Food and Agriculture Organization, Rome.

Friis, C. and Reenberg, A. (2010) *Land Grab in Africa: Emerging land system drivers in a teleconnected world*, Global Land Project, Copenhagen.

Hamilton, J.G. (1946) *Radioactive Warfare*, Memorandum to Col. K.D. Nichols, Radiation Laboratory, University of California, Berkeley.

Laishley, R. (2009) Is Africa's land up for grabs? Foreign acquisitions: some opportunities, but many see threats, *Africa Renewal*, 23(3): 4–5, 22.

Lampietti, J., Mangan, N., Michaels, S., McCalla, A., Saade, M. and Khouri, N. (2009) *Improving Food Security in Arab Countries*, World Bank/Food and Agriculture Organization/International Fund for Agricultural Development, Washington.

Levy, C.J. (2010) Ukraine Woos Russia With Lease Deal, *New York Times*, 21 April.

Lough, R. (2009) Madagascar's new leader says Daewoo land deal off, *Reuters*, 18 March.

Midlarsky, M.I. (1993) *Handbook of War Studies*, University of Michigan Press, Ann Arbor.

*Oryza Rice News* (2009) South Korea to Encourage Farming Abroad, 8 April.

Park, S. (2008), Daewoo Logistics Says Farm Deal May Cost $6 Billion, *Bloomberg*, 20 November.

Pearson, G.S. (1998) The Threat of Deliberate Disease in the 21st Century. In Smithson, A.E. (ed.) *Biological Weapons Proliferation: Reasons for Concern, Courses of Action*, Henry L. Stimson Center, Washington: 10–36.

Protocol Additional to the Geneva Conventions of 12 August 1949, and relating to the Protection of Victims of International Armed Conflicts (1977), Article 54, Paragraphs 1–2.

Rice-Oxley, M. (2009) G8: Does world need new rules on food security? *Christian Science Monitor*, 8 July.

Smith, J. (2005) *The United States and Latin America: A history of American diplomacy, 1776–2000*, Routledge, Abingdon.

Stevens, C. (2000) The International Dimensions of Food Security. Paper presented at the Conference on Global and Local Dimensions of Food Security: Threats, Challenges and Responses, University College Cork.

Strauss, M.J. (2009) *The Leasing of Guantanamo Bay*, Praeger, Westport, Connecticut.

Strauss, M.J. (2010) Redistribuer le territoire des Etats pour éviter les penuries alimentaires. In Chaigneau, P. (ed.) *Enjeux diplomatiques et stratégiques 2010*, Economica, Paris: 159–166.

Strauss, M.J. (2011) Land Leasing in Africa: The Geopolitical Risks, *African Geopolitics*, 40: 189–200.

Teodosijević, S.B. (2003) *Armed Conflicts and Food Security*, ESA Working Paper 03–11, Food and Agriculture Organization, Rome.

U.S. Naval War College (1912) *International Law Situations with Solutions and Notes – 1912*, Government Printing Office, Washington.

Vasquez, J.A. (2009) *The War Puzzle Revisited*, Cambridge University Press, Cambridge.

Verwey, W.D. (1977) *Riot Control Agents and Herbicides in War: Their humanitarian, toxicological, ecological, military, polemological, and legal aspects*, A.J. Sijthoff, Leiden.

Whitby, S.B. (2002) *Biological Warfare against Crops*, Palgrave, Basingstoke.

Whitby, S.B. (2006) Anticrop Biological Weapons Programs. In Wheelis, M., Rozsa, L. and Dando, M. (eds) *Deadly Cultures: Biological Weapons since 1945*, Harvard University Press, Boston: 213–223.

Wise, T. (1975) *Medieval European Armies*, Osprey, Oxford.

# CHAPTER 16
## FOOD, CONFLICT AND HUMAN RIGHTS: ACCOUNTING FOR STRUCTURAL VIOLENCE

*Ellen Messer*

## Introduction

In 2010 the Food and Agriculture Organization (FAO) of the United Nations, in its annual *State of Food Insecurity (SOFI)* report made 'food security in countries in protracted crisis' its major theme (Food and Agriculture Organization 2010). This effort followed 2007–2008 public demonstrations, some of which turned violent, in dozens of countries, where protestors demanded government accountability for spiking food and fuel prices (Messer 2009). These situations prompted the United Nations (UN) Secretary General to convene their High Level Task Force (UNHLTF) to address immediate and longer term food problems (United Nations High Level Task Force 2008), and World Bank leaders to make 'Conflict, Security and Development' the theme of their 2011 World Development Report (World Bank 2011). But such responses did not necessarily translate into more conflict-sensitive food-policy actions or outlooks. On the contrary, two long-term agricultural assessments and 'future of food' exercises, the International Assessment of Agricultural Knowledge, Science and Technology for Development (IAASTD) (2008) and the UK Foresight Project on the Future of Food and Farming (Foresight 2011), addressed mainly the technical issues that agricultural, food and nutrition scientists or economists could solve, leaving social and political conflict issues to diplomats, other political actors or for a later stage of research and policy discussions (Albrecht *et al.* 2013; but see also United Nations High Level Task Force on World Food Security Crisis 2008; Allouche 2011; Grebmer *et al.* 2011; World Bank 2011). Most food-security planning still does not sufficiently consider the legacy of conflict, either when considering how to deliver humanitarian or development rations, or when considering how agriculture might be used to build livelihoods in areas that are conflict-prone. What anthropologists can add to these efforts are project and literature reviews, which elaborate connections between food and conflict, as well as political-geographic-ethnic-religious (PGER) and human rights analysis, which can situate projects and programmes in the more holistic context of historical structural violence. This chapter argues for greater attention to 'food wars' (FW), defined as situations of organised armed political violence, where combatants on one or both sides use hunger as a weapon, and where destruction of farming populations, infrastructure, waterworks and markets result in disruptions to agricultural production, food markets, health services and human nutrition long after formal fighting had ceased. In many of these FW places, persistent food and livelihood insecurity raises risks of renewed conflict, as witnessed in Food and Agriculture Organization (2010) case studies. These causal, often cyclic, linkages connecting conflict and hunger in both directions, are rooted, historically, in underlying socioeconomic inequalities, political exclusions and human rights violations that render populations ripe for conflict. These PGER conditions, which, in relation to conflict, anthropologists and others label 'structural violence', are an important part of the context, influencing who has preferred access to or is excluded from land, seed, water, humanitarian relief and economic development assets. For those designing assistance programmes for agriculture, food and nutrition, conflict history matters and PGER matters. There are conflict-sensitive methods that can help break pernicious cycles of conflict and hunger. The sections below briefly describe the development of this FW concept, conflict-sensitivity methods and food-security programmes in conflict contexts, and then how PGER and rights-based approaches to development can assist such efforts.

## Food Wars (FW): Evolution of the Concept

FW, as a construct, was developed by Brown University World Hunger Program (WHP) researchers studying the causes and consequences of *Hunger in History* (Newman *et al.* 1990), and mapping the overlap of famine and conflict countries in *Hunger Reports* (Messer 1990, 1994, 1996a). Later FW reports included critical commentaries summarising advances in the principles and practice of humanitarian assistance and the significance of food security in human rights and development indicators. They also created brief PGER histories in FW countries, including who fought whom and why and with what food-insecurity outcomes, constructed from ethnographic, historical and food-agency reports and media sources (Messer 1990, 1994, 1996a).

Bringing this FW concept and analysis into the mainstream, the International Food Policy Research Institute (IFPRI) participated in and published WHP's mid-1990s report, *Food From Peace: Breaking the Links Between Conflict and Hunger* (Messer *et al.* 1998). This FW synthesis, drawing on anthropological among other literatures, summarised the theoretical and historical dynamics through which conflict causes hunger, food insecurity and a popular sense of unfair agricultural appropriations. All these pose risk factors for rebellion (e.g., Wolf 1969), or exacerbate conflict, where human rights violations and structural violence underlie both hunger and conflict. It also presented a model quantifying the losses to food production and to rate of increase in food production in Sub-Saharan African (SSA) war-torn countries.

Thereafter IFPRI encouraged additional FW studies that would address the influences of globalisation on FW, which FW research suggested were mixed. On the negative side, evidence could be marshalled to demonstrate that agricultural export commodities, such as sugar cane, coffee, cotton and cocoa, served as 'war commodities' in places such as Colombia, Chad and Côte D'Ivoire. Especially in SSA, contending parties fought to control land, crops and revenues, which they used to fund armies and arms. But it was also possible to show that global norms and social movements, including fair trade, human rights and environmental sustainability, could have positive impacts on the lives and livelihoods of small farmers and others. These views (Messer and Cohen 2007, 2008) formed part of IFPRI's millennium research into agriculture, food policy and poverty (alleviation), and also responded to a separate stream of 'causes and correlates of conflict' research, which debated whether the causes of war were principally resource scarcities: 'need' (Homer-Dixon 1999); identity politics: 'creed'; or desire to exert control over precious resources: 'greed' (de Soysa 2002; Collier 2003). FW analyses showed that all three were implicated in aetiologies of war-related hunger (Messer et al. 2001). Later research added a 'climate change' dimension (Messer 2010), indicating where food insecurity figured in the assertion, 'climate change causes conflict' and in the wake of the 2007–2008 world food price crisis, added PGER and human rights analyses (Messer 2009). Marchione and Messer (2010), calling for a human rights basis for US food-aid policy, drew additional attention to underlying human rights violations that could contribute to subsequent rounds of violence, particularly in post-conflict countries, such as Ethiopia and Zimbabwe. As anthropologists, they hypothesised that PGER preferences versus exclusions would unfairly distort access to development assistance and fan tensions, and suggested that aid programmes should always consider such factors in their design, implementation and monitoring. They also drew connections between food-price spike riots and the wider structural violence of PGER-based exclusions and human rights violations in FW situations (Messer 2009), where food-related entitlement scarcities could present both a trigger and a root cause of conflict. Drawing on almost two decades of FW research, they recommended more PGER and conflict sensitive food policy.

## Conflict Sensitivity

Most food-security agencies working in war or post-conflict situations pay some attention to conflict background, because local conditions affect the safety and operations of their personnel. Conflict acknowledgment, however, does not mean that agencies invest many additional resources to identifying the forces that connect or divide communities where projects operate; nor do they consistently employ conflict-transformation methods or professionals in their field operations, beyond some initial field trainings.

In the case of the Rwandan genocide, Uvin (1998) even calls for development workers to stop 'aiding violence'. He points out the many ways in which agricultural development programmes, through insensitive property appropriations and skewed benefit distributions, exacerbated PGER tensions, which in Rwanda led to genocide, and he demanded that future projects always begin by asking:

- Who controls the land, water and building resources where the project will operate?
- Who will staff the project, at what salary?
- How might the identities of project staffers stoke PGER tensions and affect project outcomes and inter- or intra-community tensions and social relations?

Lange (2004), contributing to the comprehensive set of peace-building trainings for International Alert, a London-based, peace-building non-governmental organisation (NGO) that works with affected populations, policy makers and practitioners, elaborates additional directives that can help organisations make the transition to conflict sensitivity:

- Be aware of the conflict context
- Do no harm
- Do some good
- Understand why wars were fought in particular places at particular times and the tensions that remain
- Identify the key contenders (e.g., military and civilian political parties, gangs and suppliers of arms and food) and focus on where contending parties may find it productive to work side by side
- In food or other economic interventions, don't circumvent constraints, but try to improve the situation and to avoid causes of division such as treating parties unequally.

In operational terms, these mean: analyse the background to conflict conditions, assess how programme components will affect the conflict context and how that context might constrain programme operations, and apply these findings so that projects should moderate rather than aggravate tensions among target beneficiaries. Acknowledge grievances and tensions, then find ways to work with and around them to build trust and peaceful outcomes.

Anderson (1999) offers additional 'do no harm' guidance on what kinds of cultural behaviours might be necessary, and recommends respectful participation in customary local rites of hospitality, including aid-workers bringing gifts of food and drinking endless cups of tea with local authorities to build the respect and trust that allow projects to go forward. Such food-exchange or hospitality rituals, other than state dinners, however, are rarely reported.

Lange (2004) notes that an increasing number of inter-governmental and non-governmental aid agencies have adopted conflict-sensitive strategies for planning fieldwork, but do not necessarily apply them in practice. Conflict sensitivity at the World Bank is a case in point. The past President, Zoellick, passionately endorsed special World Bank programmes for working in 'fragile states' and reorganised its bureaucracy to incorporate conflict-sensitivity lines. Assessing procedures and processes, Bell (2008), however, found few connections tying the Bank's business-as-usual lending programmes and assessments to its conflict-sensitive research, infrastructural changes and indicators in conflict-affected countries. One example of this is in Burundi, where the Bank experts recommended reform of the coffee sector. While technically not wrong, such (mis)guidance considered only the formal dimensions of managing coffee production and trade in a more transparent and equitable way. It did not consider the politics that would make their plan (un)acceptable both to government officials, who depend on coffee for revenues, and to all levels of producers and traders, whose lives would be disrupted by such major transformations (Bell 2008).

This raises the question: are there case studies demonstrating the value added of conflict sensitivity in food or agricultural projects, either better food security or more peaceful outcomes or cases where food-focused projects function as conflict-transformation tools for peace? What is the evidence, or what evidence might be required?

## Food in Conflict Situations

In war situations, food is a fungible, lootable commodity. Regarding the Somalia crisis of 1990–1991, de Waal berated the international humanitarian aid community for introducing lootable dry rations, whereas wet food rations were more likely to reach starving civilians (de Waal 1997). This wet versus dry distinction contrasts with the focused, technical nutritional targeting, which asserts that certain nutritional mixes are most appropriate for particular vulnerable groups, wherever located. For instance, lipid-based pastes should feed severely malnourished children in all disaster situations and fortified foods should be targeted toward malnourished populations whether in peace or war (Webb *et al.* 2011).

Emergency food sourcing sometimes changes food habits (see also Shepler this volume). In the protracted crisis in Darfur, Sudan, for example, food habits have shifted from millet to sorghum, as food-aid sorghum has been feeding conflict-affected people directly or through market mechanisms, whereas the production and marketing of local millet were disrupted by violence (Young *et al.* 2009). Farmers also adjusted cropping and food-storage patterns to grow quicker-maturing grain varieties and to sell crops immediately, in order to avoid losses due to looting (Young *et al.* 2009; Feinstein International Center 2011 to 2013). Projects for the security of food and livelihood here are grounded in human rights approaches and historical and ethnographic analysis of PGER dynamics.

## Agriculture and Food-Security Programming in Countries in Conflict

Food-security targets and indicators were incorporated into the goals of the World Food Summit (1996) and into the Millennium Development Goals (MDGs) (United Nations Millennium Development Project 2005), both of which aimed to reduce hunger by half. MDGs, at a global level, do not incorporate explicit 'peace' goals or conflict resolution targets. However, at the national level, some leaders do insert such goals into their poverty-reduction strategy plans. Cambodia and Angola, for instance, include landmines as a major agricultural constraint and foster their removal in their MDG poverty-reduction and food-security plans.

Meeting immediate nutritional needs and building future food-system capacities in places ripe for conflict are also a principal theme of the United Nations High Level Task Force on the Global Food Security Crisis (UNHLTF) (2008). Some food-security and other 'basic needs' documents emphasise that a major constraint to meeting MDGs is violent conflict (e.g., UNICEF 2009; Food and Agriculture Organization 2010; Millennium Development Goals Report 2011); these writings, along with all the responses to the food price crisis riots in 2007–2008, emphasise that lack of food security undermines human security and potentiates conflict (e.g., United Nations High Level Task Force 2008).

In conflict zones, UNICEF, FAO, the World Food Programme (WFP) and their multiple partners have been trying to develop conflict-sensitive food security programmes since the late 1980s. To date, there is one outstanding success story, which is the 1990s–2000s eradication of rinderpest in southern Sudan through the Operation Lifeline Sudan livestock livelihood programme (Catley *et al.* 2008). This operation, which involved universities and UN agencies (UNICEF, then FAO), plus local pastoralists as the main facilitators, demonstrated the wisdom of understanding the full context, using local connections, connectors and accountability to reach everyone with the necessary livestock pharmaceuticals to achieve disease eradication. The programme, which involved multiple ethnic groups during planning, implementation, mid-course correction and monitoring, was able to operate on the basis of building awareness and technical capacities among regional networks of local agents and avoid destructive politics.

In multiple places, but at a smaller scale, NGOs, such as Mercy Corps (www.mercycorps.org), intentionally work mainly in conflict or post-conflict places, building capacities for conflict transformation as well as infrastructure, livelihoods and food security. NGO projects which are conflict sensitive help war-affected populations develop agricultural cooperative structures and infrastructure and negotiate with government and international market stakeholders. They also help integrate human rights and PGER concerns into food-value chains that can promote political and economic stability and peace (see Messer and Cohen 2007, 2008). Yet, many examples of conflict-sensitive food-security programming, however well conceived and successful on a local scale, have been overwhelmed by large-scale political violence. The Nuba Mountains Community Empowerment Project (NMPACT) showed conflict sensitivity in all its stages (planning, implementation, monitoring and mid-course corrections to include community-based interventions), leading to increased food production and marketing and reduced tensions (Pantuliano 2008). This outcome is sustainable only so long as other external violence does not erupt (see Bennett *et al.* 2010).

Additional projects that anticipate or claim food and livelihood security outcomes from conflict-sensitive approaches include coffee cooperatives in Uganda and Rwanda, grain and potato producer associations in Rwanda and the Progressive Safety Net Programmes in Ethiopia. Nevertheless, in this last case, evaluations report food continues to be manipulated as a political tool (Sharp *et al.* 2006). The Ethiopian government's forced resettlement of food-insecure populations, whose political allegiance lies with the opposition, raise again, as in 1974 and 1984, questions about Ethiopia's leaders' use of humanitarian food aid as a weapon (see also Talton, this volume).

## A Humanitarian or Development Context Makes a Difference

The humanitarian versus development context influences whether particular intervention agencies find it appropriate and within their mission to address conflict situations. UN international interventions are constrained by an institutional division of labour that directs development agencies, such as the United Nations Development Programme (2009) to work for conflict prevention or post-conflict reconstruction, but not in conflict zones, which are the mandate of WFP, as it is responsible for humanitarian food aid. Currently, FAO and WFP are trying to bridge this divide which separates relief from development, and to rethink ways of delivering food and development aid more effectively, especially in protracted crisis countries. WFP, through its Purchase for Progress (P4P 2011) initiative, situated especially in post-conflict countries, is active, from delivering emergency food aid to incentivising and integrating local food producers, processors and markets to supply nutritionally enhanced food as food aid, in order to build capacities for commercial market production. Humanitarian NGOs, such as Oxfam, are also at the fore-front, deploring the political uses of food and aid in war and natural disaster situations, asserting a right to feed, assist and protect as part of their mission. They are also very active on the development front, negotiating agreements between local agencies, government and private-sector partners, as they seek to advance peaceful development through fair trade, no-slave labour, agricultural production and marketing agreements, and help local communities negotiate more environmentally just deals with mining companies. They pay attention to who owns the land, water and resources to be mobilised in agricultural development projects. Their human rights, food and livelihood security actions emphasise social justice and conflict-prevention (see www.oxfam.org). Other mainstream agricultural development programmes, by contrast, simply avoid places of conflict, as they partner with governments and their national agricultural agencies. The Bill and Melinda Gates Foundation, for example, works to build national agricultural infrastructure in post-conflict Ethiopia, but not in active-conflict places in the Democratic Republic of Congo.

Official US defence agencies and contractors that actively engage conflict in either humanitarian or development situations frame their missions as security, rather than conflict prevention. Such security-framed efforts involve military and related strategic thinking (e.g., Perry and Borchard 2010; see also the non-combat humanitarian and development agenda of US Africa Command (AFRICOM) at www.africom.mil). These security strategists ostensibly respond to critiques that humanitarian and development aid tends to ignore politics and operate as if there is or has been no war going on (e.g., Duffield 2001), as do recent UNHLTF (2008, updated 2011) and World Bank (2011) efforts. These developments, overall, demonstrate increasing official concern that numerous, predominantly SSA, countries are food-insecure and violent (Food and Agriculture Organization 2010). However, leaders continue to think and act like economists, who privilege economic-growth models with analysis of technical and market factors. They persist in their economic analysis of conventional indicators despite growing evidence that those involved in food-security or conflict-prevention planning might benefit from closer attention to anthropological analyses of structural violence, human rights violations and PGER-based preferential treatment or exclusions.

## Value Added of Human Rights and PGER Perspectives

Human rights analyses offer a principled, legal approach to address and redress the causes of food insecurity and conflict, and also ways to improve access to food, just livelihoods and political participation (see Messer 1996b; Messer and Cohen 2009; Marchione and Messer 2010). The Office of the UN Special Rapporteur on the Right to Food has documented legal obligations of governments to protect access to adequate food as a human right over market forces. The latter are often prioritised in World Trade Organization actions, direct foreign investments in agricultural land (also known as 'land-grabs') (see also Strauss this volume) and programmes which seek to modernise agriculture through larger-scale, modern plantings, which threaten to replace traditional small-holder agriculture rights to land and subsistence (United Nations Human Rights Council 2009; De Schutter 2010, 2011).[1] Such legal notes are available to all who are fighting unjust land seizures, unfair wages or working-conditions in agriculture, food-processing and/or food-marketing; they can also serve as a reference point for those working on safe production and marketing standards. These documents thus help raise awareness of conflict and human rights issues that influence the ways products are produced and marketed, and help consumers make more informed consumption choices which respect and protect human rights, the dignity of the human being and other paths that affirm life and peace. Such actions transform normative frameworks for the human right to food (HRF) into substantive institutions and practice, which help HRF advocates negotiate the political-economic and socio-cultural terrain where positive changes, toward fairer trade, no slave labour, environmentally protective food production, marketing and consumption can happen.

Oxfam, Global Exchange and other NGOs also work in this rights-based food-security and advocacy arena. They keep the pressure on for regular monitoring and evaluation of social protection and other food-security programmes, to ensure equity and non-exclusion and also possibilities of appeals. They try to report accurately and elicit donor interventions in contexts where, as expected, governments privilege their political supporters, marginalise their political opponents and try to circumvent the conditions donors impose, such as gender inclusiveness for qualifying to receive project aid.

Humanitarian NGOs, which deplore the political uses of food aid in wars and natural disasters and assert a 'right to feed' in conflict zones, are considering how to restore livelihoods, on a principled humanitarian basis (Sphere project 2000; Young *et al.* 2009), which integrates human rights and refugee rights. The humanitarian community, including NGOs, has also formulated and affirmed additional principles (Jaspars 2000; Sphere project 2000, 2011), voluntary codes of conduct and a 'right to assist', or 'right to protect', which is asserted mainly in conflict situations (Messer and Cohen 2008).

PGER analyses provide additional ways to bring attention to social discrimination and unfair land and labour practices, even where there is not a strong advocacy or legal tradition to build on. Most developing countries are multinational states, with stateless nations within them seething for recognition. Until international donors and interveners learn to deal effectively with horizontal as well as vertical inequalities (Stewart 2008), MDG poverty reduction is likely to be partial, unsustainable and prone to structural violence leading to conflict. Repeated cycles of ethnic violence and civil war in Côte D'Ivoire provide a case in point. There, attention strictly to technical factors, including poverty monitoring, transparent state budgets and 'free and fair' elections, has not effectively addressed the continuing ethnic tensions of past regimes, and such demands may make political-economic tensions worse. The World Bank's decision to invest in improving technical capacities to produce Poverty Reduction Strategy plans and reports does little to address the underlying structural violence regarding citizenship, access to land, child and other violent labour practices associated with cocoa and coffee production, or even to recognise non-Ivoirian exclusions (Fruchart 2011). The World Bank's food-security background papers to their 2011 World Development on conflict, security and development also signal that there is much work to be done to integrate PGER dimensions into their efforts; these papers were authored by economists and conflict specialists (Bora *et al.* 2010; Brinkman and Hendrix 2010), who largely dismissed PGER factors as outside their disciplinary frames of reference.

PGER sensitivity is more routine in humanitarian assistance, which uses local leadership structures to distribute emergency food. Humanitarians are aware, however, that this targeting can skew allocations against those who are marginal or external to the chosen leaders, and in particular may omit unprotected women and children (Maxwell *et al.* 2011). Integration of PGER understandings into livelihood strategies sometimes involve conflict-transformation components (e.g., Pantuliano 2008). 'Do no harm' conflict-sensitive methods can keep local leaders from fighting, joining or renewing conflicts, but they cannot necessarily keep at bay forces of violence beyond the local (Bennett *et al.* 2010). Implementing these codes is tricky, however, and it is hard to pinpoint situations where attention to PGER factors has helped transform conflicts or build new understandings, sustainable livelihoods and durable peace (see Pantuliano 2008; Bennett *et al.* 2010).

PGER awareness is also intrinsic to food-sovereignty advocacy movements, which help mobilise farmers on their own behalf to assert their right to food. The most important activist organisation on this front is FIAN (Food First Information and Action Network), allied with *Via Campesina* (Peasant Way), which works in conflict and post-conflict countries, helping farmers and consumer unions put food justice on to political agendas. Significantly, these activists favour conflict, but of the non-violent kind, as a constructive tool for social change.

## Summary and Conclusions

International agricultural and food-security planning and projects emphasise mainly technical and institutional indicators, targets and goals. They may address the challenges of good governance, including accountable, efficient and effective resource management, but they leave conflict issues, including land reform or land allocations, to other experts or host governments, or for a second stage in planning. Emphasis on livelihoods (Food and Agriculture Organization 2010) and rights-based development (the framing of Oxfam and other NGOs) are the latest approaches to helping populations break out of protracted crises and improve food security. In addition, technical agencies like the World Bank and WFP are investing more in conflict-sensitive framings and trainings at multiple social levels: national, regional, local. However, two challenges loom large in situations where 'conflict sensitivity' means sketching the conflict background, in preparation for business as usual. First, how to motivate agricultural and food-security interventionists to pay greater attention to PGER factors and conflict-sensitive methods in all food-security and agricultural programmes? Second, and as a corollary, how to incentivise agricultural experts and policy makers to construe the social complexities of landholding and water access that influence project participation and distribution of costs and benefits? It should be noted in this regard that anthropologists who study food, nutrition and human rights offer a more holistic understanding of PGER, gender and the dynamics connecting local populations to wider and longer-distance social networks, regional and national governance structures and country- and global-level political economic systems.

Food insecurity as a result of conflict and conflict resulting from food insecurity are dual sides of food war analysis. PGER factors and human rights violations underlie FW causation in both directions. A difficulty some scholars and policy makers might have with the FW concept is that they like to keep their independent and dependent variables separate in analysis, whereas that concept asserts causation flows in both directions. Exploring the PGER factors and human rights violations underlying both sets of variables or flows, can help food-security and conflict-transformation professionals sort and use FW and PGER analyses for their respective purposes.

## Notes

1   From the trade liberalisation perspective, problems of high and volatile food prices can be attributed mainly to market imperfections, unequal knowledge, lack of transparency and temporary fluctuations in agricultural supply and demand. Left alone, the market can rectify them, and the WTO presents an actionable, robust legal framework to adjudicate matters of unfair agricultural subsidies, dumping and taxes, which prevent low-income producers in economically disadvantaged countries from fairly accessing superior markets and gaining livelihoods. Correcting these flaws, according to WTO principles, will create a level playing field and self-correcting system that will enable the world in all its parts and peoples to feed itself. Its rules and regulations are designed to increase the flow of accurate information based on more transparent institutions.

    Countering this position, or the way this position is implemented, are not only political progressives, who assert that it is the capitalist global market system that is flawed, and not its workings. There is also a highly principled, expert human-rights legal office, which is vetting economic developments in food, nutrition, and agriculture, and producing position papers, concept notes, briefings, and reports on human right to food (HRF) issues. These publications are not only updates on which governments have or have not signed the International Covenant on Economic, Social and Cultural Rights, and implemented HRF legal principles in their Constitutions and codes of law. They are also detailed reports and human rights analyses of the legal implications and obligations stemming from controversial agricultural and food-security behaviours and directives (UN Human Rights Council 2009; De Schutter 2010, 2011).

# References

Albrecht, S., Braun, R., Heuschkel, Z., Mari, F. and Pippig, J. (eds) (2013) *Future of Food. State of the Art, Challenges and Options for Action*, Brot für die Welt, Vereinigung Deutscher Wissenschaftier. Published at: http://www.academia.edu/5086604/Future_of_Food_State_of_the_Art_Challenges_and_Options_for_Action_by_S._Albrecht_R._Braun_Z._Heuschkel_F._Mari_J._Pippig_Editors. Accessed on 2nd March 2014.

Allouche, J. (2011) The Sustainability and Resilience of Global Water and Food Systems: Political Analysis of the Interplay between Security, Resource Scarcity, Political Systems, and Global Trade, *Food Policy*, 36: S3–S8.

Anderson, M.B. (1999) *Do No Harm. How Aid Can Support Peace – Or War*, Lynne Rienner, Boulder, Colorado.

Bell, E. (2008) *The World Bank in Fragile and Conflict-Affected Countries. 'How', Not 'How Much'*, International Alert. Published at: http://www.international-alert.org/sites/default/files/publications/WBank_in_fragile_and_conflict-affected_c.pdf. Accessed on 27th Februrary 2014.

Bennett, J., Pantuliano, S., Fenton, W., Vaux, A., Barnett, C. and Brussett, E. (2010) *Aiding the Peace. A Multi-donor Evaluation of Support to Conflict Prevention and Peace-Building Activities in Southern Sudan, 2005–2010*, ODI Research Reports and Studies. Published at: http://www.odi.org.uk/resources/details.asp?id=5488&title=aid-effectivenes-south-sudan. Accessed on 27th February 2014.

Bora, S., Ceccacci, I., Delgado,C. and Townshend, R. (2010) *Food Security and Conflict*. Published at: http://www-wds.worldbank.org/external/default/WDSContentServer/WDSP/IB/2011/06/01/000333037_20110601012349/Rendered/PDF/620340WP0Food00BOX0361475B00PUBLIC0.pdf. Accessed on 27th February 2014.

Brinkman, H.-J. and Hendrix, C. (2010) *Food Insecurity and Conflict: Applying the WDR Framework*. Published at: https://openknowledge.worldbank.org/bitstream/handle/10986/9106/WDR2011_0025.pdf?sequence=1. Accessed on 27th February 2014.

Catley, A., Leyland, T. and Bishop, S. (2008) Policies, Practice, and Participation in Protracted Crises: The Case of Livestock Interventions in South Sudan. In Alinovi, L., Hemrich, G. and Russo, L. (eds) *Beyond Relief: Food Security in Protracted Crises*, Practical Action Publishing, Rugby: 65–96.

Collier, P. (2003) *Breaking the Conflict Trap: Civil War and Development Policy*, World Bank Policy Research Report, World Bank, Washington, D.C.

De Schutter, O. (2010) *Food Commodities Speculation and Food Price Crises. Regulation to Reduce the Risks of Price Volatility*. Briefing Note 2, September 2010. United Nations Rapporteur on the Right to Food.

De Schutter, O. (2011) *The World Trade Organization and the Post-Global Food Crisis Agenda. Putting Food Security First in the International Trade System*. Briefing Note 4, November 2011. United Nations Rapporteur on the Right to Food.

de Soysa, I. (2002) Paradise is a Bazaar? Greed, Creed, and Governance in Civil War, 1989–1999, *Journal of Peace Research*, 39(4): 395–416.

de Waal, A. (1997) *Famine Crimes: Politics and the Disaster Relief Industry in Africa*, University of Indiana Press, Bloomfield, Indiana.

Duffield, M. (2001) *Global Governance and the New Wars*, Routledge, New York.

Feinstein International Center (2011 to 2013) *Market Monitoring Bulletins: Darfur*. Published at: http://fic.tufts.edu/research-item/markets-and-trade-in-darfur/. Accessed on 20th March 2014.

Food and Agriculture Organization (FAO) (2010) *The State of Food Insecurity in the World*, FAO, Rome.

Foresight (2011) *The Future of Food and Farming*. Government Office of Science, London. Published at: http://webarchive.nationalarchives.gov.uk/+/http://www.bis.gov.uk/foresight/our-work/projects/current-projects/global-food-and-farming-futures/reports-and-publications). Accessed on 27th February 2014.

Fruchart, V. (2011) *The PRS as an Entry Point for Improving Governance in Fragile States*, Conflict, Crime and Violence Issue Note, Social Development Department, The World Bank Group. Published at: http://siteresources.worldbank.org/EXTCPR/Resources/PRS-Governance-Fragile-States.pdf. Accessed on 27th February 2014.

Grebmer, K. von, Torero, M., Olofinbiyi, T., Fritschel, H., Wiesmann, D., Yisehac, Y., Schofield, L. and Oppeln, C. von (2011) *Global Hunger Index 2011. The Challenge of Hunger. Taming Price Spikes and Excessive Price Volatility*, IFPRI, Washington DC. Published at: http://www.ifpri.org/sites/default/files/publications/ghi11.pdf. Accessed on 27th February 2014.

Homer-Dixon, T. (1999) *Environment, Scarcity, and Violence*, Princeton University Press, Princeton, New Jersey.

International Agricultural Assessment for Knowledge, Science, and Technology in Development (IAASTD) (2011) *Beyond the Crossroads: New Issues, Persistent Problems. Linking Food Security, Sustainability, Science and Sustainability Politics*. Conference Reader. International Conference Urania, Berlin, 9–10 November 2011. Abstracts available at: http://www.vdwev.de/images/stories/vdwdokumente/aktuelles/iaastd2_konferenz_programmflyer.pdf. Accessed on 27th February 2014.

Jaspars, S. (2000) *Solidarity and Soup Kitchens: A Review of Principles and Practice for Food Distribution in Conflict*, Humanitarian Policy Group (HPG) Report 7. Published at: http://www.odi.org.uk/resources/docs/301.pdf. Accessed on 27th February 2014.

Lange, M. (2004) Building Institutional Capacities for Conflict-Sensitive Practice. The Case of International NGOs. Published at: http://www.conflictsensitivity.org/sites/default/files/Building_Institutional_Capacity.pdf. Accessed on 27th February 2014.

Marchione, T.J. and Messer, E. (2010) Food Aid and the World Hunger Solution: Why the US Should Use a Human Rights Approach, *Food & Foodways*, 18: 10–27.

Maxwell, D., Young, H., Jaspars, S., Burns, J. and Frize, J. (2011) Targeting and Distribution in Complex Emergencies. Participatory Management of Humanitarian Food Assistance, *Food Policy*, 36(4): 535–543.

Messer, E. (1990) Food Wars. In Chen, R.S. (ed.) *The Hunger Report, 1989*, The Brown University World Hunger Program, Providence, Rhode Island: 27–36.

Messer, E. (1994) Food Wars: Hunger as a Weapon of War in 1993. In Uvin, P. (ed.) *The Hunger Report, 1993*, Gordon & Breach, Publishers for the Brown University World Hunger Programs, Yverdon, Switzerland: 43–69.

Messer, E. (1996a) Food Wars: Hunger as a Weapon of War in 1994. In Messer E. and Uvin, P. (eds) *The Hunger Report: 1995*, Langhorne, Pennsylvania: 19–48.

Messer, E. (1996b) Hunger and Human Rights (1989–1994). In Messer, E. and Uvin, P. (eds) *The Hunger Report: 1995*, Langhorne, Pennsylvania: 65–82.

Messer, E. (2009) Rising Food Prices, Social Mobilizations, and Violence: Conceptual Issues in Understanding and Responding to the Connections Linking Hunger and Conflict, *NAPA Bulletin*, 32: 12–22.

Messer, E. (2010) Climate Change and Violent Conflict. A Critical Literature Review. Oxfam Backgrounder. Published at: http://www.oxfamamerica.org/static/oa3/files/climate-change-and-violent-conflict.pdf. Accessed on 28th February 2014.

Messer, E. and Cohen, M.J. (2007) Conflict, Food Insecurity, and Globalization, *Food, Culture, and Society*, 10(2): 297–316.

Messer, E. and Cohen, M.J. (2008) Conflict, Food Insecurity, and Globalization. In Braun, J. von and Diaz-Bonilla, E. (eds) *Globalization of Food and Agriculture and the Poor*, Oxford University Press and International Food Policy Research Institute, New Delhi: 299–336.

Messer, E. and Cohen, M.J. (2009) US approaches to food and nutrition rights, 1976–2008, *World Hunger Notes: The Right to Food is a Basic Human Right*. Published at: http://www.worldhunger.org/articles/08/hrf/messer.htm. Accessed on 27th February 2014.

Messer, E., Cohen, M.J. and D'Costa, J. (1998) *Food from Peace: Breaking the Links Between Conflict and Hunger*, 2020 Vision for Food, Agriculture, and the Environment. Paper 24, International Food Policy Research Institute, Washington, D.C.

Messer, E., Cohen, M.J. and Marchione, J. (2001) Conflict: A Cause and Effect of Hunger, *Environmental Change and Security Project Report*, 7: 1–38.

Millennium Development Goals (2011) The Millennium Development Goals Report 2011. Published at: http://mdgs.un.org/unsd/mdg/Resources/Static/Products/Progress2011/11-31339%20%28E%29%20MDG%20Report%202011_Book%20LR.pdf. Accessed on 27th February 2014.

Newman, L.F., Crossgrove, W., Kates, R.W., Matthews, R. and Millman, S., eds. (1990) *Hunger in History*, Basil Blackwell, Cambridge, Massachusetts:

Pantuliano, S. (2008) Responding to Protracted Crises: The Principled Model of NMPACT in Sudan. In Alinovi, L., Hemrich, G. and Russo, L. (eds) *Beyond Relief: Food Security in Protracted Crises*, Practical Action Publishing, Rugby: 25–65.

Perry, J. and Bouchard, J. (2010) *African Security Challenges: Now and Over the Horizon. Food Security and Conflict: Current and Future Dimensions of the Challenge in Africa*, Working Group Discussion Report. Defense Threat Reduction Agency. Advanced Systems and Concepts Office. Report Number ASCO 2010–009.

Sharp, K., Brown, T. and Teshome, A. (2006) Targeting Ethiopia's Productive Safety Net Program (PSNP), Overseas Development Institute. Published at: http://www.odi.org.uk/sites/odi.org.uk/files/odi-assets/publications-opinion-files/3966.pdf. Accessed on 27th February 2014.

Sphere Project, The (2000, 2011) *The Sphere Handbook: Humanitarian Charter and Minimum Standards in Humanitarian Response*. Published at: http://www.spherepro-ject.org/handbook. Accessed on 27th February 2014.

Stewart, F, (2008) *Horizontal Inequalities and Conflict. Understanding Group Violence in Multiethnic Societies*. Palgrave Macmillan, New York.

United Nations Human Rights Council (2009) *Promotion and Protection of All Human Rights, Civil, Political, Economic, Social and Cultural Rights, Including the Right to Development. Report of the Special Rapporteur on the Right to Food, Olivier de Schutter: Crisis into opportunity: reinforcing multilateralism*, 21 July 2009, A/HRC/12/31. Published at: http://www.unhcr.org/refworld/docid/4a9d1bee0.html. Accessed on 27th February 2014.

United Nations Development Programme (UNDP) (2009) *Governance in Conflict Prevention and Recovery*. Guidance Note, published at: http://www.undp.org/content/undp/en/home/librarypage/democratic-governance/dg-publications/governance-in-conflict-prevention-and-recovery-a-guidance-note/. Accessed on 27th February 2014.

United Nations High Level Task Force on Global Food Security Crisis (UNHLTF) (2008, updated 2011) *Comprehensive Framework for Action*. Published at: http://www.un.org/en/issues/food/taskforce/docs.shtml. Accessed on 27th February 2014.

United Nations Millennium Project (2005) *Halving hunger. It Can be Done*. Task Force on Hunger, published at: http://www.unmillenniumproject.org/documents/Hunger-highres-frontmatter.pdf. Accessed on 27th February 2014.

UNICEF (2009) *Children and Conflict in a Changing World*. Published at: www.unicef.org/publications/index_49985.html. Accessed on 27th February 2014.

Uvin, P. (1998) *Aiding Violence. The Development Enterprise in Rwanda*, Kumarian Press, Bloomfield, Connecticut.

Webb, P., Rogers, B., Rosenberg, I., Schlossman, N., Wanke, C., Bagriansky, J., Sadler, K., Johnson, Q., Tilahun, J., Reese Masterson, S. and Narayan, A. (2011) *Delivering Improved Nutrition: Recommendations for Changes to U.S. Food Aid Products and programs*, Tufts University, Boston, Massachusetts. Published at: http://nutrition.tufts.edu/documents/DeliveringImprovedNutrition.pdf. Accessed on 27th February 2014.

Wolf, E. (1969) *Peasant Wars of the Twentieth Century*, Harper and Rowe, New York.

World Bank (2011) *World Development Report 2011: Conflict, Security, and Development*, World Bank, Washington, D.C. Published at: http://siteresources.worldbank.org/INTWDRS/Resources/WDR2011_Full_Text.pdf/. Accessed on 27th February 2014.

World Food Programme (2011) Purchase for Progress (P4P) 2011, published at: http://www.wfp.org/purchase-progress. Accessed on 27th February 2014.

World Food Summit (1996) Rome Declaration on World Food Security and World Food Summit Plan of Action. Published at: http://www.fao.org/wfs/index_en.htm. Accessed on 27th February 2014.

Young, H., Osman, A.M., Abusin, A.M., Asher, M. and Egemi, O. (2009) *Livelihoods, Power, and Choice. The Vulnerability of the Northern Rizaygat, Darfur, Sudan*, Feinstein International Center, Tufts University, Medford, Massachusetts.

# INDEX

........................................................................................

**A**

access (to food), x, 2–4, 6–7, 15, 19, 56, 62, 72, 74, 77–78, 116, 131, 171–172, 175, 187–188, 206, 210, 216

access, accessible, inaccessible (to land, fields, areas, markets, etc.), 12, 17, 39, 42, 45, 65–67, 70–72, 74, 119, 171, 197, 199, 210, 218–219

Action Contre la Faim (ACF), 12, 65

Action for Peace summit, 79, 83

adaptable, adaptability, 8, 10–11, 13, 18, 22

Afghanistan, 4, 18, 25, 58, 64

Africa, 2, 4, 6– 7, 11–12, 16, 19–24, 29, 34–51, 53, 55, 77–83, 186, 194–195, 198, 206– 207, 216, 221–222

AFRICOM (*see* United States Africa Command)

agency, -ies, 2, 7–8, 16, 18, 25, 28, 33, 46, 54, 58, 65, 74, 81–82, 137–138, 142, 145–146, 153, 210–216, 219, 222

agribusiness, 199

agriculture, agricultural, 2–6, 13, 16, 18–24, 41–44, 47, 49–50, 60, 62, 69–70, 72–73, 75, 77, 81, 83, 90, 93, 97, 108–109, 112, 116, 121, 129, 173, 175, 185–187, 189, 197, 199–207, 209–222

aid (humanitarian, food, etc.), x–xi, 5, 7–9, 12, 15–23, 25, 28–29, 32, 49, 55, 58, 63, 80–82, 166, 190, 195, 198, 201, 211, 213, 215–216, 220–221, 223

AIDS (*see* HIV/AIDS)

alcohol, alcoholic, alcoholism, liquor, 69–70, 74, 139–141

Allied Translator and Interpreter Service (ATIS), 141–142

allotment, -s (*see also* garden, -s), 13, 110–111, 116, 120–121

Amnesty International, 17, 19

Angola, 4, 42–45, 47–48, 58, 214

animal, -s 59, 79, 87, 89–91, 97, 102–103, 108–111, 118, 130, 145, 150, 202
  disease, 97,
  feed, feeding, (*see* feed)
  protein, 118

animism, animist, 80

anthropology, anthropological, anthropologist, -s, 9–10, 13, 16, 20, 22, 29, 35–38, 62, 92, 98, 121, 132, 146, 153, 171, 173, 209–211, 219

anti-personnel ordnance (APO), -s, - mines, etc., 11, 40–50

army, -ies, armed forces, 2, 10, 14, 16–17, 49–50, 69, 79, 97–98, 101–102, 109, 123–125, 128–129, 131–143, 179, 191, 193–194, 200, 207, 211

Australia, 138, 143

available, availability (of food, nutrients, rations, etc.), 2, 5–6, 12, 36, 54, 56, 59, 61, 74, 77, 111, 115, 117–119, 124, 128–129, 131, 133, 156, 206

available, availability (of land) 70, 72, 74, 200, 203

**B**

Bahai, 79

Balkans, 13, 95

Bamako, 17

Bangladesh, 2, 36
battle, -s, 4, 129, 132–133, 138, 140, 147,
    165
beef, 85, 89, 91, 103, 124–125, 148
Belgium, 6, 198
biological weapons, (*see* weapons)
biscuit, -s, 59, 124–125, 131, 138
blockade, blockaded, 107, 155–156
Bolshevism, -ist, 159–161, 163, 165
bomb, -s, bombing, 6, 39–41, 43, 46, 49–50,
    99–100, 102, 111, 134–136, 144, 202
  cluster, 39–43, 46 (*see also* Convention
    on Cluster Munitions)
bomblet, -s, 40–42, 46–47
border, -s, 13, 15, 17, 44, 54–55, 63, 67,
    69–70, 74, 83, 85–87, 90–92, 146, 171,
    173–174, 179–182, 199
  crossing, -s, 85–87, 90–91, 93
Bosnia-Herzegovina, Bosnian, -s, 19, 95,
    97, 105
Botswana, 3
bread (*see also* flatbread), 13, 33, 95,
    98–103, 109, 111, 115–116, 119,
    123–124, 129, 131, 137, 148, 155–167
Britain, United Kingdom (UK), British,
    x, 5, 7–8, 13–15, 17–19, 21–25, 29, 31,
    38, 45, 50–51, 53–54, 56–57, 63–64,
    77–78, 81, 83, 98, 107–126, 129–130,
    132, 139, 155–156, 167, 171, 173–176,
    178, 180–183, 188, 192, 209, 214–215,
    217, 221, 223
Buddhist, 79
bulgur, 29, 31
Burkina Faso, 5
Burundi, 3–4, 21, 43, 45, 47, 82–83, 213
bush meat (*see* meat)

**C**
calorie, -s, calorific, 4, 14, 19, 44, 68, 109,
    123–125, 138, 147
Cameroon, 5, 32
cannibal, cannibalism, 14, 142
Cape Verde, 43, 45
Care International, 42
Caritas International, 79, 82, 98
cassava, 29, 34, 44–45, 50, 80
Catholic, 75, 78–79, 82, 98, 173–174, 180

cattle, cows, 6, 13, 20, 22, 29, 31–33, 79,
    85–92, 102–103, 147, 187
Central African Republic (CAR), 4–5, 17,
    19, 22, 41, 43, 45, 53
cereal, -s, 55, 58–61, 63, 108–109, 118, 138,
    162–163, 197, 201
Chad, 4, 43–45, 54, 211
charity, -ies, charitable, 8, 104, 178, 182
Chechnya, 8
chemical weapons, (*see* weapons)
Chihuahua, 85–90
child, children, childhood, 4, 6, 9, 27–28,
    36–37, 41–42, 55–59, 62–63, 69, 73–75,
    78, 80–82, 99, 110, 115–119, 121, 126,
    156, 158–161, 163–164, 166, 174, 193,
    213, 218, 223
China, Chinese, 2, 40, 50, 134, 154, 199
chocolate, -s, 103, 126, 138, 147
choice (in relation to food or
    consumption), 23, 28, 35, 92, 131, 146,
    150
Christian, 12, 78–80, 82, 207
Chronic Poverty Research Centre
    (CPRC), 4, 20
civil war, -s, (*see* war, -s)
civilian, -s, 1, 10, 15, 24, 31, 43, 69, 81, 95,
    98, 104, 123, 127, 129, 131, 133,
    141–142, 152, 191–192, 202–203,
    212–213
class, -es (social, socioeconomic), 116,
    126, 130–131, 161, 174–176, 187–189,
    191, 195
climate, 45, 96, 133, 205, 211, 222
  change, 3, 6, 18, 22–24, 205, 211, 222
cluster bomb, -s (*see* bomb)
coffee, 97, 109, 111, 138, 211, 213, 215, 218
Colombia, 211
colonial, colonialism, 35–36, 57, 143, 146,
    153, 171, 177, 180, 183, 188, 197
Communism, Communist, 98, 157, 163,
    165–166
community, -ies, 2–3, 8–12, 15, 18, 20,
    22–24, 28, 33, 45, 54, 60, 66, 74–75,
    80, 110, 116, 127, 130, 154, 172–174,
    178–181, 187, 189, 204, 212–213,
    215–217
comrade, -s, comradeship, 128, 157

conflict
   resolution (*see* resolution)
   sensitive, sensitivity (*see* sensitive, sensitivity)
   transformation, 212–213, 215, 218–219
   zones (*see* zones of conflict)
Congo, the Democratic Republic of (DRC), 2, 4, 39, 40–45, 47–48, 50, 78, 80–82, 199, 214
Congo-Brazzaville (Republic of Congo), 4, 39, 41, 43, 45
consumption, 9, 11, 13–14, 28, 34, 55–56, 65, 67–68, 70–73, 77, 86, 90, 112, 117–119, 121, 134, 140–141, 145–146, 148, 150–154, 217
Convention on Cluster Munitions (CCM), 46, 50–51
cook, cookery, x, 10, 27, 29–31, 58–60, 68, 80, 97, 100, 113, 116, 119–120, 125, 136, 139–140, 148–149, 158–159, 191
   pre-cooked, 140
   uncooked, 61
corruption, 6, 32, 34, 41, 185, 188, 193
Côte d'Ivoire, 4–5, 34, 45, 211, 217
coup, -s, 16–17, 185–188, 191, 194, 203–204
Croatia, Croatian, -s, x, 13, 95–98, 102, 104–105
crop, -s, cropping, 4, 6, 8, 47, 58, 67, 70–71, 73–74, 80, 109–110, 135, 171, 174, 180, 201–204, 207, 211, 214
   -land, 3
   losses, 39, 45
   misses, 39, 45
cross-disciplinary, xii, 9, 53, 62
cuisine, 14, 97, 143, 145–146, 149–152
culinary, 35, 130, 134, 153
cultivate, cultivation, 4, 8, 12, 13, 29, 42, 45, 47, 55, 67, 73–74, 102, 110, 126, 176, 185, 198, 203

**D**
Daewoo, 16, 203–204, 207
dal, 68
Darfur, 7–8, 17, 21–22, 25, 53, 82, 213, 221, 223
deficiency, -ies (of food, nutrition), 54–57, 60, 63, 68–69, 117, 134, 138, 188

de-mining, 45–50
democracy, -ies, democratic, democratically, 36, 39, 156–157, 165, 189, 223
demographic, 171, 205
denial (of food), 7, 9–10
Derg, 186, 189, 192–193
Derry, Londonderry, 173, 175
develop, development, developmental, 1, 4, 7–10, 12, 14–16, 18, 20–22, 24–25, 31, 36, 38–40, 45–47, 49–50, 57–61, 65, 68, 75, 92, 95, 107, 116, 121, 136, 138, 147, 177–179, 181, 197, 201–203, 205–207, 209–212, 214–216, 218–223
developed countries, nations, economies 12, 49, 55, 61
developing countries, 5, 54–55, 59, 75, 197–198, 217
dictatorship, 155, 167
diet, dietary, dietetics, 9, 13, 15, 29, 32, 34, 55–56, 60, 63, 68, 72–74, 77, 81, 102–104, 107, 112, 114–115, 117–121, 123–125, 130, 133–134, 147, 153–154, 156, 174–176
Dig for Victory, 13, 110
Disarmament, Demobilisation and Reintegration (DDR), 49
disaster, -s, disastrous, 3, 5–6, 21–23, 25, 63, 77, 103, 146, 181, 195, 213, 216–217, 221
displace, displacement, x, 4–5, 11, 17–18, 20–22, 25, 32–34, 36, 39, 42, 45, 50, 53, 57, 63–64, 79–80, 82–83, 103
distribute, distribution, -s (of food, aid, etc.), 7, 13–14, 44, 49, 60, 78–81, 86, 88, 97, 99, 102, 108–109, 111–112, 114, 116, 119, 131, 136–137, 141, 163, 187, 190, 218, 221
distribute, distribution (of land), 6, 176, 199, 212
Donegal, 172–175, 178–183
donor, -s, 8, 126, 217, 220
drought, -s, 3, 45, 186–187, 189, 192, 204
drug, -s, drug-related activities, 13, 85, 87–90, 92
   cartels 85, 87, 89, 92
   wars, conflict, 13, 85, 87–90

**E**

East Africa, 3, 6, 20, 22–24, 194

economic, -s, economically, economy, -ies, x, 1, 3, 5, 10, 16, 20–24, 28, 37, 47, 49, 54, 62, 66, 75, 78, 81, 87, 89–90, 120–121, 150, 153, 164–165, 171, 174–175, 178–179, 182, 185, 188–189, 193, 200–204, 210, 212, 215–220

socio-economic, 12, 18, 37, 85, 89, 107, 210

economist, -s, 21, 171, 199, 206, 209

education, educational, 12, 37, 101, 112, 158, 160, 185, 190

Egypt, 5, 46, 53

elect, election, -s, electorally, 157–158, 165–166, 168, 218

emergency, -ies, 18, 23, 25, 56–57, 63–64, 97, 103, 108, 112, 138, 140, 192, 213, 215, 218, 221

emigration, 171, 176, 182

Emperor (*see also* Haile Selassie), 15, 142, 185–192, 193, 195

employment, 90, 179

unemployment, 4

enemy, -ies, 14, 19, 40, 42, 45, 95, 99–100, 102–103, 107, 133, 136, 140–141, 146, 149–152, 155, 163, 200–202, 204

energy, 19, 47, 55–64, 114–120, 147, 191, 193

environment, -s, environmental, -ly, 3, 6, 9–10, 14, 18–19, 22–24, 45, 91, 110, 130, 206, 211, 216–217, 221–222

Eritrea, 4, 43–48, 193

estaminet, -s, 125, 130–131

Ethiopia, xi, 2, 4, 15–17, 19, 43–48, 54, 63, 82, 185–195, 211, 215–216, 222

ethnic, ethnicity, 12, 17, 19, 24, 32–33, 35, 53, 67, 83, 95, 152, 182, 187–189, 210, 214, 217, 218

multiethnic, 213

ethnography, ethnographic, 7, 13, 35, 37, 78, 98, 104–105, 172, 182, 210, 214

Europe, European, 107–108, 119, 156, 171, 173, 178, 185, 188, 207

exchange, -s, exchanged, 62, 87, 128, 132, 139, 198, 203, 213, 217

explosive, -s, 40–41, 46, 50, 126

export, -s, exportation (of food, feed, etc.), 15, 85–87, 92, 108, 157, 174–175, 183, 189, 198, 201, 203, 211

**F**

famine, -s, x–xi, 6–7, 10, 15, 20–24, 83, 107, 119, 121, 155–156, 161–162, 164–165, 167, 171–190, 192–195, 201, 210, 221

farm, -s, farming, 4, 16, 32–33, 37, 45, 70, 81, 110, 111, 125, 160, 173, 179, 182, 197, 199–203, 205–207, 209–210, 221

animals, 111, 130

-land (*see* land)

feed, feeding (of humans), 3, 13, 24, 35, 39, 57–60, 62–63, 67, 79, 81, 112, 116, 123, 133, 137, 151, 153, 158, 192, 213, 216–217, 219

feed (of animals), 90, 102, 108–109

Feinstein International Center, 214, 221, 223

fertiliser, 45, 156

fieldwork, 15, 28, 33, 66, 98, 171, 213

First World War, (*see* war, -s)

fish, fishing, 29, 34, 59, 66–67, 70, 73, 102, 108–109, 111, 115, 120, 130, 136, 140, 174

fisherman, -men, 100, 102

flatbread, 14, 145, 147–14

food

access to (*see* access to food)

aid (*see* aid)

as a weapon (*see* weapon)

availability (*see* available, availability)

choice (*see* choice)

deficiency (*see* deficiency)

denial (*see* denial)

export, -s (*see* export, -s)

fortification (*see* fortify, fortification)

import, -s (*see* import, -s)

insecurity (*see* insecure, insecurity)

security (*see* secure, security)

staple (*see* staple)

Food and Agriculture Organization (FAO), 2–4, 16, 19, 21, 24, 41–43, 50, 77, 83, 199, 203, 206–207, 209–210, 214–216, 219, 221 fortify, fortification (of food, nutrients, etc.), 55, 57–58, 62–64, 115, 213

**G**
Gambia, 3
game (*see also* wild food), 112, 121, 129
gathering (of food, *see also* wild food), 136,
gender, 11, 45, 83, 217, 219
Geneva Convention, -s, 7, 188, 203, 207
Geneva Protocol, 202
genocide, 180, 212
Germany, German, 14–15, 37, 40, 51, 79, 107–108, 119, 124, 129, 155–159, 161–164, 166–168, 198
Ghana, 5, 20, 24, 57
gift, -s, 29, 73, 125–128, 130–132, 134, 140, 213
global, globalisation, 2–5, 16, 18–19, 21–23, 25, 28, 32, 41, 50, 53, 63–64, 93, 193, 197–198, 206–207, 211, 214, 217, 219, 220–223
Global Food Security Crisis, 214, 223
governance, 82, 218–219, 221, 223
government,-s, governmental x-xi, 2, 5–7, 9–11, 13, 15–17, 19, 21, 28, 35, 40, 42–46, 54, 66, 69, 72, 74, 78–79, 86–87, 108–110, 112–114, 120, 143–144, 149, 155–158, 166, 174, 178, 181, 185–192, 194, 198–199, 201–203, 205, 207, 209, 213, 215–218, 220–221
grain, -s, 88, 99–100, 115, 163, 174, 189, 214–215
Great Hunger (An Gorta Mór), 171, 183
Great Lakes, 49, 79, 82
Guinea, 4, 33–34, 36, 43, 45, 136, 142–143

**H**
Hague Regulations, 202
Haile Selassie (*see also* Emperor), 15, 185, 187–190, 192–193
Haile Selassie I University, 185, 188, 190–191
Haiti, 4
harvest, -s, 12, 44–45, 67, 70–72, 79–81, 110, 176

health, healthy, 12–13, 16, 22, 24, 54–58, 62–64, 72, 74–75, 77–78, 81, 83, 88, 91, 97, 107–108, 114–121, 210
ill-health, 12
history, historic, -al, historian, 1, 8–10, 15, 18, 23, 37, 99, 103, 107, 110, 120–121, 132, 135, 142–145, 152–154, 157–158, 161, 164, 166, 168, 171, 173, 176–177, 178–183, 185–186, 193–195, 201, 203, 205, 207, 210, 214, 222
HIV/AIDS, 39, 81
holism, holistic, 11–13, 62, 113–114, 210, 219
homemade, 103, 127
horse, -s, 13, 85–89, 125, 130, 141
household, -s, 4, 12, 17, 42, 65, 66–75, 126, 130
Household Economy Analysis (HEA), 66
human right, -s, 42, 49, 52, 189, 206, 209–211, 214–223
Human Right to Food (HRF), 217, 220
Human Rights Watch (HRW), 40–44, 47–48, 50
human security, 24, 29, 34–35, 214
humanitarian, -s, x-xi, 2, 5, 7–9, 17, 18, 21–25, 28, 49–50, 63, 78, 98, 186, 189–190, 194–195, 207, 209–210, 213, 215–218, 221, 223
hunger, hungry, x, 2, 9, 11, 12, 15–16, 18–20, 23, 29–30, 34–35, 37–38, 40, 57, 65, 100–104, 123, 125, 128–130, 133, 146, 157–158, 160–161, 163–166, 177, 182–183, 185–, 190, 192–194, 203, 210–211, 214, 221–223
hunt, hunting (*see also* wild food), 66–67, 70, 74, 136
Hutu, -s, 43–44, 78

**I**
identity, -ies, 10, 14, 28, 35–36, 96, 111, 127, 143, 145–146, 151–154, 164, 172, 174, 177, 183, 211–212
ideology, -ies, 150, 152–153, 159, 176, 183, 189
Imperial Japanese Army (IJA), 14, 134–138, 140–141

Imperial Japanese Navy (IJN), 136–137
Imperial War Museum, 120–121, 127, 132
import, -s, importation, importer (of food, feed, etc.), 4–5, 85–87, 91–92, 107–109, 111, 115–116, 120, 157, 197–202, 204–205
India, Indian, 2, 83, 109, 146, 153, 175
Indonesia, 2
infant, -s, 4, 58, 60, 115–116, 118–119
informant, -s, 12, 29–32, 36, 66, 78–81, 85, 88–92, 98–99
insecure, insecurity (of food, nutrition), 2, 4–7, 9, 12, 16, 18, 20–24, 39–40, 42, 45, 49, 65–66, 69–70, 73–74, 77, 81, 83, 85, 209–211, 215–216, 219–22
insecure, insecurity (re. danger), 85, 88–89, 91
interdisciplinary, interdisciplinarity, 9, 16, 182–183
Internally Displaced Person (IDP), -s, 17, 33, 39, 53, 63, 79, 80, 82–83, 103
International Alert, 20, 212, 220
International Assessment of Agricultural Knowledge, Science and Technology for Development (IAASTD), 209, 221
International Commission on the Anthropology of Food and Nutrition (ICAF), xi, 35, 62
International Food Policy Research Institute (IFPRI), 23, 50, 210–211, 221–222
International Institute of Tropical Agriculture (IITA), 44, 50
international law, -s, 200, 202, 207
intervention, -s, 7–9, 12–13, 17, 40, 43–44, 46, 49, 63, 65–66, 72, 129, 166,194, 204, 212, 215, 217, 220
Iraq, Iraqi, x, 4–5, 14–15, 18, 20, 24, 53, 55, 145–153, 201
Ireland (island of ), xi, 101, 171–177, 180–183
    Northern Ireland (see also Ulster), 173, 178–183
    Republic of Ireland (see also Donegal), 171, 174, 178–179, 181–183
Irish Land League, 15, 176–177

irrigation, 65–66, 203
Islam, Islamic, Islamist, Muslim, 17, 66–67, 69–70, 73, 79–80, 82

J
Japan, Japanese, 6, 14, 108, 134–144
Java, 134

K
Kenya, 3–5, 17, 20–24, 28, 36–37, 43, 45, 54, 58, 63
Kigali, 79
Korea, 134, 143
    North Korea, North Korean, 4, 16, 198, 204
    South Korea, South Korean, 3, 16, 134, 198, 203–204, 207
kwashiorkor, 57

L
labour, labourer, -s, 42, 66–67, 69–70, 72, 108–110, 116, 136, 157, 179, 186, 192, 215–218
land, -s, 5–6, 13, 15–16, 21, 24, 39–43, 45, 47–49, 66–67, 70–75, 109, 129, 135–136, 140, 166, 171, 173–174, 176–177, 179, 181, 183, 185, 187, 189, 197–207, 210–212, 216–219
    access, (see access to land)
    de-mined, 47
    grab, 21, 197, 206–207, 217
    leasing, 16, 207
    -lord, -s, 15, 176
    -mine, -s, 39–43, 49–50, 214
    Mine Action (see United Nations Mine Action)
    ownership, 15
    reform, -s, 6, 176, 193, 218
    tenure, 41, 185, 187, 206
lease, leasing, 16, 73, 197–200, 203, 205–207
Lesotho, 45
Liberation Tigers of Tamil Elam (LTTE), 66, 72
Liberia, -n, 3–5, 20, 24, 34, 36, 41, 43, 45, 82
Libya, 43–44, 46

liquor (*see* alcohol)
livelihood, -s, 5, 8, 16, 21–25, 66, 70–71,
   73–74, 176, 199, 209–211, 214–219,
   223
livestock, 13, 33, 42, 45, 85–93, 95, 103,
   136, 174, 176, 203, 214, 220
Londonderry (*see* Derry)
loot, looting, lootable, (*see also* steal), 31,
   80, 129, 133, 135, 213–214
Lutheran World Federation, 79, 83

**M**

Madagascar, 3, 16, 43, 45, 79, 198,
   203–204, 207
Malaya, 134
Mali, 17, 25, 45, 53
malnutrition (*see also* undernutrition,
   protein-energy malnutrition), 4, 9,
   14–15, 24, 40, 49, 54, 56–59, 61, 63–65,
   72, 74, 81, 114, 117, 120, 142, 153
Manila, 139
Manos Unidas, 49, 79
marasmus, 57
market, -s, 5, 13, 16, 27, 34, 36, 40, 44–45,
   58, 66, 74, 77, 121, 125, 156, 164, 169,
   175, 197, 203, 210, 213, 215–216, 219,
   221
Marxism, Marxist, -s, 164, 189
Mauritania, 5, 44–45
Meals Ready to Eat (MREs), 145–148
meat, 29, 31, 33, 59, 68, 86, 90–91, 103,
   108–109, 111–112, 115–117, 124, 130,
   134, 138, 142, 145, 148, 169
   bush meat (*see also* wild food) 29
media, 1, 45, 90, 92, 137, 210
Mediterranean, 63, 108
memory, -ies, memorial, -s, 10, 15, 28,
   30–31, 34, 36–38, 98, 107, 114, 127,
   132, 151– 153, 155–157, 161, 163–164,
   167–168, 173
   (*see also* remember)
Mercy Corps, 215
Mexico, 13, 85–93
micronutrient, -s, x, 9, 12, 14, 54–59,
   62–63, 81, 115, 119
Middle East (*see also* separate countries),
   18, 23, 63, 151

migration, -s (*see also* emigration), 5, 20,
   22, 50, 62, 85, 89, 92
military, x, 3, 9, 13–14, 17, 41, 43, 80–81,
   91–92, 95, 98, 108–109, 123–124, 127,
   129, 131–134, 136, 138–143, 146,
   149–151, 155, 161, 185–186, 190–194,
   198, 200, 204–205, 207, 212, 216
militia, -s, 17, 79
milk, 57, 59, 68, 103, 109, 111, 115–119,
   124, 130, 163, 174
   -less, 113
Millennium Development Goal (MDG),
   -s, 4, 214, 217, 222
mine, -s (*see also* landmine), 11, 39, 43, 46,
   49, 50–51
Mine Ban Treaty (MBT), 46
   (*see also* United Nations Mine Action)
Ministry of Agriculture, UK, 108–109
Ministry of Food (MOF), UK, 107–112,
   114–116, 120–121
Missio Aachen, 79, 82
Morocco, 5, 44, 46
mortality, 4, 6, 9, 118–119, 171
Mozambique, Mozambican, 43, 45, 47–48,
   50, 55, 63
multidisciplinary, x, 9, 11, 51
munition, -s (*see also* bomb, ordnance), 1,
   6, 39–40, 46, 49–51, 109, 136
Muslim (*see* Islam)

**N**

narrative, -s, 11, 27–28, 34–35, 145
National Socialism, -ist, 155, 164–168
nationalism, nationalist, 24, 28, 150–152,
   173, 177–178, 180, 188, 193
natural disaster, -s, 3, 5–6, 23, 77, 216–217
Navy, Army and Air Force Institute
   (NAAFI), 139, 143
New Guinea, 136, 142–143
New Mexico, 85–87, 90, 92
newspaper, -s, 22, 90, 96–97, 111, 143, 164,
   182
Niger, 41, 45
Nigeria, Nigerian, 29, 33, 37, 41, 43–44, 83
non-governmental organisation (NGO),
   -s, agencies, 4, 8, 12, 40, 54, 65, 79,
   212–213, 215

Nuba Mountains Community Empowerment Project (NMPACT), 215, 222

nutrient, -s (see also micronutrient), x, 12, 55–56, 61, 63, 114–115, 117–120, 201

nutrition (general) xi, 9–10, 12–13, 16, 21, 23, 25, 50, 62–64, 75, 77, 98, 101, 105, 125–126, 133, 182, 206, 209–210, 219–220, 222–223
  of refugees, 53–64
  in UK Second World War, 107–121
  (see also malnutrition, undernutrition)

nutritional, nutritive, nutritious, xii, 9–10, 12–14, 39–40, 49, 53–55, 58–59, 61–63, 67–68, 71–73, 75, 77–78, 81, 97, 124, 127, 174, 176, 213–215
  deficiency (see deficiency)

nutritionist, -s, 9, 62

**O**

Occupied Palestinian Territories (OPT), 8

Operation Lifeline Sudan, 214

ordnance, -s (see also bomb, munition), 6, 11, 39–42, 125

Overseas Development Institute (ODI), 8, 21–23, 29, 37, 50, 220, 222

Oxfam, 63, 83, 216–217, 219, 222

**P**

Pacific, 14, 109, 133–134, 136–140, 142–143

Pakistan, 2

parcel, -s, 14, 123, 125–128, 131

pastoralist, -s, 6, 22, 24, 214

peace, peacetime, peaceful, 7, 19, 22–24, 36–37, 39–43, 54, 78–83, 103, 138, 142, 152, 158–159, 161, 173, 178–181, 190, 195, 210, 212–218, 220, 222
  corps, 28
  country-with-relative-peace, 39–41
  -keeper, -s, -keeping, 33–34, 36

peasant, -s, peasantry, 185–190, 192–195, 218, 223
  Via Campesina (Peasant Way) 218

Philippines, 134, 143

pig, -s, 29, 33, 109–110, 125, 130

political, -ly, politics, 4, 6–10, 15–16, 18–24, 28, 32, 35–38, 41, 47, 49, 54, 62, 81–82, 96, 99, 133, 142, 153, 155–156, 158, 161, 163, 165–168, 172–173, 175–176, 178, 180–181, 183, 185–195, 198, 200–201, 204–205, 209–221, 223
  geopolitical, 206–207

political-geographic-ethnic-religious (PGER), 210–212, 214–219

pollution, 204

Post Exchange (PX), 14, 139, 143

poster, -s, 15, 21, 110, 113, 155–168

potato, -es, 29, 68, 79, 102, 111, 113, 115–116, 119, 138, 162–164, 171, 174, 215

poverty, 4, 7, 9, 18, 20, 22–24, 38, 75, 82, 159, 161, 178, 187, 189, 211, 214, 217–218

press (see also newspaper), 97, 103–104, 156, 161

price, -s, x, 3–5, 21, 23, 36–37, 44, 88, 91, 102, 108, 112, 117, 130–131, 187, 197, 209, 211, 214, 219, 221–222

procure, procurement, 1, 12, 14, 70, 72, 114, 134–135, 137–138, 140

productive, productivity, 4, 42, 81, 85, 212–222

propaganda, 15, 112, 118, 155–158, 160, 162–168, 190

protein, -s, 29, 58–61, 64, 115, 117–118

protein-energy malnutrition (PEM), 56–57, 64

Protestant, -s, 173–174, 176, 179–180

**R**

radio, -s, 31, 96, 100, 112, 179, 191–192

radioactive, 6, 201–202, 206

ranch, -es, rancher, -s, 13, 85, 88–92

rape, 79–81, 83

Rastafari, -an, 79

ration, -s, rationing, x, 12–14, 19, 54–56, 63, 81, 97, 100, 107, 111–112, 115–117, 119, 121, 123–125, 128, 131, 133, 138–140, 143, 145, 149, 153, 161–162, 209, 213

Ready to Use Therapeutic Food (RUTF), -s, 12, 58–62

rebel, -s, rebellion, 4, 8, 17, 27–28, 30–34, 39, 41– 43, 45, 177, 180. 183, 191, 211
recipe, -s, 33, 58, 60, 103, 112–113, 124, 136, 181
reconstruction (*as in* post-war, post-conflict), 35, 39, 49, 165, 215
Recreation and Amusement Association (RAA), 141
Red Cross, Red Crescent, (ICRC), 8, 22, 42, 46, 50, 98
reform, -s, reformer, -s, 6, 176, 185, 187, 189–191, 193, 213, 218
refugee, -s, 5, 12, 17–18, 20, 23–25, 33, 36, 39, 45, 53–58, 61–64, 79–82, 98–99, 101–102, 104, 217
religion, -s, religious, 10, 12, 16, 53, 77–83, 95, 172–174, 179, 210
remember, remembrance (*see also* memory), 10, 14, 30, 34, 38, 67, 101, 103, 108, 113–114, 128, 132, 139, 145–146, 150–151, 177, 181
resource, -s, 6, 18, 21–25, 32, 37, 39, 49–51, 66, 74–75, 77, 82, 90, 92, 111–112, 126, 128, 134–136, 161, 201–202, 204, 211–212, 216, 218, 220–223
retail, retailer, -s, 13, 108, 111–112
revanchism, revanchist, 161
revolution, -s, revolutionary, -ies, 16, 20, 31, 36, 157, 185–187, 191–195, 205
Revolutionary United Front (RUF), 31, 36–37
rice, 29, 31, 34, 36–37, 60–61, 67–74, 103, 109, 124, 134–137, 140, 198–199, 203, 207
rural, 15, 20, 31, 36–37, 42, 45, 66, 74–75, 77, 85, 102, 112, 116, 130, 178, 186–187
Rwanda, 39–43, 45, 78–79, 82–83, 212, 215, 223

**S**
Sahel, Sahelian, 3, 53, 186, 190
salt, 27, 30, 55, 103, 138, 166
sanitation, 12, 58, 62, 72, 74, 77, 104
scarce, scarcity, -ies, 1, 3, 6, 10, 24, 29, 35, 54, 83, 90, 100, 107–109, 112, 138, 211, 220–221

scrounge, scrounging, 14, 123, 125, 128–129, 131, 145
scrumping, 125, 131
(*see also* steal, stealing)
season, -s, seasonal, 17, 68, 70–71, 73, 102, 201
Second World War, (*see* war)
secure, security
  *re.* danger, 88, 90, 97, 200, 214
  of food, nutrition, 2–3, 5–7, 12, 16–25, 29, 34–35, 37–38, 40, 49–50, 65–75, 77–83, 134, 197, 199–200, 203–207, 209–211, 213–223
  of funding, 178–179
Senegal, 5, 195
share, -s, sharing, 14, 25, 2–28, 31, 34, 99, 108, 112–113, 123, 126, 128, 131, 151, 173, 178–179, 188, 200
shortage, -s, 6, 10, 13–14, 17–18, 29, 34–35, 45, 47, 65, 67–71, 73, 100–101, 108, 121, 124, 126, 128–129, 131, 135, 138, 167, 204
*Shuho*, 14, 139
Sierra Leone, -an, 4, 11, 24, 27–29, 31–38, 41, 43–45
soldier, -s, 13–14, 28, 36, 37, 80, 102, 123–138, 140, 142–143, 146–149, 151, 153, 157, 167, 186, 191–192
Somalia, Somali, 4–5, 8, 39, 41, 43, 45–49, 80–81, 193, 213
South Africa, 21, 43–44, 79, 83
South Sudan, 5, 8, 17, 25, 41, 45, 49, 54, 78–80, 220
Sphere Project, 217, 223
Sri Lanka, x, 8, 12, 65–70, 74–75
staple (of food, diet, etc.), 13, 29, 45, 59, 61, 130, 174, 176
starve, starvation, x-xi, 9, 14, 15, 101, 103, 120, 142, 148–149, 156–161, 164, 167–168, 175–176, 178, 180, 187, 189, 192, 195, 203, 213
steal, stolen, 88, 123, 125, 128–129, 131, 134, 148, 162–163, 166
(*see also* scrumping)
(*see also* theft)
stockpile, 11, 46, 50
stress, 3, 6, 10–13, 15–16, 87, 120

Sub-Saharan Africa, -n (SSA), 4, 6, 12,
    19–21, 53, 77–79, 81–82, 211, 216
Sudan, Sudanese, 4–6, 8, 17, 21, 24–25, 41,
    44–48, 54, 78, 80, 82–83, 213–214, 220,
    222–223
Sudan People's Liberation Movement
    (SPLM), 80
sugar, 55–57, 59–60, 103, 108–109, 111,
    115–116, 124, 138, 140, 163, 211
supplement, -s, supplementation, 22, 55,
    57–59, 62, 71, 81, 112. 116–117, 123,
    130, 136, 138, 174, 180
supply, -ies, 2, 4, 40, 54, 78, 81, 95, 97, 99,
    100–101, 107–108, 110, 115–117, 119,
    124–126, 129, 131, 134, 136–138, 140,
    147, 155–156, 158, 162, 164, 167, 175,
    197, 198, 203, 215, 219
survival, survivalism, x-xi, 22, 37, 99,
    104–105, 128, 133, 146, 149, 153, 178,
    195, 201, 203
sustainable, sustainability, 3, 5, 12, 16,
    21–22, 77–78, 79, 82, 91, 121, 174, 206,
    211, 215, 218, 220–221
  unsustainable, 189, 217
Swaziland, 3, 45
symbol, -s, symbolic, symbolise,
    symbolism, 2, 10–11, 13–15, 27–28,
    32, 34–35, 38, 101, 155–156, 163,
    171–173, 176, 179, 181, 193
Symposium of Episcopal Conferences of
    Africa and Madagascar (SECAM),
    79, 82
Syria, 4–5, 8, 18, 22, 25, 53


**T**
Tajikistan, 4
Tamil, 66–67, 69, 71–73
Tanzania, 3, 45, 58, 63
taste,-s, tasting, x, 14, 37, 59, 100, 102, 125,
    127, 133–134, 138–142, 147–148, 151,
    153
territory, -ies, territorial, 6, 8, 16, 49, 104,
    134–136, 162, 191, 197–201,
    204–206
Texas, 86–87, 90–91
theft (see also steal), 88–89, 123, 129
Tigray, 187, 192

transport, transportation, 13, 33, 45, 59,
    80, 85–91, 111, 125, 130, 138, 146, 200
treaty, -ies, 11, 40, 46, 50, 161–163, 166,
    199, 202–203, 205
Tutsi, -s, 43–44, 78


**U**
Uganda, Ugandan, 3–4, 17, 22, 44–45, 49,
    54, 56, 63, 80, 83, 215
Ulster, 171–175, 179, 181–183
underdevelopment, 2, 7, 9, 179, 193
undernutrition (see also malnutrition),
    108, 114
unemployment, 4
unexploded (of ordnance) (UXO), 6, 11,
    40, 42, 45
UNICEF, 17, 25, 74–75, 83, 214, 223
United Kingdom (UK) (see Britain)
United Nations (UN), 5, 7, 12, 17–19,
    21–25, 31, 36, 38, 43, 45–46, 49, 51,
    53–54, 63, 64, 77–78, 81, 83, 98, 182,
    188, 198, 206, 209, 214–215, 217,
    220–223
United Nations Development
    Programme (UNDP), 18, 24–25, 31,
    38, 45, 51, 215, 223
United Nations High Commissioner for
    Refugees (UNHCR), 5, 12, 18, 25,
    53–54, 62, 63–64, 9, 223
United Nations High Level Task
    Force (UNHLTF), 209, 214, 216,
    223
United Nations Human Rights Council,
    217, 220, 223
United Nations Mine Action, 43, 46
United States Africa Command
    (AFRICOM), 216
United States of America (USA), US,
    (North) America, -n, 13–16, 22, 29,
    35–37, 40–41, 47, 50–51, 86–91, 121,
    124, 134–144, 147, 149–152, 154, 179,
    183, 187–189, 195, 200–203, 207, 211,
    216, 221–223
university, 114, 185, 189–190, 192
urban, urbanisation, urbanism, 3, 15, 17,
    36, 77, 100, 154, 158, 161, 187–189,
    194, 197

**V**

veterinary, veterinarian, -s, 87, 90, 97, 103–104

Via Campesina (*see* peasant)

Vietnam, 188, 202

violence, violent, 1, 6–7, 13, 16–21, 23–25, 28, 31, 34–35, 37, 78, 80–83, 88–90, 92, 104, 161, 183, 188, 190–191, 209–212, 215–218, 221–223

vitamin, -s, 55–56, 58–61, 63, 83, 115–118, 125

**W**

war, -s, warfare (general), x–xi, 1–3, 6, 10–11, 13–14, 19, 21–22, 24, 40, 50, 53, 75, 80, 82–83, 95, 195, 200–204, 206–207, 211–213, 215–217, 220–223
  in the Balkans, 95–105
  civil war, -s, 3–5, 9, 11, 13, 18, 20, 24, 27–38, 39–45, 53, 65, 79–80, 82, 217, 220–221
  Cold War, 3, 18
  drug wars, 13, 85–93
  First World War, x, 6, 13, 107–108, 114, 123–132, 155–169
  food war, -s, 10, 16, 39, 210–211, 219, 222
  in Iraq, 145–154
  in Ireland, 171–183
  Pacific War (*see* Second World War)
  Second World War, xi, 13–14, 19, 40, 95, 107–121, 133–144, 167–168, 202
  in Sierra Leone, 27–38

wartime, 27–28, 32, 34, 105, 107, 110, 112–113, 115, 120–121, 129, 134–135, 142, 144–145, 150–151, 153, 167, 201

water, 3, 12–13, 57–62, 74, 77–78, 95, 97, 99–101, 138, 140, 147–148, 199, 202–204, 210, 212, 216, 219, 220
  buffaloes, 135
  supply, 100
  -mills, 102–103
  -ways, 40
  -works, 16, 210

weapon, -s (as ordnance), 40, 46, 49–51, 140, 147, 152, 155
  anti-crop, 202
  biological, 40–41, 201–203, 207
  Biological and Toxin Weapons Convention, 203
  chemical, 40–41, 201–203
  Chemical Weapons Convention, 203
  food or hunger as a weapon, x, 2, 10, 15–16, 103, 107, 133, 155, 163, 168, 203, 215, 222
  radioactive, 201

Weimar Republic, 15, 155–156, 159, 161, 164–168

Wello, 187, 190, 192

wheat, 29, 56, 97, 100, 109, 115, 134, 158, 175

wild (of food and plants), 33, 97, 105, 112
  bush meat, 29
  -life, 6

woman, women, 6, 27, 29, 33, 36, 42, 66, 69, 75, 77–83, 89, 103, 109, 112, 115–118, 120, 126, 130–131, 133, 146, 149, 158–164, 166, 218

Women's Land Army, 109

World Bank, 20, 198, 205–207, 209, 213, 216, 218–223

World Food Programme (WFP), 4, 16–18, 20, 25, 58, 214–215, 219, 223

World Food Summit, 77, 214, 223

World Hunger Program (WHP), 210, 222

World Trade Organization (WTO), 217, 219, 221

**Y**

Yugoslavia (*see also* Croatia, Bosnia), 95–97, 104

**Z**

Zambia, 3, 36, 44, 58, 64

Zimbabwe, 4, 45–46, 211

zones of conflict, combat zones, conflict zones, war zones, x, xii, 1–2, 8–10, 35, 57, 77–78, 80–83, 85, 91–92, 96, 98, 138, 142, 214–215, 217